Baedeker Paris

Baedeker's
PARIS

Imprint

109 colour photographs
Map of Paris, plan of the métro, 12 plans and diagrams

Conception and editorial work:
Redaktionsbüro Harenberg, Schwerte
English language edition: Alec Court

Text:
Madeleine Cabos, Manfred Kottman, Christa Sturm
Continuation: Baedeker-Radaktion (Madeleine Cabos)

General direction:
Dr Peter Baumgarten, Baedeker, Stuttgart

English translation:
Babel Translations, Norwich and Alec Court

Cartography:
Gert Oberländer, Munich
Hallwag AG, Bern (Map of Paris)

Source of illustrations:
Cabos (91), dpa (5), Historia Photo (3), Messerschmidt (3), Rogge (2), Rudolf (1), Stetter (4)

Following the tradition established by Karl Baedeker in 1844, sights of particular interest and hotels and restaurants of particular quality are distinguished by one or two asterisks.

To make it easier to locate the various sights listed in the "A–Z" section of the guide, their coordinates on the large map of Paris are shown in red at the head of each entry.

Only a selection of hotels, restaurants and shops can be given; no reflection is implied, therefore, on establishments not included.

In a time of rapid change it is difficult to ensure that all the information given is entirely accurate and up to date and the possibility of error can never be entirely eliminated. Although the publishers can accept no responsibility for inaccuracies and omissions they are always grateful for corrections and suggestions for improvement.

5th Edition

© Baedeker Stuttgart
Original German edition

© 1991 Jarrold and Sons Ltd
English language edition worldwide

© 1991 The Automobile Association
United Kingdom and Ireland

US and Canadian edition
Prentice Hall Press

Distributed in the United Kingdom by the Publishing Division of The Automobile Association, Fanum House, Basingstoke, Hampshire, RG21 2EA.

The name Baedeker is a registered trademark
A CIP catalogue record for this book is available from the British Library.

Licensed user: Mairs Graphische Betriebe GmbH Co., Ostfildern-Kemnat bei Stuttgart

Reproductions: Golz Repro-Service GmbH, Ludwigsburg

Printed in Italy by G. Canale & C. S.p.A – Borgaro T.se – Turin

0 7495 0284 3 UK
0-13-094798-9 US & Canada

Contents

Arc de Triomphe · Arc du Carrousel · Arènes de Lutèce · Bagatelle · Bastille · Bois de Boulogne · Boulevards · Boulevard Saint-Michel · Bourse (des Valeurs) · Catacombes · Cemeteries · Centre Pompidou/Beaubourg · Champ-de-Mars · Champs Elysées · Chantilly · Châtelet · Cité · Collège de France · Conciergerie · La Défense · Dôme des Invalides · Ecole Militaire · Etoile · Eurodisneyland · Faubourg Saint-Germain · Faubourg Saint-Honoré · Fontainebleau · Fontaine des Innocents · Grand Palais · Les Halles · Hôtel de Ville · Ile Saint-Louis · Institut de France · Invalides · Jardin d'Acclimatation · Jardin des Plantes · Jeu de Paume · Louvre · Luxembourg · Madeleine · Maisons Laffitte · Malmaison · Marais · Marché aux Puces · Monnaie · Montmartre · Montparnasse · Mosquée · Musée Carnavalet · Musée Condé · Musée d'Art Moderne de la Ville de Paris · Musée de la Marine · Musée de l'Armée · Musée de l'Homme · Musée de l'Hôtel de Cluny · Musée des Monuments Français · Musée d'Orsay · Musée Giumet · Musée Picasso · Musée Rodin · Notre-Dame · Opéra · Palais Bourbon · Palais de Chaillot · Palais de Justice · Palais de la Découverte · Palais de Tokyo · Palais Royal · Panthéon · Pavillon de l'Arsenal · Petit Palais Place de la Concorde · Place des Vosges · Place du Tertre · Place Vendôme · Quais · Quartier Latin · Rambouillet · Rue de Rivoli · Rue Royale · Sacré-Cœur · Saint-Denis · Sainte-Chapelle · Saint-Etienne-du-Mont · Saint-Eustache · Saint-Germain-des-Prés · Saint-Germain-en-Laye · Saint-Germain-l'Auxerrois · Saint-Julien-le-Pauvre · Saint-Pierre-de-Montmartre · Saint-Séverin · Saint-Sulpice · Saint-Vincent-de-Paul · Seine Bridges · Sorbonne · Théâtre Français · Thermes · Tour Eiffel · Tour Saint-Jacques · Tuileries · UNESCO · Val-de-Grâce · Vaux-le-Vicomte · Versailles · Vidéothèque de Paris · La Villette · Vincennes · Zoo de Paris

Advance Booking · Airports · Antique Shops · Banks/Exchange Bureaus · Boat Trips · Breakdown service · Cafés/Salons de Thé · Calendar of Events · Camping · Car Rental · Chemists · Church Services · Cinemas · Circus · Curiosities · Currency/Currency Regulations · Customs Regulations · Department Stores · Diplomatic and Consular Offices · Electricity · Excursions · Fashion Houses · Galleries · Help for Handicapped · Hotels · Information · Libraries · Lost Property · Markets · Medical Emergencies · Museums · Music · Night Life · Parking · Parks and Gardens · Pets · Police · Post · Programme of Events · Public Holidays · Public Transport · Railway Stations · Restaurants · Shopping · Sightseeing · Sightseeing Programme · Sont et Lumière · Sport · Swimming Baths · Taxis · Telephone · Theatres · Time · Times of Opening · Tipping · Traffic · Travel Bureaus · Travel Documents · Travelling to Paris · Useful Telephone Numbers at a Glance

The Principal Sights at a Glance

Preface

This Pocket Guide to Paris is one of the new generation of Baedeker guides.

These pocket-size guides, illustrated throughout in colour, are designed to meet the needs of the modern traveller. They are quick and easy to consult, with the principal sights described in alphabetical order and practical details about opening times, how to get there, etc., shown in the margin.

Each guide is divided into three parts. The first part gives a general account of the city, its history, prominent personalities and so on; in the second part the principal sights are described; and the third part contains a variety of practical information designed to help visitors to find their way about and make the most of their stay.

The new guides are abundantly illustrated and contain numbers of newly drawn plans. At the back of the book is a large city map, and each entry in the main part of the guide gives the coordinates of the square on the map in which the particular monument, building, etc. is situated. Users of this guide, therefore, will have no difficulty in finding what they want to see.

Facts and Figures

Arms of the
City of Paris

General Information

Paris is the capital of France, the seat of the President of the Republic, of the Government and both Chambers of the French Parliament (National Assembly and Senate).

Capital

Northern France (Région Ile-de-France).

Region

Latitude 48° 50′ N; longitude 2° 20′ E; altitude 27–127 m (90–415 ft) (highest point: Montmartre, 127 m – 415 ft).

Geographical location

To Paris: from Great Britain: 010 33 1; from USA: 011 33 1; from Canada: 011 33 1.
From Paris: to Great Britain: 19 44; to USA: 19 1; to Canada: 19 1.

International dialling codes

The historic heart of Paris – rive droite, rive gauche, the area from Notre-Dame to the Etoile, from Montmartre to Montparnasse – extends over 20 sq. km (7·72 sq. miles) and in it live some half a million people. The extension of the town led to the establishment of a municipal area (ville and département) where in 1982 2,186,243 people lived in an area covering 105 sq. km (40·5 sq. miles). Today Greater Paris (agglomération parisienne) together with its suburbs and satellite towns covers an area of 1800 sq. km (695 sq. miles) and has a population of about 10 million. It is, therefore, one of the most densely populated cities in the world.

Area and Population

Paris is divided up into 20 "arrondissements" (precincts or wards) which are each further subdivided into four "quartiers" (quarters). When the poet Jean Cocteau called Paris a town made up of individual townships and villages he was alluding to the districts of the city which are also known as "quartiers" (or in many cases "faubourgs"). These traditional quartiers, whose popular names do not necessarily coincide with their official designation for administrative purposes, have in many cases retained their individuality and derive their names from villages that have subsequently been absorbed into the city (Montmartre, Chaillot), from churches (Saint-Germain de Prés), from buildings (Les Halles, Opéra) or from some special characteristic (Quartier Latin).
"Faubourg", literally "outside the town", means suburb, and as a rule these suburbs were named after the nearest village (hence Faubourg Montmartre was the suburb on the approach to the village of Montmartre). The suburbs outside today's city boundaries are called "banlieues".
A handy tip for finding your way around is that the arrondissements are arranged in a spiral that starts at the Louvre (1st arr.) then circles twice round the historic heart of Paris moving outwards from the Ile-de-la-Cité and ending (in the 20th arr.) at the Place de la Nation.

Arrondissements and quartiers

◀ *July Column in the Place de la Bastille*

General Information

Redevelopment

The 1960s saw the great wave of redevelopment in Paris – that is everything that was old was pulled down, whether it was necessary or not, and replaced by concrete "silos" serving as offices and dwellings. Areas of architectural monotony appeared coupled with a considerable alteration in the structure of the population. Today sanity has returned. Redevelopment means renewal on grounds of preservation. The most ambitious project of redevelopment was begun in 1985 in the east of Paris. By specific structural measures Mayor Chirac is trying to improve the quality of life and stimulate economic activity in this previously neglected area which extends over 40 sq. km (15·5 sq. miles). One million people live in this area and one-third of all the jobs in Paris are located here. The aim is to raise the status of the east of Paris and make it the equal of the west. A few facts will exemplify the size of the problem: 10,000 old dwellings are to be restored, 20,000 new ones are to be built, 45 ha (111 acres) of parks and gardens are to be laid out, 30 crèches and 50 primary schools will be provided. Some 300,000 sq. m (3,229,200 sq. ft) of office space and 200,000 sq. m (2,152,800 sq. ft) of space for trade and industry are planned. To improve transport facilities a bridge over the Seine is to be widened and a new one is to be built.

"banlieues 89"

An improvement in living conditions is also being actively sought in the suburbs where President Mitterand's plan "banlieues 89" is being put into effect. Building of satellite towns with publicly owned dwellings, controlled as to size but being individually designed, is intended to further community life and communications. Coming into being are Marne-la-Vallée in the east, Melun-Sénart in the south-east, Evry in the south, St-Quentin-en-Yvelines in the south-west and Cergy-Pontoise in the north-west. The unusual architecture of the Palacio d'Abraxas (1982) by Ricardo Bofill in Marne-la-Vallée and of his Belvedère de St-Christophe (1985) in Cergy-Pontoise has aroused lively comment.

Although the dimensions of the buildings may be controlled, this is no longer true of their extent; the area of Marne-la-Vallée alone extends over 18,000 ha (44,478 acres) and comprises 26 parishes – Paris has only 10,500 ha (25,945 acres). The banlieues and the existing territory of the city will later combine to become "Greater Paris", and the population in the year 2000 is expected to be some 15 million.

Administration

Together with the départements Hauts-de-Seine, Seine-St-Denis, Val-de-Marne, Yvelines, Essonne and Val d'Oise, Paris forms the Région Ile-de-France. Since 1977 the town has been both commune and département. The head of the civic administration is the elected maire (mayor) and leading each of the départements is a préfet (prefect) appointed by the government, as well as a prefect of police. The Conseil de Paris (city council) numbers 109 members and is at the same time the responsible Conseil Général of the département.

The Prefect of Paris is also Prefect of the Ile-de-France and in this capacity heads the Regional Council (Conseil Régional) which determines the budgetary plan of the region.

International organisations

Among the many international institutions which have their headquarters or are represented in Paris the three best known are: UNESCO (see Paris A–Z), here since 1946; the Secretariat of the Organisation for Economic Cooperation and Develop-

Hôtel de Ville

ment (OECD); and the European Headquarters of INTERPOL, the organisation of national criminal police forces.

Population and Religion

France is concentrated in Paris. Here on 2·2 per cent of the total area of the country, lives 18·8 per cent of the French population. The population of the actual core of the city (ville-département) is decreasing considerably because, especially in the city centre, very old buildings are being pulled down and less – but more expensive – living space is being created. On the other hand the density of population in the bordering départements has been growing at the rate of 3–4 per cent annually. Paris is not France, but the city is a magnet for workers from the whole of the country, the overseas départements and from abroad. Sixty per cent of Parisians are incomers, 6 out of 10 of these come from the provinces. Every French region is represented by its own people. Many suburbs are "firmly in the hands" of newcomers from the south-west, the Auvergne, and from eastern France. They celebrate their regional festivals and almost all of them publish their own newspaper. The proportion of foreign workers amounts to 12 per cent. First come the Algerians, then the Portuguese and Spaniards. In the Goutte d'Or in the east (now a region of redevelopment) the 20,000 people who live here belong to 40 different nationalities, most of them, however, are North African.

Paris is also a city of refugees and those seeking asylum from every country in the world. Very many people seeking asylum here come from South America and Indo-China. The 13th

Population

arrondissement is already called "Chinatown". Here there live predominantly Chinese and other Asians from Cambodia (70 per cent) and Vietnam (20 per cent) but also from Laos.

Religion

France is predominantly a Catholic country. Since 1905 the Church and the State have been officially separated. Paris is the See of an Archbishop and has 94 Catholic parishes. In addition there are 15 Greek and Russian Orthodox churches, 7 synagogues (over 220,000 orthodox Jews). There are 2 mosques for the 50,000 Muslims.

Communications

Port

Although the Port of Paris (Port Autonome) is declining in importance, as industry moves out of the city and freight has largely switched to road and rail, it is still France's major inland port. As the main transhipment areas now lie outside the city, the port installations on the Seine and the canals play nowadays only an ancillary role.

The pleasure boats, on the other hand, which cater entirely for the tourist trade, ply from moorings in the centre of the city.

Airports

The State Airports Company – Aéroport de Paris – administers Paris's three airports: Orly (in the S) and Le Bourget and Roissy-Charles de Gaulle (in the N). Altogether they represent Europe's second largest airport complex after London. Orly continues to handle the most passenger traffic (14·2 million passengers), having weathered the steep fall in numbers that followed the opening of Roissy-Charles de Gaulle Airport in 1974, while the latter has in the meantime become the largest handler of air freight. The importance of Le Bourget in this field has almost come to a standstill.

Rail, Métro, RER

Although it lies on the western edge of the continent of Europe Paris is a hub of international communications. Thanks to the siting of its rail terminals and the building of its underground system, the Métro (Chemin de Fer Métropolitain), Paris has managed to avoid the fate of other major cities that have seen their historical centres carved up by railway tracks.

Two large companies are responsible for carrying the 10 million· people or more that travel every day into, out of and through Paris by public transport. The State Railway Company (Société Nationale des Chemins de Fer), carries annually over 83 million long-distance travellers and over 500 million commuters. The RATP – which is part-owned by the State – records annually over 1·9 billion passengers using the Métro and almost a billion bus passengers. The RER, or Regional Express Network (Réseau Express Régional), a relatively new transport subsidiary of the RATP, carries each year over 240 million passengers. It operates four lines. The junction of the RER lines running from E to W and from N to S is the vast station of Châtelet-Les Halles. By the year 2000 three further RER lines and additional Métro stations will improve communications between the suburbs and the centre of Paris.

The Métro network, which has steadily been extended, has 15 lines, the longest stretch (Balard–Créteuil) is 22·1 km (14 miles) and the shortest (Gambetta–Porte des Lilas) is 1·3 km (0·8 mile). The average distance between stations is 543 m (592 yd) and the trains run at 1½-minute intervals in the rush hour and at 2–7-minute intervals at other times.

Bateau-Mouche on Seine

L'Etoille – La Défense

Gare du Nord

13

Fountains by Niki de St Phalle and Jean Tinguely outside the Pompidou Centre

Motorways

Paris is the hub of the French motorway network, its system of "autoroutes", almost all of which start (or finish), as they have always done, in Paris. The Autoroute du Nord (A1/E15) goes to Lille, with the A2/E19 branching off near Péronne to Belgium (for Brussels); the Autoroute de l'Est (A4/E50) leads to Germany via Reims–Metz–Strasbourg; the Autoroute du Sud (Autoroute du Soleil A6/E15) leads down to the South of France via Lyon while South-western France is served by the Autoroute l'Aquitaine (A10/E05), via Orléans–Tours–Poitiers–Bordeaux. Linking Paris with the West of France via Chartres and Le Mans is the Autoroute Océanie (A11/E50), and the Autoroute de Normandie (A13/E05 and E46) to Rouen and Caen.

The autoroutes all enter or leave Paris by the Boulevard Périphérique Extérieur, the outer ring-road encircling Paris and carrying between six and ten lanes of traffic. The autoroutes are built and operated, as in Italy, by private companies and are subject to tolls.

The other long-distance highways, the "routes nationales", are well engineered, often more direct and free of charge.

Culture

General

Despite an upsurge in the seventies of public interest in France's provinces and regions, Paris remains the focal point of power, knowledge, learning, employment opportunities, culture and pleasure. Here are found the major universities, the most extensive and interesting museums and libraries (La Bibliothèque Nationale with 11 million books the number increases every year by some 70,000), the greatest concentration of theatres and cinemas, all the larger and many of the smaller publishers of books and newspapers, the national radio and television stations.

From the time of the Impressionists until the beginning of the Second World War Paris was the art capital of the world and gave birth to or set the seal on the art movements of Impressionism, Symbolism, Fauvism, Cubism, Futurism and Surrealism in the École de Paris. Artists from all over Europe were involved: Picasso, Miró, Gris and Dali from Spain, Chagall and Soutine from Russia, Pascin from Bulgaria, Modigliani from Italy and Max Ernst and Hans Hartung from Germany.

After the Second World War New York took over from Paris as the internationally recognised headquarters of avant-garde art, but Paris remained in the top flight as an art centre. This is attested by the museums and the retrospective exhibitions of the collected works of important artists, as well as the three great exhibitions (salons) that take place; in the spring the Salon des Indépendants (paintings) and the Salon de Mai (sculpture) and in the autumn the Salon d'Automne (paintings). In 1985 the New Parisian Biennial took over from its predecessor the Biennial of Contemporary Art as another forum of modern art.

In addition there are the newly founded culture and museum centres which have contributed to the reputation of Paris as an art metropolis. In 1977 the Centre Pompidou (see A–Z) was opened as a cultural and art centre and it has since been altered and extended. Its influence and attraction remain unbroken. In 1984 Cartier founded in Jouy-en-Josas an artistic park as the centre of contemporary art for sculptors and painters; in the same year the Zénith concert hall was dedicated as the first part of a new cultural centre, the Parc de la Villette (see A–Z). Between 1985 and 1988 "La Grande Halle", the futuristic cinema "La Géode" and the huge "Musée des Sciences et Techniques" (nucleus of the Cité des Sciences et de l'Industrie) were all opened. In 1985 the Musée de Picasso (See A–Z) was inaugurated and in the following year the Musée d'Orsay opened its doors. By 1989 external work should be complete around the glass pyramid of the "Grand Louvre", where a vast underground leisure complex is being constructed (see A–Z, Louvre). The work of past and contemporary artists is on view all the year round in the Galeries which are concentrated in and around the districts of Saint-Germain-des-Prés, the Faubourg Saint-Honoré and Beaubourg.

Situated in the latter is the Centre Pompidou, the new centre for art and culture – known by most Parisians as the "Centre Beaubourg" after the name of the quarter – and it is undoubtedly the "Beaubourg" which is currently having the most vibrant impact and exerting the greatest pulling power on the Parisian art scene.

In addition to the 13 universities (the Sorbonne itself was split up into four universities in 1968), in which c. 300,000 students are enrolled, Paris also has its "Grandes Ecoles". Entry to these colleges is by competitive examination only and their graduates are sure of subsequently obtaining top posts in industry or the Civil Service. Among the most important are the École Polytechnique (engineers), École des Hautes Etudes Commerciales (managers), École Nationale d'Administration (Civil Ser-

Palais des Congrès

Théâtre Français

vice experts; many subsequent professional politicians), École Normale Supérieure (teachers, lecturers).

The most outstanding of the many research institutions is the Centre National de la Recherche Scientifique (national centre for scientific research).

There is also the Institut de France which, although not a college as such, is an immensely respected authority in the intellectual and scientific field. Rich in tradition, the Institut has five scientific academies of which the best known is the Académie Française.

Theatre

There are a great many theatres (see Practical Information) in and around the capital – about 150 according to the weekly programme published in "Pariscope", but for many years the productions did not awaken much interest in the rest of Europe. Then suddenly directors became household names, especially Ariane Mnouchkine with her "Théâtre du Soleil" in the "Cartoucherie" in the Bois de Vincennes. Among the most prominent directors who now work from time to time in Paris are Roger Planchon and George Lavandant from the Villerurbanne Theatre in Lyons and Patrice Chereau, who directed Alban Berg's "Lulu" at the Paris Opera. Claude Regy became especially well-known for his productions with linguistic perfectionists such as Marguerite Duras and Natalie Sarraute. Under President Mitterand artistic initiative was encouraged by generous state subsidies.

Since the 70s many well-known European figures have directed productions in Paris. Most of them work at the Comédie Française or at the Opera, which is also known as the

"Palais Garnier" after its builder. The names of Claus Peymann and Peter Stein are well known, as are Peter Brook in the "Bouffes du Nord" and Giorgio Strehler in the classical "Théâtre de l'Odéon".
Besides the many theatres with a classical repertoire there are several experimental theatres, particularly in the suburbs. The "boulevard-théâtres" and the "café-théâtres" are characteristic of Paris, particularly the latter which are experimental stages for the very new generation of theatrical groups.

For decades the Parisian music scene was considered old fashioned; but Rolf Liebermann, Director of the Opéra (see A–Z) from 1973 to 1980 was setting new trends and under Mitterand things really began to happen. First came Pierre Boulez, appointed as leader of IRCAM, a centre for research into the foundations of music, which was set up in the Centre Pompidou. Then in 1984 building of a new People's Opera House at the Bastille was begun, in the very place where once stood the notorious prison which was destroyed on 14 July 1789. The new Opera House was dedicated on 14 July 1989 for the bicentenary of the French Revolution. The Latin American Carlos Ott has designed a building with 2700 seats, where everyone will be able to see and hear equally well, which is not the case in the present Opera House which has 2200 seats (and 500 have no view of the stage) and which is considered too small. Therefore the new theatre will be devoted entirely to opera, and the Palais Garnier will be the home of ballet. Whether the new theatre will also contain video rooms and have film performances has not yet been decided; however there is no doubt that the Bastille Opera House will be the most modern in the world. A number of great concert halls (Auditorium de Radio-France, Salle Gaveau, Palais des Congrès, Salle Pleyel, Théâtre des Champs-Elysées and others) provide a wide range of classical music performed by well-known orchestras (Orchestre national de France, Orchestre de Paris, Nouvel Orchestre Philharmonique de Radio-France). New music can be heard at the annual Festival d'Automne. The popular Sunday concerts given by the Orchestre des Concerts Lamoureaux, the Concerts Colonne and the Orchestre Pasdeloup are permanent features of the Parisian musical scene (see Practical Information – Music).
Lovers of classical ballet are recommended to visit the ballet performances staged at the Opéra and other theatres, depending on the season. While many churches are venues for excellent concerts and recitals of Church music, such as Notre-Dame on Sunday evenings, a different audience is catered for in the popular music halls, Olympia and Bobino, the Théâtre de la Ville and the Palais des Congrès, with their varied programmes of entertainment by the top names in French and international light music.
Spectacular combinations of music and dancers are the speciality of the Revues staged by the world-famous Moulin Rouge, Follies Bergère and the Lido, the last strongholds of the traditional French "can can".
Claiming to be more exclusive, esoteric, exotic and erotic are the "way-out dragshows" at the Alcazar and Paradis Latin and the stylish striptease at the Crazy Horse Saloon (see Practical Information – Night Life).

Music and Dance

Place de la Défense

Industry and Commerce

Economic Structure

Over 4.5 million people work in Greater Paris, that is one in five of all employed in France. About one million commute daily from the suburbs. However, since the end of the war the number of jobs available has tended to favour the surrounding départements of the Ile-de-France Région. In 1954 Paris accounted for 55% of the Région's jobs; in 1982 it was still as high as 39·1%. In 1986 the percentage of unemployed in Paris was 10% whereas in the Ile-de-France Région it was 8·4%. Between 1972 and 1985 about 70,000 jobs disappeared in the Région.

Employment figures have been falling as industry moves out of the capital and is replaced by companies in the constantly expanding service sector. Over 73% of all employees are engaged in this sector, 20% in industry, 6% in the building trades and barely 1% in agriculture.

Modern architecture reflects the increasing importance of the tertiary sector. Examples of this fashion include: the office complex of "Le Grand Ponant" (1989; architect Olivier Clément Cacoub), a huge glass and metal construction on the site of the former Citroën factory; "La Grande Arche", also completed in 1989, the bicentenary of the Revolution; and the still unfinished "Tour de Folie" in the expanding commercial district of La Défense.

Industries and Crafts

Industries traditionally located in Paris are those concerned with electronics, precision engineering, timber, textiles, pharmaceuticals, chemicals, aircraft and motor manufacturing – the

Renault works at Boulogne-Billancourt are the largest in the Région.

The metal and engineering industries, timber, textiles and chemicals have been particularly affected by the drift away from the City, although most companies still retain their head offices in Paris. Their reasons for leaving include measures aimed at decentralisation, environmental protection costs and companies' inability to expand when necessary because land prices are too high.

Those left are mainly the small and medium-sized firms, often midway between a craft and an industry, which still largely determine the look of their "quartier"; ready-to-wear trade (2nd arr.), newspapers and printing (2nd and 9th arr.), publishers (6th arr.), metalworking and precision engineering (10th, 11th and 12th arr.).

Craftsmen's products are traditionally to be found in the furniture workshops in the Faubourg Saint-Antoine (11th and 12th arr.) and the leatherworking district in the Marais (3rd arr. – see entry) while jewellery is fashioned in the Marais and the quarter between Opéra, Rue Royale and Place Vendôme (see entries). The highly lucrative "haute couture" trade is centred in the Faubourg Saint-Honoré (see entry).

In France the services sector (financial and insurance institutions in the 8th and 9th arr., public administration in the 7th and 8th arr., transport, real estate and other service industries) also includes the wholesale and retail trade.

Services

There are four centres for trade fairs and exhibitions – Parc des Expositions, CNIT, Parc des Expositions Paris-Nord, Parc des Expositions du Bourget. In addition to the Stock Exchange (see A–Z Bourse) there is also the Commercial Exchange.

Congresses, Trade Fairs and Exchanges

Since the market halls of Les Halles in the centre of Paris were demolished in 1969 the "stomach of Paris" is located outside the city in the southern suburb of Rungis where it occupies 600 hectares (1483 acres) and daily supplies the City and Greater Paris with thousands of tonnes of fresh fruit and vegetables, meat and other foodstuffs. Rungis also stores 25 million hectolitres (565 million gallons) of wine, 6 million (136 million gallons) of them for Paris. Over 12,000 buyers come here annually, and approximately 2½ million tonnes of produce account for a turnover of about 45 billion francs every year.

Rungis

Famous People

Honoré de Balzac
(20.5.1799–18.8.1850)

Honoré de Balzac is regarded as being the founder of social realism in literature: eschewing the Romantic style of his period, he brilliantly described his characters and their settings in minute and realistic detail, and portrayed them caught up in the interplay of social forces and human passions.

His great work is "La Comédie Humaine", a series of 40 novels spanning French society from the Revolution to the Restoration. The most important novels in this series include "La Peau de Chagrin" (1831), "La Femme de Trente Ans" (1831–44), "Le Colonel Chabert" (1832), "Eugénie Grandet" (1833), "Le Médecin de Campagne" (1833), "Père Goriot" (1835), "Le Lys dans la Vallée" (1836), "César Birotteau" (1838), "Les Illusions Perdues" (1837–43), "Splendeurs et Misères des Courtisanes" (1839–47), "La Cousine Bette" (1846), "Le Cousin Pons" (1847). His other great work is the collection of short stories, "Contes Drolatiques" (1832–7). However, his few plays (including "Mercadet ou le Faiseur" (1845) earned little acclaim.

In all Balzac was the author of 90 novels, 30 short stories and 5 (unsuccessful) plays. Driven by business failures, risky speculations and an extravagant life-style to produce this enormous literary output, he ruined his health and died, worn-out, when only 51. Shortly before his death he married his great friend, the Polish Countess Evelina Hanska-Rzewuska.

Jean Cocteau
(5.7.1889–11.10.1963)

Jean Cocteau was an artist of great versatility, able to express and combine a number of different talents. Not only was he a successful author ("Le Grand Ecart", "Les Enfants terribles"), film director ("La Belle et la Bête", "L'Eternel Retour"), scriptwriter ("Les Enfants du Paradis"), playwright ("Orphée"), painter, choreographer and librettist (for operas and ballets scored by Honegger, Stravinsky and Milhaud), he also embodied to a particular degree that quality of "esprit" – lightness, sharpness and brilliance of wit – for which others so admire the French.

In the vanguard of radical and literary movements, Cocteau played a decisive part in every manifestation of the avant-garde and was for decades one of the most fascinating celebrities on the French literary scene. His work encompasses Futurism and Dadaism but is more likely to be classified as a whole under the later heading of Surrealism.

In 1955 he became a member of the Académie Française.

Victor Hugo
(26.2.1802–22.5.1885)

Victor Hugo, the son of an officer in the Napoleonic armies, was, with his plays, novels, writings and lyric and epic poetry, the leading figure among the French Romantics, whose programme he framed in the prologue to his play "Cromwell" (1827) and whose journal "La Muse Française" he founded and published. After the success of his poems ("Odes et Ballades", 1826) and his play "Hernani" (1830), his novel "Notre-Dame de Paris" (The Hunchback of Notre Dame) brought him fresh triumphs and its colourful and lively portrayal of life in medieval Paris inspired a sympathetic reappraisal of Gothic architecture (see Saint-Denis). In 1841 Hugo was made a member of the Académie Française.

After his daughter's suicide in 1843 Hugo temporarily lost his

Honoré de Balzac

Victor Hugo

Napoleon I

creative writing powers. He turned to politics (member of the Constituent and Legislative Assemblies, Presidential Candidate 1848) and although at first a sympathiser of Louis-Napoleon, he later became his bitter enemy when Louis seized power in 1851 and had himself proclaimed Emperor. Hugo was then forced into exile in the Channel Islands and became the idol of the radical Opposition.

After his return (1870) he completed "La Légende des Siècles" (1859–83), a masterly collection of epic poems.

In 1885 his remains were disinterred, in a State ceremony, from their resting-place at the Arc de Triomphe and re-interred in the Panthéon.

Other works: "Les Orientales" (poems), "Les Feuilles d'Automne" (poems), "Marion de Lorme" (play), "Lucrèce Borgia" (play), "Les Voix Intérieures" (poems), "Les Burgraves" (play), "Les Misérables" (novel), "William Shakespeare" (writings), "Les Travailleurs de la Mer" (Toilers of the Sea), "L'Homme qui rit" (novels).

Henri IV, still known today as "le Bon Roi Henri" (good King Henry), became King of Navarre in 1562 and was the leader of the Huguenots. Through his marriage with Margaret, the sister of Charles IX, he sought to reconcile the Catholics and the Protestants. This was prevented by the Massacre of St Bartholomew when, on the night of 23 August 1572, the flower of the Huguenot nobility, in Paris for the wedding, were murdered, together with thousands of fellow Protestants, on the orders of Catherine de Medici, the Queen Mother. Henri only saved his own life by renouncing his faith and he was held prisoner at the Court until he fled in 1576.

After the death of King Henri III (1589) Henri was the rightful successor to the throne but it was not until 1594, after long and bitter opposition and Henri's acceptance of Catholicism ("Paris is well worth a Mass"), that he was crowned the first king of the House of Bourbon.

Once king, Henri IV strove to restore French prosperity after the religious wars by promulgating the Edict of Nantes (1598), which secured religious freedom and equality of civil rights, reorganising the State's finances and opening up his country through the building of roads. As legend has it, his wish was that "in his kingdom every peasant should have a chicken in the pot on Sundays".

Henry IV
(Henry of Navarre,
13.12.1553–14.5.1610)

His reign saw the start of the colonisation of Canada and, with the restoration of central power to the monarchy, France was well and truly set on the road to absolutism.
Henry was assassinated in 1610.

Napoleon I
(15.8.1769–5.5.1821)

Napoleon Bonaparte, the son of a Corsican noble, won rapid promotion in the French Revolutionary Army to become a brigadier at the age of 24. As Commander-in-Chief in France and in the Italian and Egyptian campaigns he achieved a position of power that enabled him to overthrow the Directory (which after Robespierre's Reign of Terror was the supreme governing body of the State) and to seize power for himself as First Consul. Supported by plebiscite he made himself Consul for life in 1802 and finally, in 1804, France's first Emperor (Napoleon I).
The traditional enmity with England led him into wars with the Grand Alliance, the coalition led by England, and the conquest of Prussia and Austria. He seized Portugal and Spain in order to bring England to her knees through a continental blockade and finally he aimed at mastery of the whole of Europe by planning to conquer Russia which opposed the continental blockade.
The failure of the Russian campaign, defeat at the Battle of Leipzig (1813) and the occupation of Paris by the Allies forced Napoleon to abdicate (1814) and go into exile on the island of Elba. In 1815 he attempted to win back power in the famous 100 days but his troops were finally defeated at the Battle of Waterloo. He was banished to the British island of St Helena in the South Atlantic where he died in 1821. In 1840 his remains were brought back from St Helena to Paris to be interred, with great pomp and ceremony, under the Dôme des Invalides (see entry). Unlike his nephew, Louis-Napoleon (Napoleon III), Napoleon has lived on in the hearts of the French. His image as saviour of the Revolution was glorified by the Romantic movement (especially Victor Hugo) and monuments to him can still be seen today in every French town (in Paris he stands, in the garb of a Roman Emperor, on the column in the Place Vendôme (see entry)).
In fact the "Code Civil" (the first civil legal code) which Napoleon drew up in 1804, codified the laws relating to property and society that were the fundamental achievements of the Revolution.

Edith Piaf
(19.12.1915–11.10.1963)

Known as the "Paris Sparrow" ("Piaf" is Parisian slang for Sparrow), the diseuse Edith Piaf (actually Edith Giovanna Gassion) began to earn money as a singer at the age of nine because of her distinctive voice. She was a child of the people and for the whole of her life she indulged in the typical "gouaillerie parisienne", the banter of her native city. With her father she entertained in the bars of Parisian suburbs, and as she grew older she performed first in the streets and later in night clubs. Ultimately she rose to fame, and the little chanteuse, who had numerous lovers and friends, among whom were Charles Aznavour, Yves Montand, Eddie Constantine and Jean Cocteau (see entry), had her greatest success when she appeared at the Carnegie Hall in New York in 1956.
In her chansons, which combined suburban romanticism with the inimitable tendency of the Parisian towards mockery, Piaf sang of love, of sailors, of prostitutes and of Foreign Legionaries. Among her best-known songs are "La Vie en Rose", "Milord" by Georges Moustaki, and last but not least "Je ne

regrette rien" which the singer, prematurely aged by drink and drugs, called her personal creed.

The Spaniard Pablo Picasso (actually Ruiz y Picasso), who was born in Malaga, was not only a painter and sculptor but also a graphic artist and a writer. He is considered the leading artist of modern times and for more than eight decades he set his seal on 20th century art. He first studied with his father; at 15 he entered the Barcelona art school and from 1896 he attended the Academy at Madrid. There followed several visits to Paris and in 1904 he made France his adopted country. A melancholy feeling stamps his early work which, according to the principal colours that he used, can be divided into a "blue" period (1901–4) and a "pink" period (1906).

With his epoch-making work "Damoiselles d'Avignon", completed in 1907, Picasso laid the foundations which enabled him and Georges Braques – and later also Juan Gris and Fernand Léger – to develop the cubist movement.

Although he was still occupied with cubist and geometric forms, Picasso returned in the years following the First World War to figurative representation. He was now approaching the art of the Surrealists. For a long time his representation of form had been geometric, but now it was organic and his pictures were characterised by themes of movement, with figures bursting with vitality. At the end of the 1920s he was also increasingly occupied with sculpture.

Cycles of pictures based on ancient texts, works concerned with the Spanish Civil War, with destruction caused by armed conflict and with mutilation – "Guernica" (1937) – were a further climax. Representations of bullfights, portraits and variations on the theme of "artist and model" now became his principal subjects. Parallel with his protest at the brutality of war which he expressed in his pictures, his political activity also increased and this led to his becoming a member of the Communist Party from 1944 until 1956.

Pablo Picasso
(25.10.1881–8.4.1973)

The existentialist writer and philosopher Jean-Paul Sartre was the son of middle-class parents in Paris, where he went to school and university. In the thirties he taught philosophy in Le Havre and Berlin; then during the Second World War, after a period as a prisoner of war in 1940–1, he became an active member of the French Resistance. In 1945 he abandoned his teaching career and founded a literary and political review, the "Temps Modernes". In 1973 he was one of the founders of the newspaper "Libération". He became a member of the French Communist Party, but left it in 1956 after fiercely criticising the Soviet intervention in Hungary. His political commitment grew stronger in the late sixties and early seventies, when he attacked the Warsaw Pact intervention in Czechoslovakia, chaired the Vietnam Tribunal initiated by Bertrand Russell and defended various left-wing organisations.

Jean-Paul Sartre
(1905–1980)

History of the City

300 B.C.–A.D. 360	From 300 B.C. onwards Celtic Gauls have settlements on the island in the Seine (today: Ile-de-la-Cité). Their settlement "louk-teih" (place of the marsh) is conquered and destroyed by the Romans (first mention of "Lutetia Parisii" in Caesar's "De Bello Gallico" 53 B.C.). The Gallo-Roman town of Lutetia is founded and renamed Parisia after its inhabitants, the Parisii, by the Roman Caesar Julian Apostata in A.D. 360.
A.D. 508	After defeating the Alemanni in the east and the last of the Romans in northern France, and conquering western France up to the Pyrénées, Clovis I, the King of the Franks, chooses Paris for the capital of his kingdom.
987	Hugh Capet becomes king of France. After being neglected under the rule of the Carolingians (Charlemagne's Court was in Aachen), the Capetians make Paris the capital of the kingdom of France.
1163	Under Louis VII work is begun on parts of the Early Gothic choir of the Cathedral of Notre-Dame.
1180–1223	Philippe II (Philippe-Auguste), considered the founder of France as a nation and great power, drives the English out of their French territories. In his reign Paris becomes a large residential city (c. 100,000 inhabitants).
1200	Philippe II builds the fortress of the Louvre to protect Paris as the seat of his Court.
1226–70	Saint Louis (Louis IX) strengthens his power base against the feudal nobles, establishes an effective administration and a supreme royal court of justice (Parlement) in Paris and allows the burghers of the capital to form their own (police) force instead of the royal guard. After the death of the last "Staufer" emperor (Frederick II, d. 1250) Louis IX becomes Europe's most powerful ruler and makes Paris the most important metropolis of the High Middle Ages.
1253	Robert de Sorbon, the cathedral Canon, founds a college (later to become the Sorbonne) for poor theological students.
1358	Murder of Etienne Marcel, Provost of the Paris merchants, who had led the first civil uprising against the monarchy. The revolt collapses with his death.
1337–1453	During the Hundred Years War with England Paris is occupied twice by the English and is not finally recaptured until 1436.
1527	François I makes the City of Paris once more the seat of the royal court after its long absence from the city. He brings many Italian artists to France (including Andrea del Sarto, Leonardo da Vinci) and is responsible for building Paris's first Renaissance buildings (Town Hall).

Catherine de Medici, widow of Henri II and the Regent of France, has plans drawn up for the Palace of the Tuileries.	1564
The religious wars reach their peak with the Massacre of St Bartholomew when on the night of 23 August 3000 Huguenots are murdered in Paris alone.	1572
Founding of the Académie Française by Cardinal Richelieu, Chief Minister of Louis XIII.	1635
Louis XIV moves the Court to Versailles.	1682
The French Revolution begins with the storming of the Bastille on 14 July – the present national holiday.	1789
The first French Republic is proclaimed on 21 September. Four months later Louis XVI is guillotined in the Place de la Révolution (now the Place de la Concorde).	1792
Under Napoleon Bonaparte, first Consul of the Republic, France is divided up into 90 "départements", each headed by a Prefect appointed by the Minister of the Interior. Paris comes under the Département de la Seine.	1800
Napoleon Bonaparte crowns himself Emperor Napoleon I in Notre-Dame.	1804
The Allies occupy Paris, Napoleon is defeated. The monarchy is temporarily reinstated with Louis XVIII.	1814
Napoleon manages to regain power but the 100 days are soon ended with his defeat at Waterloo.	1815
First railway line in France – from Paris to Saint-Germain-en-Laye.	1837
The February Revolution finally abolishes the monarchy and the Second French Republic is proclaimed. Prince Charles Louis-Napoleon Bonaparte (later Napoleon III) is elected President of the Republic by plebiscite on 10 December.	1848
A fresh plebiscite (97 per cent in favour) grants Louis-Napoleon the title of "Emperor of the French by the Grace of God and the Will of the Nation" (Emperor Napoleon III).	1852
Baron Haussmann, Prefect of Paris, begins the massive undertaking of replanning Paris (boulevards, stations, parks, sewers).	1853
France loses the Franco-Prussian War. The Third French Republic is established in Paris (4 September 1870).	1870–1
The workers' uprising, the Paris Commune (March–May 1871), is bloodily suppressed (30,000 dead).	
Completion of the Eiffel Tower for the World Fair in Paris.	1889
Opening of the first métro line (Porte Maillot–Porte-de-Vincennes) for the World Fair.	1900

History of the City

1940–4	Occupation of Paris by the German Army. The City is liberated by the troops of the Allies on 26 August 1944.
1962	As Minister of Culture, the French writer and scholar André Malraux promulgates a law (the "Loi Malraux") for the conservation and rehabilitation of historical buildings whereby the monuments are given a face-lift and the Marais Quarter is rediscovered and reinstated.
1964	The number of France's départements is increased to 95 by the administrative reorganisation of the Région Parisienne.
1968	Student protest in the Sorbonne and the Latin Quarter against the cultural and social policies of President de Gaulle. As workers join in the demonstrations and wild-cat strikes take place, the trade unions declare their solidarity and a General Strike brings the whole of France to a standstill.
1976	Greater Paris has its name changed from Région Parisienne to Région Ile-de-France.
1977	The City of Paris, previously administered by a government-appointed Prefect gets its first elected Mayor (his 11 predecessors in office were appointed by the government of the day). The Centre National d'Art et de Culture Georges Pompidou is opened on 31 January.
1981	The super-modern shopping complex Forum des Halles opens on the site of the former Les Halles (market halls).
1982	Work on renovating the Eiffel Tower begins. The work is to be finished in 1989.
1983	New market halls are completed between the Paris airports of Le Bourget and Roissy – Charles de Gaulle. A concert hall, the first part of the new cultural centre of La Villette, is dedicated; one year later the exhibition hall is finished and in 1986 the technical museum.
1984	President Mitterand approves the plan for a glass pyramid in the Court of Honour of the Louvre as a new entrance to the museum. There is violent argument between supporters and opponents. Walls of old fortifications are discovered during work on the Louvre.
1985	The city administration begins the redevelopment of the east of Paris. The Picasso Museum is opened. Building of the new Opera House in the Place de la Bastille. Opening of the "Grande Halle" in the Parc de la Villette.
1986	The Conservative Jacques Chirac is elected Prime Minister. He has to "co-exist" with the Socialist President Mitterand who remains in office until 1988. In December there are violent protests by students against the planned university law (which includes "numerus clausis" and competition between individual French universities. Bloody conflicts lead to a postponement of the new proposals. The Musée d'Orsay on the left bank of the Seine opens its doors.

Great Jubilee exhibition in the centre Pompidou "Ten years of Beaubourg". The Impressionist paintings from the Jeu de Paume are again on view in the new Musée d'Orsay. A start is made with the planned extension of the Gare Montparnasse.

1987

François Mitterand is re-elected President (April/June). He names Michel Rocard as the new Prime Minister. As a result of elections to the National Assembly both the Socialists and the centre coalition of the URC (Union du Rassemblement et du Centre) of Gaullists and the middle-class centre parties lose their absolute majority.
A new Arab cultural centre, the Institut de Monde Arabe, is opened, and in December another museum of Parisian history opens in the Pavillon de l'Arsenal.

1988

Bicentenary of the French Revolution. Opening of the huge new opera house at the Place de la Bastille and dedication of the "Grande Arche" (triumphal arch of human rights) at La Défense.

1989

Paris A–Z

Académie Française

See Institut de France

⚓* Arc de Triomphe (triumphal arch)   E4

The Arc de Triomphe de l'Etoile is dedicated to the glory of the
victorious French armies of the Revolution and of the First
Empire.

Napoleon ordered the building of this mighty edifice in 1806
but did not live to see its completion (in 1836, architect: Chalgrin). In 1920 the triumphal arch became the site of the Tomb of
the Unknown Soldier.

The arch is 50 m (164 ft) high and 45 m (148 ft) wide and its
façades are covered with huge sculptures and friezes depicting
the departure, the victories and the glorious return of the
armies. (The inner surfaces bear the names of the generals and
of other battles.)

From the viewing platform (lift) there is a remarkable pan-
oramic view of the 12 avenues converging on the star-shaped
square (see Place de l'Etoile, today officially Place Charles de
Gaulle) and the straight line of the Champs-Elysées–Concorde–
Louvre on one side and, on the other, the tower blocks of La
Défense, (NE) Montmartre with Sacré-Cœur, (SE) the Eiffel
Tower, the Dôme des Invalides and the Maine-Montparnasse
tower.

Every evening at 6.30 a small delegation crosses the square. It
consists of members of the Old Soldiers' Association who
rekindle the flame at the Tomb of the Unknown Soldier. (On
11 November, the anniversary of the Armistice of 1918, re-
membrance services are held here for the Fallen of both
World Wars.)

A little museum below the platform houses an exhibition on the
history of the building of the monument and mementoes of
Napoleon and from the First World War.

Location
Place Charles de Gaulle
(16th arr.)

Métro
Charles de Gaulle (Etoile)

Buses
22, 30, 31, 52, 73, 92

Times of opening
1 Oct.–31 March 10 a.m.–
5 p.m.; 1 April–30 Sept.
10 a.m.–6 p.m. (except public
holidays)

Entrance fee

Arc du Carrousel   H5

The Arc de Triomphe du Carrousel, the former gateway to the
courtyard of the Tuileries Palace, is a copy of the triumphal arch
of Septimius Severus (Rome).

It was erected (1806–8), to commemorate Napoleon's glorious
victories, by the architects Percier and Fontaine. The Quadriga
(team of four horses) on the top is the work of the sculptor F.-J.
Bosio (1828).

When the Tuileries Palace was destroyed the arch ceased to be
the gateway to the Palace and today looks rather isolated.

Location
Place du Carrousel, between
the two wings of the Louvre
(1st arr.)

Métro
Louvre, Palais-Royal

Buses
27, 39, 48, 81, 95

◀ Arc de Triomphe

Arènes de Lutèce (Roman amphitheatre) J5

Location
Rue des Arènas,
Rue de Navarre
(5th arr.)

Métro
Monge

Buses
47, 67

The remains of the Roman amphitheatre give an idea of the huge size of the original structure: the elliptical arena (56×48 m – 184×157 ft) is almost the same size as the interior of the Colosseum in Rome. Gladiator and animal fights as well as theatrical performances were staged here.

It was built about A.D. 200 and although it had only 36 rows of seating, its 17,000 seats could hold almost the entire population of what was then the Roman town of Lutetia. The individual seats have the names of the "season ticket holders" scratched on them.

Assemblée Nationale

See Palais Bourbon

*Bagatelle (Bagatelle park and castle) B4

Location
Bois de Boulogne
(Sèvres–Neuilly road,
16th arr.)

Métro
Pont de Neuilly

Buses
43, 144, 244

Times of opening
Park: daily 8.30 a.m.–
7 p.m.;
in winter 6 p.m.

In the NW part of the Bois de Boulogne (see entry) lies a small château in an English garden, both bearing the name "Bagatelle".

These charming grounds date from the end of the 18th c. The young Count of Artois (later Charles X) bet his sister-in-law Marie-Antoinette that he could have the little château built and the park landscaped in only three months. An international competition for rose-growers is held here each June. Besides the Orangerie, with its evergreens, and a Japanese watergarden, the northernmost of the four lakes with its splendid display of water-lilies is of especial interest for visitors who can also visit the park on summer evenings when it is floodlit (between 9.30 and 11). Entrance Fee

Bastille (Place de la Bastille) K5

Location
centre–E (3rd arr.)

Métro
Bastille

Buses
20, 29, 65, 69, 76, 86, 87, 91

Today there is a huge square on what was the site of the hated fortified prison of La Bastille. Anyone hoping to find the remains of the Bastille is in for a disappointment; it was completely demolished within a few months of being stormed on 14 July 1789.

The Bastille (small bastion) was built between 1370 and 1382 in the reign of Charles V. The fortifications of the bastion of Saint-Antoine protected Charles V's newly built city wall at this point. The Bastille proved poor protection and was captured on several occasions. The people began to hate the fortress when Cardinal Richelieu, Louis XIII's Minister, made it the State prison, where prisoners (including the Marquis de Sade) were held without trial merely by order of the King ("lettre de cachet").

The Bastille was often "full up", but on 14 July 1789, when the French Revolution began with the storming of the Bastille, the liberators could find only seven prisoners in the cells. These were petty criminals and a couple of madmen, but the mob gave them a triumphant reception.

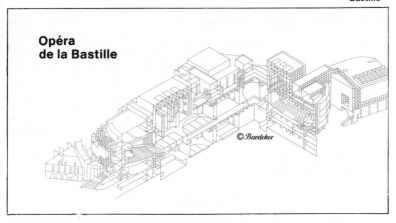

**Opéra
de la Bastille**

© Baedeker

François René, Vicomte de Chateaubriand describes the taking
of the Bastille in his "Mémoires d'Outre-Tombe": "On 14 July
the Bastille was stormed. As an observer I was a witness to this
act against a couple of veterans and a faint-hearted governor:
had the gates been locked the people would never have forced
their way into the fortress. I saw how two or three cannon-shots
were fired, not by the veterans but by the Gardes Françaises
who had already occupied the towers. De Launay (the Governor) was fetched from his hiding-place and after much man
handling was slaughtered on the steps of the town hall;
Flesselles, leader of the merchants, had his skull shattered by a
pistol-shot; this was a spectacle much enjoyed by the heartless
onlookers. As in the Roman street-fights under Otto and Vitel-
lius, people abandoned themselves to un-bridled orgies in the
midst of this slaughter. The victors of the Bastille, drunk with
happiness and hailed as conquerors in the taverns, were driven
round in carriages, prostitutes and Sans-culottes began to hold
sway and keep them company.
"Passers-by raised their hats with the respect of fear to these
heroes, some of whom died from exhaustion at the height of
their triumph. The number of keys to the Bastille was constantly multiplying, such keys sent to pompous nincompoops
in every corner of the world. . . . The experts proceeded to
conduct the post-mortems on the Bastille. Temporary cafés
were set up under canvas; the crowds came as to the fair . . .
countless carriages drove past or stopped at the foot of the
towers, whose stones were pulled down amidst great clouds of
dust. . . . It was a rallying-point for the most famous speakers,
the best-known writers, the most celebrated painters, the most
distinguished actors and actresses, the most popular dancers,
the most aristocratic foreigners, the great lords of the Court and
envoys from all over Europe; the old France had come here to
say farewell for ever, the new France had come here to make its
début."

The July Column (with a statue of Liberty regilded in 1989)   Colonne de Juillet
stands today in the Place de la Bastille. It does not, however,
commemorate 14 July, the French National holiday, but the
Republicans killed during the July Revolution of 1830 whereby

Bastille

Opéra de la Bastille

Charles X was deposed and the Citizen-King Louis-Philippe brought to power.

Bastille quarter

Since the mid-80s several galleries have opened in the Bastille quarter. Well-known gallery owners such as Leif Stähle, president of the Swedish art fair, exhibit in the Rue de la Charonne, and works by Andy Warhol and Mimmo Rotella are shown here by André Lavignes. In the Rue de la Roquette, opposite the avant-garde Théâtre de la Bastille, the Donguy brothers and others exhibit experimental art and photography.

A free interpretation of the flag of the Revolution in the national colours of blue, white and red can be seen in the huge mosaic (1988) by Pierre Guerchet-Jeannin in the Bastille Métro station. (picture page 194).

A model of the former Bastille is on view in the Musée Carnavalet (see entry).

*Opéra de la Bastille

Information
11 bis Rue Daumesnel
(12th arr.)
tel. 43 42 92 92

The new Opera House on the site of the former prison was opened on July 14th 1989. It was designed by Uraguay-born Canadian Carlos Ott. The prestigious rectangular building with curving sides occupies a space of 15 hectare (37 acres). The stepped lattice-work glass façade has a cool and functional appearance. The bright foyer forms a kind of semicircle around the auditorium, the tent-like ceiling of which harmonises well with the rows of white seats below. The main opera house has 2700 seats and a huge stage which is surrounded by five subsidiary stages of identical dimensions on the sides and at

the rear. In addition the complex includes an amphitheatre accommodating an audience of 500, a studio with 280 seats, as well as rehearsal stages, a library and a videothèque.
Immediately adjoining the opera house is the "Tour d'Argent" restaurant which had been destroyed but which has been rebuilt as an historic replica.

Beaubourg

See Centre Pompidou

* Bois de Boulogne

A–D 3–6

The 865 hectare (2137 acre) park is one of the most popular recreation areas in the immediate vicinity of Paris. It is right on the western edge of the city, bounded on the E by the Boulevard Périphérique and on the W by the Seine. It is criss-crossed by footpaths, bridle-paths and roads.

The name of the park comes from a church (Notre-Dame-de-Boulogne-le-Petit) built by the inhabitants of a village on this spot in the 14th c. in honour of their place of pilgrimage, Boulogne-sur-Mer.

For a long time a royal hunting ground as well as a bandits' hideout, the forest had a wall built round it in the 16th c., during the reign of Henri II. Louis XIV ordered his Minister Colbert to have a park laid out with paths converging in the form of a star, and opened it to the public. During the Regency (early 18th c.), and again from the middle of the 19th c. onwards, the park was a meeting-place for the fashionable world. This was mainly due to the building of racecourses at Longchamp and Auteuil (c. 1850) and to the new landscaping of the park at about the same time by the Prefect, Baron Haussmann. (Napoleon III had given the park to the city.) Nowadays many people spend their leisure hours here going for walks, picnicking in the meadows, rowing or simply doing nothing. As evening falls there is a different public with different interests: night-time prostitution is well established (and so is voyeurism).

Anyone who is short of time for their visit to Paris should take a drive through the Bois de Boulogne by car.

The main things to see are:
1. Bagatelle (see entry – park and castle).
2. Grande Cascade (large waterfall) at the Carrefour de Longchamp.
3. Auteuil racecourse: this adjoins the western end of the upper lake. Its grandstand is on the slope of a small hill (Butte Mortemart) made when the two lakes were excavated. Only steeplechasing takes place here (see Practical Information – Sport).
4. Longchamp racecourse (1857): one of the best known in the world (room for 10,000 racegoers, see Practical Information – Sport).
5. See Jardin d'Acclimatation (children's amusement park with Musée des Arts et Traditions Populaires (see entry) (Museum of Folklore).
6. Lac Inférieur (lower lake): this is over 1000 m (1100 yd) long and 1·5 m (5 ft) deep. Those not energetic enough to walk

Location
On the western outskirts of the city

Métro
Sablons, Porte Maillot, Porte Dauphiné, Porte d'Auteuil

Buses
32, 33, 43, 52, 63, PC

round the lake may like to take the ferry (from the W bank) to the two islands (café-restaurant) or hire a rowing-boat (at the northern end).

7. Lac Supérieur (upper lake): it is also possible to walk round this 400 m (438 yd) long lake (also artificial).

8. Pré Catelan: these gardens, named after a troubadour (Armand Catelan) who was murdered here about 1300, contain two small châteaux and a majestic 200-year-old copper beech. The Jardin Shakespeare (guided tours: 11 a.m., 1.30, 3, 5.00 and 5.30 p.m.) contains all the plants mentioned in the plays of William Shakespeare.

Bois de Vincennes

See Vincennes

Boulevards

The word "boulevard" (cognate with the English "bulwark") means a street built on the site of fortifications.

It is easy to see from a map of the city how Paris has grown outwards from the centre (Ile-de-la-Cité) in a ring formation: the boulevards lie round this centre like the rings for every year of a tree.

The first ring (on the line of the 14th c. city wall) is formed by the Boulevards Beaumarchais, du Temple, the "Grands Boulevards" of Saint-Martin, Saint-Denis, Bonne-Nouvelle, Poissonnière, Montmartre, des Italiens, des Capucines, de la Madeleine and – linked by the Rue Royale, Place de la Concorde (see entries) and Pont de la Concorde – the Boulevard Saint-Germain on the left bank of the Seine.

The next ring consists, *inter alia*, of the Boulevards Rochechouart, de Clichy (N), de Courcelles (W), de Grenelle and du Montparnasse (S), Picpus and de Charonne (E).

The third ring is the so-called Boulevard Périphérique Intérieur (named exclusively after Generals and Marshals) and finally the fourth ring is the Boulevard Périphérique Extérieur (ring road) which today marks the boundary of the city.

The town-planning measures (1853–70) which Baron Haussmann (1809–91), Prefect of Paris, carried out under Napoleon III completely transformed the city and saw the construction of the boulevards, stations, the first indoor markets and department stores, new bridges (5) and parks. Haussmann's town-planning (which called for the demolition of 30,000 houses and the resettlement of some 300,000 people) had several objectives. Besides improving the look of the city by making open spaces and wide streets, economic policy requirements were also of paramount importance. The new arterial roads facilitated fast transport and speeded up the circulation of goods and people between the different parts of the city in general and between the stations, markets and department stores in particular.

Finally the system of broad boulevards had strategic military advantages. It made for quicker movement and better control in the event of deployment of troops.

Boulevard Saint-Michel

The "great boulevards" (see above) have always been a great attraction for those who enjoy taking a stroll or frequenting restaurants, theatres and, nowadays, cinemas. The concept of the "théâtre du boulevard" gives some idea of their special features – noise, sensation and spectacle which nowadays means amusement halls, sensational films and discothèques. The "West End" of the Grands Boulevards in the area around the Opera House owes its worldly air to the presence of expensive boutiques and restaurants, but in the Faubourgs Montmarte, Saint-Denis and Saint-Martin, the "East End", one can soon sample the ordinary everyday life of a big city.

Grands Boulevards

Boulevard Saint-Michel

H5–7

The Boulevard Saint-Michel, on the border between the 5th and 6th arrondissements, leads southwards away from the Seine. It crosses the Boulevard Saint-Germain and passes the Place de la Sorbonne (left) and the Jardin du Luxembourg (right – see entry) on its way to the Port Royal RER Station, where it meets the Boulevard du Montparnasse and the Boulevard de Port-Royal.

The Saint-Michel métro station is a popular meeting-place and, whether the rendezvous is the Place Saint-Michel in front of the fountain (Fontaine Saint-Michel) or one of the many cafés, this is a good starting-point for walks along the Quais of the Seine, to the Cité, in the Quartier Latin, to Saint-Germain-des-Prés (see entries) or simply along the Boul' Mich' to the Jardin du Luxembourg.

Anyone looking for footwear (speciality: boots) or the latest

Location
Centre, on the Left Bank
(5/6th arr.)

Métro
Saint-Michel

Suburban station
Luxembourg (RER)

Buses
21, 27, 38, 81, 84, 85

fashion in jeans has plenty of choice in the shops on the Boul' Mich' or from the goods offered by the street traders: Indian scarves, leatherware, Far Eastern perfumes, jewellery.

During the school and university year (October–June) pupils and students from all over the world predominate on the streets. In the summer months, on the other hand, the Boul' Mich' is overwhelmingly peopled by tourists who are sometimes disappointed that all they find here are other tourists. It is a good idea to see what there is (to eat and drink) to the left and right in the narrow side streets of the Quartier Latin.

Bourse (des Valeurs) H4

Location
Rue Vivienne (2nd arr.)

Métro
Bourse

Buses
20, 29, 39, 48, 67, 69, 72

Visits
Mon.–Fri. 11 a.m.–1 p.m.

Entrance fee

Like other buildings dating from the time of Napoleon (Arc de Triomphe, Madeleine), the Paris stock exchange (1808–27) is modelled on the buildings of antiquity. The architect A.-Th. Brongniart chose the form of a single-nave Graeco-Roman temple. It was not enlarged into its present cruciform style until 1902–3.

Trading in stocks and shares reaches a peak about midday. An undisturbed view of the hectic activities of the brokers and dealers can be obtained from the gallery (reached by a staircase in the left-hand vestibule). Most visitors are in the dark about what is going on, and so information tours of introduction can be arranged (information in the gallery).

Bridges of Paris

See Seine Bridges

Catacombes H7

Location
Place Denfert-Rochereau
(14th arr.)

Métro
Denfert-Rochereau

Times of opening
Mon.–Fri. 2–4 p.m., Sat., Sun.
9–11 a.m., 2–4 p.m.

In Gallo-Roman times this was the site of underground stone quarries. Between 1785 and the mid 19th c. these old quarries were used to store skeletons from the many Parisian cemeteries which were removed to make way for new quarters of the city. The bones were arranged in the galleries according to the cemetery from which they had been removed, and stacked high against the walls of the twisting passages.
Remember to take a torch! Entrance fee.

Cemeteries (Cimetières)

Opening times

16 March–5 Nov, 7.30 a.m.–6 p.m.; 6 Nov.–15 March 8.30 a.m.–5.30 p.m., Sun. from 9 a.m.
The dog's cemetery has different opening times.

Cimetière de Montmartre
G/H2

Main entrance: Rue Caulaincourt, under the bridge (18th arr.).
Métro: Place Clichy.
Paris's third largest cemetery (1795) with the graves of Heinrich Heine (Avenue Hector Berlioz), Théophile Gautier (Avenue Cordier), Edgar Degas (Avenue Montebello), Jacques Offenbach (Avenue des Anglais), Stendhal (Avenue de la Croix) and many other famous people.

Main entrance: Boulevard Edgar Quinet (14th arr.).
Métro: Edgar Quinet, Raspail.
Second largest cemetery (1824) with the graves of Charles Baudelaire (Avenue de l'Ouest), Guy de Maupassant (in the SE), Ossip Zadkine (Avenue de l'Ouest) and André Citroën (Avenue Thierry).

Cimetière de Montparnasse
G7

Main entrance: Boulevard de Ménilmontant (20th arr.). ⬈
Métro: Père-Lachaise, Philippe-Auguste.
Paris's largest and finest cemetery, named after the father confessor of Louis XIV, Père La Chaise. Monument of the Communards who were shot here at the Mur des Fédérés in 1871 and memorial for the victims of the German concentration camps. Also park and City of the Dead where many famous people are buried: Molière, La Fontaine, Balzac, Marcel Proust, Oscar Wilde and Guillaume Apollinaire, David, Delacroix, Chopin, Bizet, Dr Guillotin (inventor of the guillotine), Edith Piaf. The rock idol Jim Morrison is buried here and since 1985 Simone Signoret as well.
(A plan of the graves is obtainable at the Gardien entrance.)

Cimetière du Père-Lachaise
M5

⬆ 3/2.

Pont de Clichy, 92-Asnières.
Métro: Porte de Clichy, Bus: 139, 140.
(At present being restored.)

Dogs' Cemetery
(Cimetière des Chiens)

---

*Centre Pompidou/Beaubourg   J5
(Georges Pompidou national centre for art and culture)

Between the Halles area (see Les Halles) and the Marais (see entry) lies the Centre National d'Art et de Culture Georges Pompidou, to give it its official name, which since it was opened in 1977 has become a major attraction, with over 8 million visitors a year. It is already being extended. The public has a choice of temporary exhibitions, two libraries, the National Gallery of Modern Art (see Musée National d'Art Moderne), a cinémathèque, a theatre and a tour of the building itself.
On the different floors, concerts, modern operas and experimental ballet take place; outside on the forecourt there is a lively mixture of street theatre and cabaret.
The idea of taking Paris into the 21st c., heralded by the tower-blocks of Défense (see entry) on the outskirts of Paris, has been taken a stage further by the Centre Pompidou (as it is known for short), or Centre Beaubourg, in the heart of the city. The international architectural competition (almost 700 schemes were submitted from 50 countries) was won by the youthful team of Richard Rogers (39, England) and Renzo Piano (34, Italy). Under their direction a structure took shape over five years and at a cost of almost a thousand million francs, which immediately sparked off a lively controversy. Its opponents call it "that monstrosity, that refinery, that gigantic gadget, a useless toy". Its advocates see in the Centre Beaubourg (Beaubourg is the name of the district) an opportunity for Paris again to become what it was from the end of the 19th c. until the Second World War: the "art capital of the world".

The Centre Beaubourg is intended to stand for a new national cultural policy, not by amassing collections of documents and

Location
Rue Rambuteau/corner of Rue St-Martin

Métro
Rambuteau, Les Halles, Hôtel de Ville 11/1/4

RER Station
Châtelet-Les-Halles

Buses
38, 47, 75

Times of opening
Mon.–Fri. noon–10 p.m.; Sat. and Sun. 10 a.m.–10 p.m.; closed Tues.

Guided tours
Weekdays 3, 3.30, 4 p.m.; Sat. and Sun. 10.30 a.m.
Contemporary Gallery:
Mon., Thurs. 5 p.m.

Entrance fee

Objective

Centre Pompidou/Beaubourg

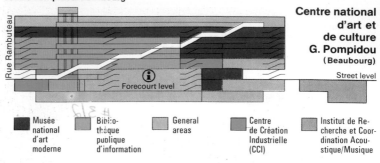

Centre national d'art et de culture G. Pompidou (Beaubourg)

Street level

Forecourt level

| | Musée national d'art moderne | | Biblio-thèque publique d'information | | General areas | | Centre de Création Industrielle (CCI) | | Institut de Recherche et Coordination Acoustique/Musique |

the usual objects to be found in museums, but by being creative, by producing works of art. This entails the regions of France being represented by exhibitions of their works and cultural events in the Centre Beaubourg, while exhibitions put together by the Beaubourg can be seen in provincial museums.

Architecture

The building, which is 166 m (547 ft) long, 60 m (197 ft) wide and 42 m (138 ft) high and is made of glass and steel, does in fact look a bit like a refinery: all the wiring and plumbing is channelled through coloured ducts on the E side of the exterior. Lifts and, in the "glass caterpillar", escalators are mounted on the main façade (W).

Leaving aside its outer aspect, the Beaubourg bears closer comparison with one of the time-honoured sights of Paris, the Cathedral of Notre-Dame (see entry). With its complicated building technique clearly visible, the "cathedral of culture", the Centre Beaubourg, is related to the Gothic architecture of Notre-Dame, particularly in so far as they share the same basic architectural principle: all load-bearing elements are contained in the outside walls. Thus the space on the ground floor and on the five upper floors (150×50 m – 492×164 ft) is not broken up by any form of support and can be arranged in any number of different ways, which is a great advantage for temporary exhibitions.

Useful information

The guided tours are in French and for individual visitors only. Groups may book guided tours in English in advance outside or during official visiting hours by writing to Centre Pompidou, F-75191-Paris Cédex O4, or by telephoning 42 77 12 33.

There is a charge for the temporary exhibitions on the 5th floor, the Musée National d'Art Moderne, the cinémathèque and for specific events (plays, concerts), but otherwise entrance is free. It is possible to buy tickets that are valid both for the museum and for the temporary exhibition.

Layout

Entrance: information desks on the right (general information) and left (that day's events). Guide booklets are available in English. Special exhibitions of large objects in the sunken central area ("forum"). Contemporary galleries (right). Sale of postcards, posters, catalogues, books (left). Bibliothèque d'actualite (left, behind the postcard and poster stall): newspapers, magazines, new books.

Bibliothèque publique d'information (open-access library): it is planned to have a million books here on shelves to which the public will have direct access. The books can only be read here,

Centre Pompidou ("Glass caterpillar" on the main façade)

they cannot be borrowed. The same applies to slides, video and audio tapes: there are sets of slides and video tapes on various themes which can be viewed *in situ* and a "médiathèque" (language laboratory) with study programmes for many languages.

Art of the 20th c. starting with the Fauves (Derain, de Vlaminck, Marquet, Dufy, Matisse) and Picasso's early 20th c. work through Cubism (Picasso, Braque, Gris), Expressionism (Nolde, Macke, Kandinsky), Constructivism (Klee, Mondrian) to Abstract Expressionism (de Staël, Hartung, Polikoff, Estère, Dubuffet), Pop-Art, Hard Edge and Minimal Art of the post-Second World War period, and a formidable collection of modern sculpture (Arp, Moore, Giacometti, Calder). The layout is chronological, starting on the 3rd floor and ending on the N side of the 5th floor.

Musée National d'Art Moderne (National Gallery of Modern Art)

Entrance on 3rd floor

Arranges temporary exhibitions, discussion groups, provides information (mezzanine, left).

Centre de Création Industrielle (CCI: Centre for Industrial Design)

Four screenings daily (from 3 p.m.) of films important in the history of the cinema.

Cinémathèque

An institute for research and development in contemporary music under the direction of Pierre Boulez, situated outside below ground level and open to the public only for concerts. Large temporary exhibitions: 5th floor.
Café-restaurant (with a view over the roofs of Paris).
Administration.

Institut de Recherche et de Co-ordination Acoustique/Musique (IRCAM)

Temporary exhibitions; workshop for children (5–12 years).

Atelier des Enfants

The Centre's underground car park is linked with the "Forum des Halles" (see entry – entrance: Rue Rambuteau).

Parking

In the northern section of the forecourt there is a small two-part building containing a reconstruction of the studio of the Romanian sculptor Constantin Brancusi and many of his works.
Times of opening: Mon. and Wed.–Fri. 10 a.m.–6 p.m.; Sat., Sun. noon–6 p.m.

Atelier Brancusi.

Times of opening
Mon. and Wed.–Fri.
10 a.m.–6 p.m.; Sat.,
Sun. noon–6 p.m.

Champ-de-Mars (field of Mars)

E–F5

The Champ-de-Mars (field of Mars), originally a military training ground, today extends like a park between the Eiffel Tower (see Tour Eiffel) and the École Militaire (see entry).
During the French Revolution this was the scene of the "Festival of the Federation" (14 July 1790) when Louis XVI and delegates from all the French provinces swore to uphold the new constitution which provided for a constitutional monarchy on the English model. It was here, too, that the mob demanded death for the royal family after their abortive flight. In 1794 the painter Jacques-Louis David organised a "Festival of the Supreme Being" (Etre suprême) which was to be worshipped as part of the new State religion decreed by Robespierre. This signalled for Robespierre the climax of his Reign of Terror. (Four months later he, too, was to lose his head on the guillotine.) World Fairs were held on the Champ-de-Mars in 1867, 1878, 1889, 1900 and 1937. Paris's first racecourse was also here for a time.

Location
W part of the city (7th arr.)

Métro
Ecole Militaire

Buses
42, 80, 82, 87, 92

**Champs-Elysées

E–G4

Famous throughout the world, this magnificent avenue, is 1·88 km (1⅙ miles) long and falls into two parts on either side of its main intersection, the Rond-Point. The upper part, towards the Arc de Triomphe (see entry), offers everything that visitors from all over the world have come to associate with the Champs-Elysées – luxury shops and hotels, countless restaurants and pavement cafés, cinemas, theatres and the offices of the big banks and international airlines. This is the meeting place of the world where one hears a mixture of languages from the passers-by.
By contrast the lower section, towards the Place de la Concorde, is flanked by gardens surrounding museums, theatres and a few restaurants. Until the end of the 16th c. this area consisted of fields and marshland. The first approach road to it was the 17th c. Cours de la Reine running from the Palace of the Tuileries but along the Seine. After the completion of the Tuileries Le Nôtre landscaped a broad shady avenue linking the palace with the hill where the Arc de Triomphe stands today. Early in the 18th c. this avenue was named the "Champs-Elysées" (Elysian Fields).
The entire Champs-Elysées forms only one section of the "voie triomphale" (the triumphal way) completed under Napoleon III

Location
Between Arc de Triomphe and Place de la Concorde (8th arr.)

Métro
George V., Franklin D. Roosevelt, Champs-Elysées-Clemenceau

Buses
28, 42, 49, 73, 80, 83

◀ *Champs-Elysées*

Château de Chantilly

and leading from the Arc de Triomphe de l'Etoile via the Place de la Concorde to the Arc de Triomphe du Carrousel.

The Marly horses, two masterly Baroque sculptures by Guillaume Coustou, were positioned between the Place de la Concorde and the Champs-Elysées in 1795.

Chantilly

Location
Chantilly, 40 km (25 miles) N of Paris on the N16

Rail
from Gare du Nord

Castle

Times of opening
Mon., Wed–Sun.
10.30 a.m.–5.30 p.m.;
closed Tues. and on
race days

Park

The little town of Chantilly (12,000 inhabitants), famous for its horse-racing and the whipped cream named after it, lies on the N16 on the same latitude as Senlis. Its château and its park in particular are popular destinations for excursions from Paris.

In the 17th and 18th c. Chantilly was the seat of the Condé family, a branch of the Royal House of Bourbon. The family bequeathed the castle to the Institut de France (see entry) in 1886. The "Grand" Château (built 1875–81) today houses the Musée Condé (see entry).

The "Petit" Château dates from the 16th c. Worth seeing: the sumptuously painted rooms, the chapel with magnificent high altar and the library (Galerie des livres) with valuable old manuscripts.

The park dates from 1663 and is the work of André Le Nôtre, the landscape-gardener of Versailles. A small hunting-lodge (Maison de Sylvie, 17th c.), an indoor court for ball games (Jeu de Paume, 1757) and a hamlet or "hameau" (for acting out the pastoral fantasies popular at that time) are all charming features of the fine park which, like Versailles, has a broad canal running across it.

To the W of the château are the Great Stables (Grandes Ecuries, 18th c.) and Chantilly racecourse (1834).

Stables
Racecourse

Châtelet

J5

The square and the enormous métro station are named after the "Grand Châtelet" which was a fortress, dating from the 12th c. and built to protect the Ile-de-la Cité (see entry), a prison and, until 1789, the law court of the chief administrator of Paris. (Prévôt des Marchands, head of the Paris merchants, see Hôtel de Ville.) Napoleon demolished the fortress in 1802 and the two theatres were built in the reign of Napoleon III. The "Châtelet" on the W side, which since 1980 has ranked as a National Theatre and is known as the Théâtre Musical de Paris, stages opera, light opera and ballet, while on the E side the "Théâtre de la Ville" (formerly "Théâtre Sara Bernhardt") mounts an ambitious programme of music recitals and modern classics.

Location
Place du Châtelet (4th arr.)

Métro
Châtelet

Buses
21, 38, 47, 69, 74, 75, 85

Cité

H/J 5/6

The Ile-de-la-Cité is the historical and geographical centre of Paris.
Here, on the island protected by the two arms of the Seine, were the first settlements in prehistoric times. Here stood the Gallo-Roman town of Lutetia. Here the inhabitants sought refuge from the onslaughts of the Teutons, the Huns and the Normans. Not until the Middle Ages was the city able to spread permanently along both banks of the Seine.
From the 6th to the 14th c. the Cité was the seat of the kings, with the secular royal palace (see Palais de Justice) and its sacral counterpart, the "Cathedral of France": Notre-Dame de Paris. When the seat of the kings was moved elsewhere the face of the town changed, as broad squares and streets were no longer needed for the festivities of the Royal Court. There grew up a closely packed huddle of alleys and houses in the shadow of the towers of Notre-Dame. Baron Haussmann, the Prefect of the Seine in the 19th c. under Napoleon III, radically altered the face of the Cité again when he established a precedent for urban redevelopment (nowadays considered unattractive) by making room for the broad N–S streets, the Prefecture of Police, the commercial court, the extensions to the law courts, the rebuilding of the Hôtel-Dieu and an unobstructed view of Notre-Dame. This involved the destruction of the historical heart of the city and the resettlement of 25,000 people. Since then the term "Cité" in the sense of the ancient nucleus of a town is hardly applicable and the only inhabitants on the island live in a few narrow streets N of Notre-Dame.
The chief attractions of a visit to the Cité are (see entries): Notre-Dame, La Sainte-Chapelle, La Conciergerie, Le Palais de Justice (Law Courts); but there are also other squares and buildings worth visiting:

Location
Centre (1st/3rd arr.)

Métro
Cité

Buses
21, 24, 27, 38, 81, 85, 96

A small area of lawn on the north-western tip of the island,

Square du Vert Galant

Notre-Dame on the Ile de la Cité

harking back to Henri IV and overlooked by his statue on horseback, this is a venue for vagrants, courting couples and musicians.

Place Dauphine

In 1607 Harlay, the wealthy Chief Justice, was given the site by Henri IV with instructions to construct a square fronted by houses sharing the same façade (only nos. 14 and 26 date from that time). The square, named after the heir to the throne (Dauphin), soon became a popular place for promenades.

Hôtel-Dieu

The hospital, looking a bit like a barracks, was built between 1868 and 1878. A convent stood here as early as the 7th c. where nuns devoted themselves to the care of the poor and the sick; thus the Hôtel-Dieu is one of the oldest hospitals in Europe.

Mémorial de la Déportation

This monument on the south-eastern tip of the island commemorates those who suffered deportation to German concentration camps (1940–5).

Parvis de Notre-Dame (Cathedral Square)

In the south-eastern corner, in front of the Pont au Double, lies the little Square Charlemagne with a statue of Charlemagne (archaeological crypt – see Notre-Dame).

A stroll across the island is very pleasant, offering fine views, virtually unmatched elsewhere, of the Seine and its bridges and the city stretching along both sides of the river.

Collège de France   J6

Location
Rue des Ecoles (5th arr.)

The Collège de France (formerly: Collège des Trois Langues) is one of the most famous academic teaching and research establishments in France. The 18th c. building was considerably enlarged in 1930.

François I established his reputation as "Father and Restorer of the Sciences" by founding in 1530 the Collège des Trois Langues (College of the Three Languages, also Collège des Lecteurs royaux=College of the Royal Lecturers). The King, an admirer of the Italian Renaissance, wanted to set up an independent scientific college where the three Classical languages, Hebrew, Greek and Latin, would be studied from the original texts (as in Italy). The lecturers were paid not by the students, as was usual elsewhere, but by the King and taught free of charge. The freedom of these men of science from academic constraints and free access to the lectures for everyone have been preserved, but the Collège de France does not issue certificates or grant titles. Lectures given currently extend to all the humanities and natural sciences.

Well-known professors in the history of the College include the physicist André Ampère, the historian Jules Michelet, the poet Paul Valéry and the philosopher Henri Bergson. Today teachers at the Collège de France include the anthropologist Claude Lévi-Strauss and the philosopher Michel Foucault.

Métro
Odéon, Maubert-Mutualité, Saint-Michel

Buses
63, 86, 87

Visits
By prior application at the main gate

Comédie Française

See Théâtre Français

Conciergerie   H/J5

The Conciergerie, part of the medieval royal palace (see Cité) and prison, is today a museum in which well-attended concerts take place. (Small sections of it are still used by the adjoining Palais de Justice (see entry) for prisoners on remand.)

About 1300 Philippe le Bel had the High Gothic halls of the Conciergerie built and these are the only parts of the old palace still left today. The "concierge" in those days was the constable of the castle and hence the chief of the royal household (nowadays "concierge" means the caretaker of a block of flats). Presumably he also had some form of jurisdiction, as the building was soon turned into a palace prison and later a State prison. Many notorious prisoners awaited sentence here, including the assassins of Henri IV and the Duc de Berry, as well as Danton, Robespierre and Marie-Antoinette.

From the opposite bank of the Seine (Quai de la Mégisserie) there is a good view of the whole building (its neo-Gothic façade dates from the 19th c.) with its three round towers and its clock-tower (Tour de l'Horloge) with the first public clock in Paris (c. 1370, destroyed in 1793, restored in the 19th c.). The entrance is to the right of this on the Quai de l'Horloge.

The following rooms are particularly interesting:

Kitchen (1353): banquets for two to three thousand royal guests could be prepared in this kitchen and it was directly supplied from the Seine (the quay did not exist at that time). The size of the open fireplaces was necessary for roasting whole oxen.

Salle des Gens d'Armes (Room of the Men-at-Arms, 1285–1314): this was used as a dining-room by the armed servants.

Location
1 Quai de l'Horloge (4th arr.)

Métro
Cité, Châtelet

Buses
21, 24, 27, 38, 81, 85, 96

Times of opening
Daily 10 a.m.–5 p.m.

Entrance fee

Viewing

Conciergerie

La Grande Arche   *P.F.A. Glass Palace*

The hall, with its ribbed vault, is divided into four aisles by three rows of pillars (dimensions: 70×30 m – 230×98 ft). It is the finest secular Gothic room still in existence in Paris.

Rue de Paris: named after the executioner ("Monsieur de Paris") to whom the condemned were handed over in this passage which is partitioned off from the Salle des Gens d'Armes.

Marie-Antoinette's cell in which the last queen of the "Old Régime" (Ancien Régime) was kept prisoner after an abortive escape attempt. Here, like thousands of other prisoners of the Revolution, she awaited execution.

Cell in which Danton and later Robespierre are said to have been held.

Women's courtyard (Cour des Femmes).

Chapelle des Girondins: the former chapel of the Conciergerie was used during the Revolution as a special prison for the supporters of the Girondist party (opponents of the dictatorship of the Jacobins). Exhibits: guillotine blade, prison rules, facsimile of Marie-Antoinette's last letter and other mementoes.

Salle des Gardes (14th c.): this was the room of the palace guards. The heavy vaults are supported by massive pillars with richly ornamented capitals (many animals fighting).

*La Défense   A/B2

Location
Western outskirts

In the W of the city, directly in line with the Champs-Elysées–Arc de Triomphe–Avenue de la Grand Armée, there has existed since the mid-sixties the business, exhibition and residential (!) quarter of La Défense. Its historical name (Defence) harks back to the war of 1870–1 when the French put up stubborn resistance to the Prussians on this spot. The name does not appear to be entirely suitable for the striking tower blocks of the quarter which herald the arrival of the French capital into the 21st century.

Métro
La Défense (RER)

To commemorate the bicentenary of the French Revolution the "Grand Arche" in white Carrera marble was dedicated here in 1989. This 110-m/360-feet-high triumphal arch was designed by a Dane, Johan Otto von Spreckeisen; housed in the arch are the French Ministry of Civic and Domestic Building, and also the headquarters of an international society of human rights.

*La Grande Arche

The "tours" (towers), as the French call the skyscrapers, are mainly occupied by large computer and oil multinationals. Thus La Défense is predominantly a quarter for business people but at the same time a residential quarter for people who like a "business-like" atmosphere, and here they have a large business centre, drugstore, restaurants, cinemas, a bank and boutiques.

Among the extravagant architectural features of La Défence are the triangular glass palace of the P.F.A., on the Esplanade Général de Gaulle, and the huge building of CNIT (Centre National de Industries et Techniques), shaped like a mussel open to the sky, in the Place de la Défense. The enormous hall (90,000 sq. m/968,400 sq. ft.) covers a greater area than the Place de la Concorde (84,000 sq, m/861,120 sq.ft.) no longer used for major events and large exhibitions, it is being converted into an hotel and conference centre. Close by stands another futuristic edifice, the Tour de la Folie (architect: Jean-Marc Ibos), a 400-m/1528-ft.-high tower, which is to provide additional office space for service undertakings.

P.F.A.

*Dôme des Invalides   F5

The Dôme des Invalides, the former "Royal Church" (see Hôtel des Invalides) of Louis XIV, is where Napoleon was entombed in 1840.
The work of the most important architect of the period, Jules Hardouin-Mansart, it is the outstanding ecclesiastical building of the French Classical period (1675–1706) and as such the counterpart of the secular masterpiece of the architecture of that period, the Palace of Versailles (see entry). With its impressive cupola (over 100 m (328 ft) in height) and façade of columns the Dôme des Invalides is an example of harmony in architecture.

The entrance is in the Place Vauban. In the open circular crypt (of the same diameter as the cupola: 11 m – 36 ft) Napoleon's red porphyry sarcophagus stands on a base of green granite. Twelve large goddesses of victory (by James Pradier) surrounding the crypt are a reminder of Napoleon's 12 major campaigns from 1797 to 1815.

Location
Place Vauban (7th arr.)

Métro
Latour-Maubourg,
St-Francois-Xavier

Buses
28, 49, 69, 82, 92

Times of opening
1 Oct.–31 Mar.: 10 a.m.–
5 p.m.
1 Apr.–30 Sept.: 10 a.m.–
6 p.m.

Entrance fee

Eglise du Dôme des Invalides

Tomb of Napoleon I

Eglise Saint-Louis-des-Invalides

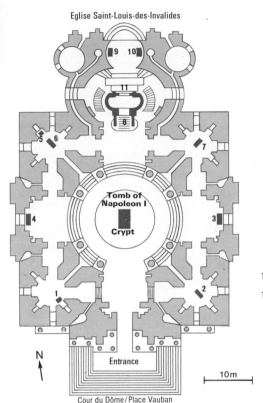

Tomb of
Napoleon I

Crypt

N

Entrance

|— 10m —|

Cour du Dôme / Place Vauban

Eglise du Dôme des Invalides
(Tomb of Napoleon)

1 Tomb of Napoleon's brother Jérôme Bonaparte (d. 1860) in the Chapel of St Jérôme
2 Tomb of Napoleon's brother Joseph Bonaparte (d. 1844)
3 Tomb of Vauban (d. 1707), containing his heart
4 Tomb of Turenne (d. 1675)
5 Heart of La Tour d'Auvergne (d. 1800)
6 Tomb of Marshal Lyautey (d. 1934)
7 Tomb of Marshal Foch (d. 1929)
8 Altar with wreathed columns and baldachin
9 Tomb of General Bertrand (d. 1844)
10 Tomb of Marshal Duroc (d. 1813)
11 Entrance to the crypt: at the entrance two large bronze statues; inside surrounding Napoleon's tomb twelve colossal figures symbolising the Emperor's victories; at the back the tomb of Napoleon's son François Charles Joseph Bonaparte (d. 1832)

Jérôme Bonaparte, King of Westphalia, one of Napoleon's brothers.
Marshal Turenne (killed near Sasbach in 1675).
La Tour d'Auvergne, military commander (killed near Oberhausen in Swabia in 1800), and Marshal Lyautey (1854–1934).
General Bertrand, Marshal of Napoleon's Household on St Helena (1773–1844).
Marshal Duroc (killed near Bautzen in 1813).
Marshal Foch (1851–1929).
Monument to Marshal Vauban, Louis XIV's master builder of fortifications (1633–1707) with his heart.
Joseph Bonaparte, King of Spain, the Emperor's oldest brother (d. 1844).

Tombs and Monument in the Side Chapel

Since 1969 there has been in a recess in Napoleon's crypt the tomb of his only legitimate son, Napoleon II. (He was King of Rome and Duke of Reichstadt and died in Vienna in 1832 at the age of 21.)

Crypt

École Militaire F5/6

Location
Boulevard de la Tour-
Maubourg (7th arr.)

Metro
Ecole Militaire, Champ-de-
Mars

Buses
28, 49, 80, 82, 87, 92

The École Militaire, the former school for officers of the royal army, at the end of the Champ-de-Mars (see entry) opposite the Eiffel Tower (see Tour Eiffel), today houses the French military academy. It is the work of the architect Jacques-Ange Gabriel in accordance with whose plans it was built in two stages between 1759 and 1782. The clear-cut, simple, unadorned construction is a fine example of Early Classicism.

In 1785 a little lieutenant left the officers' school. His superiors wrote on his certificate a meaningless phrase common at that time, "should go far". He did, and as Napoleon I became first Emperor of the French.

Behind the north façade of the main building (Place Joffre with the statue of Marshal Joffre) is the main courtyard (Cour d'honneur), its wings formed from two Doric colonnades.

The Saint-Louis Chapel in the Louis XVI style is one of the masterworks of the architect Jacques-Ange Gabriel. (Visits only on written application to: Général commandant d'armes de l'Ecole Militaire, 1 Place Joffre, 75007 Paris.)

Eiffel Tower

See Tour Eiffel

Etoile (Place Charles de Gaulle) E4

Location
16th arrondissement

Métro
Charles de Gaulle
(Etoile)

Buses
22, 30, 31, 52, 73, 92

The famous square, in the middle of which rises Napoleon's Arc de Triomphe (great triumphal arch – see entry), has, since 1970, borne the name of the former French President Charles de Gaulle. However, it is popularly known as the Place de l'Etoile.

The points of the star (étoile) are formed by the 12 avenues which meet in a circular open space, the present aspect of which owes much to Baron Haussmann's town planning (see Boulevards).

France's general rule applies here too: traffic coming from the right has priority. From the platform of the Arc de Triomphe, besides enjoying a wonderful view of the city, one is also presented with the spectacle of the traffic in the square. The drivers entering the Etoile often seem under the impression that they are taking part in a race. Any foreigner who manages to get round in his own car without incident has already gone a long way to "conquering" Paris.

Eurodisneyland

Location
Marne-la-Vallée
30 km (19 miles) E of Paris

This theme park of fairytale and adventure on the American model will be opened in 1992 in Marne-la-Vallée on a site covering 1780 ha/4398 acres.

Faubourg Saint-Germain G5

Location
7th arrondissement

The Faubourg Saint-Germain stretches from the quarter of Saint-Germain-des-Prés to the Hôtel des Invalides (see entries).

The elegant aristocrats' quarter of the 18th c. today contains the residence of the Prime Minister (Hôtel de Matignon, 54 Rue de Varenne), and many former homes of the nobility are occupied by ministries and foreign diplomatic missions.

Towards the end of the 18th c. the Marais Quarter (see entry) went out of fashion and the aristocracy and the "nouveaux riches" moved here (and into the Faubourg Saint-Honoré – see entry). Some streets still give an impression of the town-planning of that time: Rue de Lille, Rue de Grenelle, Rue de Varenne. In the Rue de Grenelle stands the magnificent fountain "Fontaine des Quatre-Saisons" (1739–46), by Edmond Bouchardon, the most important sculptor of the reign of Louis XV.

Métro
Bac, Solférino, Varenne

Bus
69

Faubourg Saint-Honoré   E–G 3–4

Bordered by the Rue Royale, the boulevards Malesherbes and Haussmann and the Champs-Elysées lie a district and a street which bear the same name: Faubourg Saint-Honoré.

Haute Couture, the Presidential Palace and the Embassy quarter are all linked with the name of the street whose most interesting section lies between Rue La Boëtie and Rue Royale. Numbers 55–7 conceal the official residence of the French President, the Palais de l'Elysée (formerly the property of Madame de Pompadour, favourite mistress of Louis XV). Almost opposite, in the Place Beauveau, is the Ministry of the Interior.

The window displays of the couturiers are a real centre of attraction: Torrente (No. 9), Lanvin (No. 22), Ted Lapidus (No. 23), Hermès (No. 34), Castillo (No. 76), Louis Féraud (No. 88). Well-known art galleries here are those of Hervé Odermatt (No. 85, contemporary) and Pacitti (No. 174, 19th and 20th c.).

The Faubourg Saint-Honoré, the Faubourg Saint-Germain (see entry) and the 16th arrondissement as a whole make up the prosperous, upper middle class West End of Paris.

Location
8th arrondissement

Métro
Saint-Philippe-du-Roulé

Buses
24, 38, 49, 52, 80, 83

Flea market

See Marché aux Puces

**Fontainebleau

The small town of Fontainebleau (20,000 inhabitants, the chief town of one of the cantons of the département of Seine-et-Marne) lies to the SE of Paris in the magnificent forest of the same name. Its great attraction is the Palace of Fontainebleau. It figures in history more than any other castle in France; the rulers from Louis VII to Napoleon III stayed here and con-tributed to the buildings.

Location
Fontainebleau, 60 km
(36 miles) SE (A6, N7)

Rail
From the Gare de Lyon

**Château de Fontainebleau

The group of buildings making up the palace, with its beautiful park and lake, dates back to a 12th c. hunting-lodge on the site

of which François I ordered Gilles le Breton, Pierre Chambiges and Philibert Delorme to construct a Renaissance palace. This was extended several times by Henri II, Henry IV and Louis XV. It was here that Napoleon, who was especially fond of this palace, took leave of his army in 1814. This is recorded in the name "Cour des Adieux" given to the present entrance court-yard. It is also called "Cour du Cheval Blanc" (Courtyard of the White Horse) after a statue of the Roman Emperor Marcus Aurelius mounted on a white horse (original on the Capitol in Rome).

The main façade of the palace as it is today is dominated by the double outside staircase in the shape of a horseshoe (1634) which, with its strong lines, announces the transition to the Baroque and overpowers the more delicate structure of the earlier (1615) central part. The outer parts of the façade date from the time of François I and are the work of the Bolognese master builder Primaticcio who worked at Fontainebleau from 1552 onwards.

The N wing of the Cour des Adieux is one of the oldest remaining parts of the palace. It was built about 1540 for François I's Court officials; the S wing (18th c.) is the work of Louis XV's architect Jacques-Ange Gabriel and contains the apartments of the royal household.

The passage under the arcades to the right of the horseshoe staircase leads into the "Cour de la Fontaine", which on the right opens on to the large carp pond. On the left there is the François I Gallery (1st floor), behind which lies the Garden of Diana (Jardin de Diane).

The most important rooms to see in the palace are the François I Gallery (Galerie François I), the ballroom and the chapel (Chapelle de la Sainte-Trinité). The outside staircase leads directly into these rooms on the 1st floor.

The François I Gallery (1534–7) was used only as a corridor between the King's apartments and the chapel. Here merchants offered their fancy goods. Visitors are consequently astonished by the sumptuous furnishings in this room. It is unique in that artists (painters, sculptors and stucco-workers) from Italy, the most outstanding of whom were Francesco Primaticcio (1507–70), Niccolò dell'Abbate (c. 1512–71) and Rosso Fiorentino (1494–1540), created a synthesis of the arts in the Mannerist style (transition between Renaissance and Baroque).

They founded the "Fontainebleau School" (as it was later known) whose showpiece this gallery is. They created a complex work of art, an ingenious unity of architecture, painting and stucco-work with delicate coloration and a multitude of allegorical references. Incorporated into the 12 wall frescoes, the small paintings, the shapes of the frames and the stucco-work are numerous symbolic references which can barely be deciphered today.

The ballroom (Henri II Gallery, 1552–6) was begun under François I (1547). The huge pilasters show that this room was to have had a vaulted ceiling (in the "medieval style"), but instead the "modern" flat ceiling was constructed which, nevertheless,

Times of opening
9.30 a.m.–12.30 p.m.,
2–5 p.m. (closed Tues.).
Admission until 11.45 or
4.15 p.m.

Entrance fee
(Wed. free)

Exterior

Interior

François I Gallery

Ballroom

◀ *Château de Fontainebleau: Cour des Adieux*

spans an area of 30×10 m (98×33 ft). The numerous mythological scenes are by dell'Abbate (after sketches by Primaticcio). The scenes of Diana, the goddess of hunting, are also a tribute to Diane de Poitiers. She was François I's last favourite and after his death the favourite of his son, Henri II (who was almost thirty years younger than she was).

Everywhere one looks in this room one finds the initials "D" and "H".

Castle Chapel

The Sainte-Trinité Chapel is the height of both storeys (entrance on 1st floor). It was started by François I, continued by Philibert Delorme for Henri II, and was decorated under Henri IV (ceiling-paintings by Frémiet).

Royal Apartments

Other rooms worth visiting on the 1st floor are the royal apartments. They consist of six rooms overlooking the Cour Ovale, including François I's suite which was altered by Louis XIV and contains the room where Louis XIII was born (Salon de Louis XIII), and 12 rooms overlooking the Jardin de Diane.

These include:
The Queen's apartments (known as the Appartements de Marie-Antoinette).
The Throne Room (Salle du Trône).
The Council Chamber (Salle du Conseil).
Napoleon's rooms, in the Empire style. It was at the small round table in the Red Drawing-room (Salon Rouge) that Napoleon signed his Abdication in April 1814.

Petits Appartements de l'Empereur

Napoleon's private rooms. These were formerly the apartments of Louis XVI and from 1806 were furnished by Napoleon in the Empire style.

Petits Appartements de l'Impératrice

The former private rooms of Marie-Antoinette. These were later occupied by Napoleon's wife Joséphine and refurbised from 1806.

Galerie de Diane

The Galerie de Diane, another wing of the palace, was constructed under Henri III and today houses a library and collection of paintings.

Gardens

A visit to the gardens should not be missed. To the W of the goldfish pond lies the Jardin Anglais (English garden) laid out by Napoleon I, and to the E the Parterre created by the landscape-gardener Le Nôtre with pools and garden figures. Northeast of this, on the far side of the canal, constructed in the time of Henri IV, extends the park with the maze and the trellised vines, the "Treille du Roi" (the King's Arbour).

Fontaine des Innocents   J5

Location
Square des Innocents next to the "Forum des Halles" (1st arr.)

Métro
Les Halles; Châtelet-Les-Halles (RER)

After the Halles district was altered the fountain "Fontaine des Innocents" (1549) was re-erected on its original site, the "Square des Innocents". Until 1786 this had been the location of the cemetery and the Church of the Innocents (Cimetière et Eglise des Innocents).

The architect of the fountain, which was converted into a temple in the 18th c., was Pierre Lescot ("Lescot-Façade" in the Cour Carrée of the Louvre – see entry). The reliefs on the older sides, the originals of which are today in the Louvre, are by the

Exhibition in the Grand Palais

master of French Renaissance sculpture Jean Goujon. The fourth side of the fountain is decorated with the figures of nymphs (1788) by Augustin Pajou.

Buses
21, 69, 75

Grand Palais   F4

Until the Centre Pompidou (see entry) was built the most important exhibitions in Paris were held in the Grand Palais, whether the collected works of individual artists (Monet, Matisse, Chagall, Miró, Picasso), periods (Impressionism, Symbolism) or countries. Today it shares this pre-eminence with the new arts centre. The Autumn Salon (Salon d'Automne), however, still takes place here all the year round. Built for the 1900 World Fair, the inside is in the Art Nouveau style of the time (iron and steel construction), but the outside has predominantly been kept in the neo-Baroque style. The noteworthy glass dome inside is 43 m (141 ft) high.

Since 1965 the S wing has housed part of one of the Universities of Paris and since 1937 the W wing has contained the natural history museum, see Palais de la Découverte.

Location
Avenue Churchill (8th arr.)

Métro
Champs-Elysées-Clemenceau

Buses
28, 42, 49, 72, 73, 83

Times of opening
Daily (except Tues.)
10 a.m.–8 p.m.,
Wed. 10 a.m.–10 p.m.

Entrance fee

Les Halles   J5

Since the demolition of the former market halls at the end of the sixties the market quarter, like the neighbouring Marias (see entry), has been in a state of upheaval.

For years there was the gaping hole of a gigantic building site

Location
Centre (1st arr.)

55

Forum des Halles

Métro
Les Halles

Suburban station
Châtelet-Les-Halles 4/

Buses
21, 29, 67, 74, 75, 85

("Le Trou des Halles") where previously there had been the "Belly of Paris" (Zola wrote a novel of the same name about it, "Le Ventre de Paris"). Since then it has been filled with concrete and become one of the biggest underground traffic junctions in Paris (two RER lines intersect a métro line and the whole complex is connected with Châtelet Station where four métro lines meet).

Above the métro and RER tunnels and underground car parks are (still underground) the commercial floors of the "Forum des Halles", opened in 1979, with cinemas, theatres, restaurants and cafés, the Centre Océanique Cousteau, opened in 1989 (deep-sea adventures in an area of 5000 sq. m (53,820 sq. ft; open Tue.–Sun. noon–7 p.m.), and the Vidéothèque de Paris (see entry). Two museums have been accommodated here, the Grevin Forum, which illustrates Parisian life about 1900 in wax figures (Paris Promenade in 1900 as a sound and light show: 10.30 a.m.– 6.45 p.m., Sun. 1–7.45 p.m.) and the Musée Français de l'Holographie (see Practical Information – Museums). The old streets surrounding the area are swarming with fashionable clothes shops, second-hand shops, cheap furniture shops and sex shops, which have sprung up in the Rue Saint-Denis as competition for the prostitutes who operate there.

Hôtel de Ville   J5

Location
Place de l'Hôtel de Ville
(4th arr.)

Since 1977 Paris, for a long time a "capital without a head", has had a mayor again. His official residence is the Hôtel de Ville (Town Hall), to which the mayor's offices (Mairies Annexes) of the 20 arrondissements are answerable. (For information on the special administrative structure of Paris and the surrounding area see General, Administration.)

The first town hall was built here in the 14th c. François I had it rebuilt in the Renaissance style. At the beginning of the 19th c. it was extended but an attempt was made to keep to the same style. In 1871 it was set on fire when the Commune was overthrown and then subsequently fully restored. The present building dates from the same period as the Opéra (see entry) and can be compared with it in so far as the neo-Baroque style of the Opéra and the neo-Renaissance style of the Town Hall resulted in unduly ornate buildings which because of their overflowing decoration are impressive, but which on closer inspection appear to lack harmony and independence.

In the Middle Ages the city's chief administrator was a provost (prévôt), the head of Paris's corporation of merchant shippers which belonged to the Hanseatic League. Though his appointment and dismissal were in the hands of the king, he still exercised considerable influence. In 1358, the provost Etienne Marcel led the first (unsuccessful) "citizens revolt" against feudalism and the monarchy. In 1789 the last provost, who as a royal official represented the monarchy, was killed by the Revolutionary mob. After the Revolution Paris had a mayor for brief periods only (1789–94, 1848, 1870–1). The rest of the time it was "governed" by representatives of the State (Prefect and Prefect of Police).

The reception office of the Town Hall can supply information on guided tours of the civic chambers where the décor matches the exterior of the building. (The Parisians think the Town Hall has more rooms for gala occasions than for work.)

Métro
Hôtel de VIlle

Buses
38, 47, 58, 67, 69, 70, 72, 74, 75, 76, 96

Guided tours
Information:
Bureau d'accueil,
tel. 42 78 13 00

Ile-de-la-Cité

See Cité

Ile Saint-Louis   J–K 5–6

In 1609, at the instigation of Cardinal Richelieu, two originally separate islands were joined together and then linked by two bridges to the right bank of the Seine. The contract for this work, and for developing the new unit as a whole, was awarded to Marie, Poulettier and Le Regrattier.

The 17th c. architecture still retains its (cold) aristocratic dignity. Besides the nobility, poets (Charles Baudelaire, Théophile Gautier), philosophers (Voltaire, Jean-Jacques Rousseau) and statesmen (Georges Pompidou) have all lived here.

If you walk along the quays you can see the Hôtel de Ville on the right bank, the Quartier Latin with the Panthéon on the left bank, and the Cité (see entries) with Notre-Dame in the distance. Smart restaurants, many of them in vaulted cellars, are an enticing setting for dining in style.

Location
Centre (4th arr.)

Métro
Pont-Marie

Bus
67

Saint-Louis-en-l'Ile (church)

The church was begun in 1664 by Louis Le Vau and completed in 1726 by Jacques Doucet. Paintings by Charles Coypel (1694–1752): "The Disciples' Meal at Emmaus", Pierre Mignard

Location
Rue Saint Louis-en-l'Ile

(1612–95): "Rest on the Flight" and Francesco Vecellio (Titian's brother): "Entombment of Christ" (16th c.).

Hôtel de Lauzun

Location
17 Quai d'Anjou

The Hôtel (1657), by the architect Louis Le Vau, belongs to the city and is used for official receptions.
The Hôtel de Lauzun (famous frescoes and sculptures) may be visited only by prior arrangement (Directeur Adjoint, Les Beaux-Arts de la Ville de Paris, 14 Rue François-Miron, 75004 Paris). The poets Baudelaire and Th. Gautier lived here for a while in the 19th c.

Hôtel Lambert

Location
2 Rue Saint-Louis-en-l'Ile

This Hôtel, built in 1640 and also by Le Vau, is privately owned and cannot be visited. With Citeits semicircular courtyard, open staircase, oval entrance hall, "Galerie d'Hercule" (depicting the legend of Hercules) and sumptuous original furnishings the Hôtel Lambert is an excellent example of the art and culture of its period.

Institut de France   H5

Location
23 Quai de Conti (6th arr.)

Métro
Pont-Neuf

Buses
24, 27

Times of opening
Guided tour (in French) on application:
Secrétariat de l'Institut,
23 Quai de Conti,
75006 Paris

The Académie Française (founded in 1635 by Cardinal Richelieu to conserve the French language) is only one of France's five scientific academies which together form the Institut de France. Its members, "les 40 Immortels" (Immortals), decide on whether a word should be admitted to their authoritative dictionary of the French language, the "Dictionnaire de l'Académie", and thus "officially" rank as a "French word". On the occasion of the 350th anniversary of the foundation, President Mitterand was presented with one of the first copies of the 9th edition. It contains 45,000 words (the 8th edition of 1935 contained about 35,000 words).

The other Academies carry out and promote research in the fields of classical history and archaeology (Inscriptions et Belles Lettres, 1663), natural sciences (Sciences, 1666), moral and social sciences and jurisprudence (Sciences morales et politiques, 1795) and art (Beaux-Arts, 1816).

In 1661 Cardinal Mazarin founded a college to take 15 young nobles from each of the four provinces which had recently become part of France – Artois, Alsace, Piedmont and Roussillon. This Collège des Quatre-Nations was given its own building (1688) with a chapel (1674) and a library (1691), all designed by the architect Louis Le Vau (1612–70). The College was in existence from 1688 until 1790. In 1805 the five former royal academies, which since 1795 had been merged together to form the Institut de France, were moved, on Napoleon's orders, from the Louvre into the college building. The Palais de l'Institut de France was designed, in town-planning terms, to offset on the left bank of the Seine the Cour Carrée of the Louvre (see entry) on the right bank. This accounts for its surprising size (for only 60 students) and imposing appearance with the typical features of "classical" French Baroque: prominent pavilions, with high-pitched roofs, that lend weight to the wings at the front of the building, alignment of the façade and the tambour at the base of the dome serried ranks of columns. A special feature is the semicircular arrangement of the façade with, in its centre, the dome of the former chapel. The chapel became the great council chamber and it is here that the individual academies and the Institut as a whole meet in plenary session. Here, too, elections are held on the death of a member and the new member is admitted.

Despite what those who are critical (and envious) of this institution may say to the contrary, membership of one of the Academies is still in France the zenith of any career. Besides the internationally renowned figures who have been members, past and present, of the Académie Française (including Victor Hugo, Prosper Mérimée, Jean Cocteau, René Clair, Eugène Ionesco), many of France's great philosophers and writers have been refused admittance and a "reception under the dome": Blaise Pascal, Molière, Rousseau, Diderot, Balzac, Zola, Proust. In 1980, for the first time in the history of the Academy, women were admitted as members: Yvonne Choquet-Bruhat (Académie des Sciences) and Marguerite Yourcenar (Académie-Française).

Inside the building, which can be visited by prior appointment only, the chief point of interest is the Great Council Chamber under the dome where one can see the memorial statue of Cardinal Mazarin by Antoine Coysevox based on Hardouin-Mansart's design.

*Invalides   F5

Hôtel des Invalides

The Hôtel des Invalides still fulfils its original function as a home for disabled ex-servicemen. Although at one time it could accommodate 7000 pensioners, there are nowadays barely 200 living in what is the finest intact complex of 17th c. buildings in Paris. Most of the rooms are museums or are used by the military authorities. The Musée de l'Armée (Military Museum – see entry) and the adjoining Musée des Plans-Reliefs (Museum of relief maps) are of great interest to the visitor interested in military history, although the main attraction for most visitors is Napoleon's tomb in the Dôme des Invalides (see entry).

Prior to Louis XIV ("the Sun King") disabled ex-servicemen (if any) were given medical attention only in hospitals or monasteries and then in most cases forced to resort to begging. With the Hôtel des Invalides the "Sun King" founded the first home for men disabled while serving in his armies. It was built in 1671–6 under the direction of the architect Libéral Bruant with the Church of Saint-Louis-des-Invalides in the centre. At that time it still lay outside the town and was surrounded by moats and bastions. Today the nave of the church is festooned with flags and standards, the booty of the victorious French armies under Napoleon. (This church is the venue for outstanding organ recitals.)

Since the church's lack of adornment was not to the King's taste

Location
2 Avenue de Tourville
(7th arr.)

Métro
Saint-François-Xavier

Bus
28, 49, 69, 82, 92

Times of opening
1 Oct.–31 March: 10 a.m.–
5 p.m.;
1 April–30 Sept.: 10 a.m.–
6 p.m.

Entrance fee

he commissioned Jules Hardouin-Mansart, one of the architects of Versailles, to build a second "Royal Church" (Eglise Royale, 1675–1706) which later became known as the Eglise du Dôme des Invalides (see entry) because of its characteristic dome.

"Son et lumière"
Performances
31 March–16 Oct:
in French 10.30 p.m.,
in English 9.30 and
11.15 p.m.
(15 May–10 Oct. only
11.15 p.m.)

In the main tourist season there are "Son et lumiére" presentations in the courtyard (Cour d'Honneur) of the Hôtel des Invalides, chiefly featuring the history of Napoleon. There is a bronze statue of Napoleon as the "Little Corporal" under the central arcade of the S pavilion.

German tanks captured in the Second World War stand at the entrance to the gardens in front of the N front of the Hôtel des Invalides. The Esplanade des Invalides extending from here to the Seine was laid out (1704–20) by Robert de Cotte.

Jardin d'Acclimatation   C3

Location
Bois de Boulogne
(16th arr.)

Métro
Sablons, Porte Maillot
(narrow-gauge railway to the
park entrance)

Bus
73

Times of opening
10 a.m.–6 p.m. daily

Children, including those of visitors to Paris, should get their money's worth, in terms of amusement, pleasure and edification, in this park where a Disneyland à la Paris has been set up on a former zoo site in the Bois de Boulogne (see entry). (Parents should accompany their children, if only to keep an eye on their spending!)

A children's zoo, donkey rides, miniature railway, mini road system, go-kart track, skate-board area, fair, children's museum and theatre are only some of the attractions on offer for eight hours every day.

For adults there is the Musée des Arts et Traditions Populaires (see entry), and obviously children are also welcome here.

Jardin des Plantes   J/K6

Location
57 Rue Cuvier (5th arr.)

Métro
Jussieu, Monge

Buses
24, 57, 61, 63, 65, 67, 89, 91

Times of opening
Daily (except Tues. and
public holidays):
Galleries: 1.30 p.m.–
5 p.m.

Tropical hothouse:
1–5 p.m.

Entomology: 2–5 p.m.

Menagerie: winter 9 a.m.–
5 p.m.; summer 9 a.m.–
6 p.m.

Entrance fee

The Jardin des Plantes offers the visitor a glimpse into the natural history research fields of botany (the school for botany has over 10,000 plant species), mineralogy, zoology, ecology and palaeontology (the study of extinct species of animals and plants). It is also a work-place for students at the nearby Paris-VII University (Jussieu).

Early in the 17th c. Louis XIII's doctors established a garden of medicinal herbs here which soon expanded into a great plant collection. A school for botany and pharmacy was set up and from 1650 onwards the garden was open to the public. Georges Louis Leclerc de Bouffon (1707–88), an aristocratic naturalist, extended the gardens and made them into a park, partly in the English and partly in the French (strictly geometrical) style. The 19th c. saw the erection of the iron and glass galleries for palaeontology, botany and mineralogy (greenhouses, bird cages and exhibition buildings) on the left of the main entrance. The acacia between the botany and mineralogy galleries is supposed to be the oldest tree in Paris (planted in 1636).

At the back (viewed from the Seine) there is a small maze.

The Parisians' first sight of the wild animals was during the French Revolution when they were moved from the royal court at Versailles to the English section of the Jardin des Plantes (beasts of prey, apes, elephants and birds). The park then became officially known as the "Musée d'Histoire Naturelle".

Jeu de Paume   G4

In the NE corner of the Tuileries gardens, on the left of the entrance in the Place de la Concorde (see entry), is the building where the ball game Jeu de Paume used to be played and which until 1986 housed the world-famous collection of Impressionist paintings from the Louvre. In that year the new Musée d'Orsay (see entry) in the former Gare d'Orsay railway station opened its doors, and the Jeu de Paume was closed. After rebuilding,, exhibitions of contemporary art will be housed here (probably from 1991). The collection of Impressionists is now dealt with under Musée d'Orsay in the A–Z section.

The Jeu de Paume (from paume=palm of hand, with which the ball was struck) was originally built in the time of the Second Empire (Napoleon III), but was considerably rebuilt in 1931.

Location
Jardins des Tuileries,
Place de la Concorde
(1st arr.)

Métro
Concorde

Buses
24, 42, 52, 72, 73, 84, 94

Times of opening
Daily (except Tues.)
9.45 a.m.–5.15 p.m.

Entrance fee

✗***Louvre**   H5

Since 1793 the former royal palace of the Louvre has been used as a museum (Musée du Louvre), which is one of the most famous in the world. Its collection of paintings ranges from the 13th to the 19th c.; the sculpture and other art treasures date back to the early history of the advanced civilisations; the valuable collections of period furniture and tableware are mainly 17th–19th c. The graphic collection of the banker James de Rothschild also is included in the stock of the Louvre; in 1936 he bequeathed to the museum 3000 drawings and 40,000 graphic illustrations. Very recently (since 1985) a fashion collection has also been housed here.

Rebuilding of this, the greatest French museum, as the "Grand Louvre" (see sketch on page 64/5) will last until the end of the century and will cost about 5½ billion francs. The north wing, which for more than 100 years, that is since the time of Napoleon III's minister, the Duke of Morny, has housed the Ministry of Trade and Finance, will also be integrated into the new scheme. Although by 1989 about half of the employees of the Ministry of Finance had already moved into the new ministry building in Bercy (architect: P. Chemetov) , the Finance Minister, M. Balladur, was successful in having his own way and remaining in the traditional offices until a centrally situated replacement building can be found. This will take a considerable time and the second building phase (Richelieu) will not be completed before the bicentenary of the Louvre in 1993.

Before building work was begun archaeologists carried out excavations in both the inner courtyard, the Cour Carrée and the Cour Napoléon when they uncovered remains of the fortress of Philippe Augustus II (c. 1200) with its keep and the palace of Charles V (14th c.).

A medieval crypt is linked directly with the new basement; here a large number of finds including part of the 15th c. tournament equipment are on show.

After completion of the "Grand Louvre" the museum has about 70,000 sq. m (753,000 sq. ft) of exhibition space at its disposal. The main entrance is formed by the Glass Pyramid, dedicated in 1989. It stands in the centre of the Cour Napoléon, is some

Location
Palais du Louvre (1st arr.)

Métro
Louvre, Palais-Royal

Buses
21, 24, 27, 39, 48, 67, 69,
72, 74, 77, 81, 85, 95

Grand Louvre

*Glass Pyramid
(main entrance)

Palais du Louvre

22 m (72 ft) high and has 675 windows. In accordance with the plan of the Chinese-American architect Ieoh Ming Pei, the visitor proceeds from the pyramid into a basement (Hall Napoléon, open daily except Tuesday 9 a.m.–10 p.m.), where are located the ticket offices, information desks, bookstalls, a café, a restaurant, auditoriums and rooms for temporary exhibitions. From here the visitor continues along corridors and up escalators to three separate art departments:

Pavillon Richelieu

On the north (Richelieu): new collections will be established from 1992 (provisional opening 1993).

Pavillon Sully

On the east (Sully): the new historical department of the Louvre, excavations from the medieval crypt, ancient oriental and Islamic art, Coptic art and Egyptian antiquities of the Pharaohs, Greek, Etruscan and Roman art objects, bronzes and terracotta articles, French painting (14th–17th c.), and Italian paintings (17th–18th c.) as well as craftwork from the Middle Ages to the 19th c.

Pavillon Denon

On the south (Denon): Greek, Etruscan and Roman sculptures, the crown jewels in the Galerie d'Apollon, French sculpture (from the Middle Ages to the 19th c.), Italian (13th–18th c.), Flemish and Dutch (15th–17th c.), German (15th–16th c.), the northern schools (18th and 19th c.) and from Spain and Great Britain. Also to be seen are the Beistegui, Lyon and De Croy collections and exhibitions of work from the department of painting.

Beneath the Cour Napoléon (reopened in 1988) are the Cour du Carrousel, with the small Arc de Triomphe, shopping arcades, restaurants galleries, conference rooms and a car park are being developed.

In addition there are plans for several workshops and, in the Aile de Flore, a scientific centre with a library, a painting studio and special facilities for the various branches of art. The Ecole du Louvre will also be situated here.

The implementation of the scheme for the Cour du Carrousel is entrusted to the S.A.R.I. (Société d'administration et de réalisation d'investissements), which also played an important role in the building of the commercial quarter of La Défense. A start was made with the construction of the huge subterranean leisure centre, when the exterior work on the "Grand Louvre" was finished in 1989.

The Palace stands on the site of a fortress (*c.* 1200) built in the reign of Philippe Augustus which was partly demolished by the "Renaissance King", François I. In 1559–74 the architect Pierre Lescot and the sculptor Jean Goujon were responsible for the converging sections of the W and S wings of the old Louvre (the Cour Carrée). These oldest parts of the present Palace were extended in 1566 in a southerly direction by adding the Petite Galerie to Lescot's S wing. At almost the same time (1564) the Tuileries Palace was built 500 m (550 yd) to the W of the old Louvre as a residence for the dowager queen Catherine de Medici (along the present Avenue du Général Lemonnier). During the reign of Henri IV this palace was joined to the Petite Galerie by the long S wing (Galerie du Bord de l'Eau) flanking the Seine. Louis XIII and Louis XIV had the Cour Carrée completed.

The old Louvre and the Tuileries Palace were only occasionally occupied by the French kings; Napoleon I then enlarged the square in front of the Tuileries castle (now the Jardin du Louvre and Place du Carrousel) where he had the Arc de Triomphe du Carrousel (see entry) erected and began to build the north wing. Finally Baron Haussmann had the Jardin du Louvre and the Place and Square du Carrousel laid out in the form in which we see them today.

The Tuileries Palace was stormed by the people on three occasions: in 1793, 1848 and 1871. The last time it was completely destroyed and never rebuilt.

Abutting on to the E side of the Cour Carrée is the Square du Carrousel with the six pavilions of the inner wings on its N and S sides. This opens on to the Place du Carrousel and further W the "Parterres" of the Jardin du Carrousel with the Arc de Triomphe du Carrousel (see entry) and 18 statues by Aristide Malllol. The Jardin du Carrousel is bordered at the ends of the S and N wings on a level with the Pavillon de Flore (in the S) and the Pavillon de Marsan (in the N) by the Avenue du Général Lemonnier; the Tuileries Gardens begin on the other side of the Avenue.

The following sections of the exterior are most worth seeing: E front/colonnades: in 1665 Louis XIV sought to get the major architects of the time to produce an especially impressive design for the E front of the old Louvre by announcing a competition (entrants included the Frenchmen Jean Marot and Jacques Lemercier and the Italian Gian Lorenzo Bernini, the architect of St Peter's Square in Rome). The winning design was a joint effort by Claude Perrault, Louis Le Vau and Charles Lebrun. The "colonnade", which today can be admired in its

Palace

Palace layout

Exterior
East Façade and
Colonnades

63

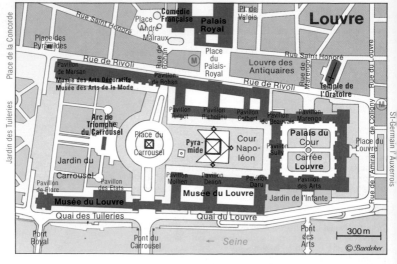

Map labels:
Rue Saint Honoré · Place André Malraux · Comédie Française · Place du Palais-Royal · Palais Royal · Pr. de Valois · **Louvre** · Place de la Concorde · Place des Pyramides · Rue de Rivoli · Pavillon de Marsan · Musée des Arts Décoratifs · Musée des Arts de la Mode · Pavillon de Rohan · Rue de Rohan · Louvre des Antiquaires · Rue Saint Honoré · Rue de Marengo · Temple de l'Oratoire · Jardin des Tuileries · Arc de Triomphe du Carrousel · Place du Carrousel · Pavillon Turgot · Pavillon Richelieu · Pavillon Colbert · Pavillon de Beauvais · Pavillon Marengo · Pyramide · Cour Napoléon · Pavillon Sully · Palais du Cour · Carrée Louvre · Place du Louvre · Rue de l'Amiral de Coligny · St-Germain l'Auxerrois · Jardin du Carrousel · Pavillon de Flore · Pavillon des États · Pavillon Mollien · Pavillon Denon · Pavillon Daru · Pavillon des Arts · Jardin de l'Infante · **Musée du Louvre** · **Musée du Louvre** · Quai des Tuileries · Quai du Louvre · Pont Royal · Pont du Carrousel · Pont des Arts · ← Seine · 300 m · © Baedeker

entirety thanks to the exposure of the base, as a result of the programme, since 1968, to refurbish Paris' monuments, represents a compromise between the styles of French Baroque and Classical Italian: the double columns and flat roof are Italian-Classical in style whereas the emphasis on the centre (triangular gable) and side sections is more typical of the French. The exposure of the base has restored to the colonnade (18 Corinthian columns) its original spatial dimensions. The "classical severity" of this magnificent façade was to have been tempered by a row of statues on the roof balustrade but this did not materialise.

All work was stopped when the court moved to Versailles, leaving its completion to Napoleon. Consequently the figures in the central pediment (Minerva, 1811) and the reliefs below it (Goddess of Victory in a chariot drawn by four horses) date from the early 19th c. The medallions on the upper left and right contain the initials of Louis XIV.

Cour Carrée

Square Courtyard: the buildings enclosing this courtyard form

Section of the Grand Louvre

Section labels: Quai du Louvre · Pavillon Denon · Great Pyramid · Little Pyramid · Seine · Salle du Manège · Accueil Napo...

the so-called Vieux Louvre (Old Louvre), the true Palace of the Louvre. This was approximately the site of Philippe Augustus' original fortress (its outline is marked out in the SW corner). Lescot's façade was begun under Henri II while work on the other wings began under Louis XIII and Louis XIV and was not finished until the time of Napoleon.

Pavillon de l'Horloge: the Clock Pavilion, designed to harmonise with Lescot's façade, is the work of Jacques Lemercier (17th c.) who also added the N section of the W wing in imitation Renaissance style.

Lescot Façade

1559–74: the southern half of the W wing of the Cour Carrée is the oldest part of the Louvre Palace. This masterpiece of Renaissance architecture was created by the architect Pierre Lescot (1510–78) and the sculptor Jean Goujon (1510–68).

With its striking harmony the Lescot façade is an expression of the concern in Renaissance architecture to revive the symmetry of its Classical models in a distinct and "unassuming" but not necessarily unadorned form (unlike, for example, the monumental ordered Classicism of the late 18th c. – see Madeleine and Panthéon). It is clearly tripartite, both horizontally, in the alternation of the door and gable sections with those of the window, and vertically (if the narrow upper floor is considered part of the roof). Thus the ratio of door section to window section and of height of storey to (projecting) storey demarcation is in each case 1:3.

The round arches of the windows on the ground floor give the impression of an arcade; in the middle storey each pair of triangular-gabled windows flanks a round-gabled window (repetition of the triple theme!); the top storey is rightly famed for the marvellous relief decoration (Jean Goujon) on the round gables, which are linked by a richly ornamented balustrade. The gable reliefs are allegories: Nature (left: Ceres for Agriculture, Neptune for Shipping, Genius with cornucopia), War (centre: Mars God of War, Bellona Goddess of War, prisoners), Science (right: Archimedes for Astronomy, Euclid for Geometry, Spirit of science).

(The Lescot wing was built at the same time as the adjoining half of the S wing which contained the royal apartments, but this façade is of little artistic importance.)

Petite Galerie

1566: this short section is at right angles to the S side of the Cour Carrée and to the long wing of the Louvre running along the Seine in a westerly direction.

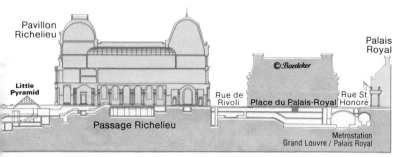

65

Louvre

Glass Pyramid in the Cour Napoleon

Pavillon Denon	The buildings added to the N and S wings date from the time of Napoleon III. There is an entrance here to the Louvre Museum.
Square du Louvre	This square was laid out by Baron Haussmann. The equestrian statue of General Lafayette which stands outside the glass pyramid was a gift from the U.S.A.
Guichet du Louvre	In the Seine wing: triple-arched gateway with gigantic allegories of the Navy and the Merchant Fleet. The entire Galerie du Bord de l'Eau (Seine wing) was restored in the 19th c.
Place du Carrousel	"Carrousel" was the name given to the equestrian games and masked balls which evolved from the medieval tournaments. The square owes its name to the "Carrousel" of 1662 which celebrated the birth of the Dauphin (crown prince) Louis XV. To the west stands the Arc de Triomphe du Carrousel (see entry).
Pavillon de Flore	The Tuileries Palace which was burned down in 1871 stood between the Pavillon de Flore and the Pavillon de Marsan. The pavilion gets its name from the relief "Triumph of Flora" (1866) by Jean-Baptiste Carpeaux (on the Seine side).
Musée des Arts Décoratifs	The west pavilion of the N wing (Pavillon de Marsan) contains the Musée des Arts Décoratifs (arts and crafts; open: Wed.–Sat. 12.30–6 p.m., Sun. 11 a.m. or noon–6 p.m.). This is a comprehensive collection of furniture and household articles from medieval to modern times.
Musée de Arts de la Mode	Since January 1896 the building has also housed a museum of fashion. Among the exhibits are exclusive dresses by Chanel, Dior, Worth, Cardin and other celebrated dress designers (open: Wed.–Sat. 12.30–6 p.m., Sun 11 a.m.–6 p.m.).
Pavillon de Rohan	The pavilion dates from the time of Louis XVIII.

****Musée du Louvre**

It is not possible to reproduce a detailed plan of the museum because it is currently being reorganised (a free plan of the present layout of the Grand Louvre can be obtained at the ticket office. Consequently only a general survey of the periods of art and exhibits can be given here.

In this context it is possible to give only a general idea of the periods, schools of painting and artefacts on display.

1. Etruscan art (inc. "Sarcophagus of Cerveteri", 6th c. B.C.).
2. Oriental antiquities (art from Mesopotamia, Persia, Phoenicia, Assyria, including a stele of Naram-Sin, king of Adge *circa* 2270 B.C.; Assyrian winged beasts of the 8th c. B.C., and the corpus of laws of Hammurabi, king of the first Babylonian kingdom).
3. Egyptian antiquities (Old, Middle and New Kingdoms including a stele of the snake-god Zet of the Thinite epoque *circa* 3000 B.C.; a stele of Antef, a high official under Thutmosis III; a bust of King Amenophis IV and a sarcophagus of the chancellor Imeneminet of the 7th c. B.C.).
4. Greek sculpture (including sculptures and fragments of friezes from the Parthenon, the temple built by Phidias 447–438 B.C. on the Acropolis of Athens; metopes from the Temple of Zeus at Olympia 5th c. B.C.; the "Venus de Milo", a statue of Aphrodite found on the Island of Melos – in French Milo – which dates from the 2nd c. B.C.; the "Lady of Auxerre", "Winged Nike of Samothrace" – see picture page 68 – the statue of an ancient Greek goddess of victory *circa* 200 B.C.; "Apollo Sauroktónos" and the "Knidish Aphrodite", copies of sculptures by Praxiteles of the 4th c. B.C.).
5. Classical bronze figures (inc. the "Athlete of Benevento" and the "Ephebe of Agde").
6. Roman sarcophagi, 2nd and 3rd c. B.C., frescoes and mosaics from Rome and Greece.
7. Greek ceramics.
8. Sculpture, 12th–19th c. (including the famous statue of Cupid by Edme Bouchardon; Michelangelo's "Slaves", Donatello's "St John the Baptist" and "Mary and Child" the "Annuciation" by Tilman Riemenscheider and the funerary monument of Philippe Pot).
9. Spanish painting, 14th–18th c. (inc. El Greco, Francisco Zurbarán, Estaban Murillo, José Ribera, Diego Velázquez, Francisco Goya).
10. Late-Gothic and Renaissance paintings from Germany and the Low Countries, 15th and 16th c. (inc. Dürer's "Self-portrait", works by Hans Holbein the Younger and Lucas Cranach).
11. Flemish and Dutch painting, 16th and 17th c. (inc. works by Peter Paul Rubens, Jan van Eyck, Hieronymus Bosch, Breughel the Elder, Frans Hals, Rembrandt's "Disciple of Emmaus" and Van Dyck's portrait of Charles I of England).
12. Italian painting, 13th–15th c. (inc. works by Giotto, Filippo Lippi, Botticelli, Mantegna).
13. Italian painting, 16th c. (the highlights are the "Mona Lisa" – in Italian "La Gioconda", in French "La Joconde" – world

Location
Palais du Louvre (1st arr.)

Métro
Louvre, Palais-Royal, Musée du Louvre

Buses
21, 24, 27, 39, 48, 67, 69, 72, 74, 77, 81, 85, 95

Times of opening
Thur.–Sun. 9 a.m.–6 p.m., Mon and Wed. 9 a.m.– 9.45 p.m.
Times subject to alteration because of rebuilding.

Entrance free on Sundays

Mona Lisa

Louvre

Venus de Milo

Nike de Samothrace ("Winged Victory")

Jardin and Palais du Luxembourg

famous for her smile, and the "Virgin of the Rocks", both by Leonardo da Vinci; also Paolo Veronese's "Marriage Feast at Cana" and the portrait of the courtier and writer Baldassare Castiglione by Raphael).

14. Italy, 17th c. masters ("Virgin Mary" by Caravaggio, Tiepolo, Caracci).

15. French 16th c. paintings (Jean Clouet, François Quernel).

16. French 17th c. painting (Lebrun, Poussin, La Tour, Le Nain).

17. French 18th and 19th c. painting (including "Freedom on the Baracades" by Eugène Delacroix, "The Gleaners" by Jean-Dominique Millet and "The Turkish Bath" by Jean-Dominique Ingres).

18. Applied art and furniture.

19. Remainder of the French Crown Jewels.

Luxembourg H6

*Jardin du Luxembourg

Children and students (from the nearby Quartier Latin – see entry) are regular visitors to the Jardin du Luxembourg, which is the best-known park in Paris after the Tuileries. It dates from the 17th c. (coinciding with the Palais du Luxembourg – see entry) and owes its present appearance to the 19th c. architect J. F. Chalgrin (1739–1811).

The large octagonal pond with fountain is flanked by two terraces. This central part of the park is laid out in the French Classical style (straight lines, symmetry), while the outer sections are closer to the less formal English style of garden (winding paths, occasional stands of trees).

A number of statues of prominent men and women from the worlds of art and politics are dotted around the terraces and paths. The "Fontaine des Médicis", in its picturesque setting among the trees (opposite the E front of the Palace), is worth looking at. The basin of the fountain with its Renaissance statuary of the river gods of the Rhône and Seine dates from around 1620 and is a reminder of the former owner, Marie de Médicis, mother of Louis XIII.

The large pond is usually besieged by children who sail their boats here (these can also be hired at a stall); smaller children sit entranced in front of the "Grand Guignol" (Punch and Judy show) near the tennis courts in the SW part of the garden.

There are chairs and benches to rest on free of charge. (Until a few years ago elderly women still did the rounds collecting the city's charges for these.) At dusk the park-keeper's whistle indicates that the gates are about to be closed for the night.

Location
Main entrance:
Place Edmond Rostand
(Boulevard St-Michel,
6th arr.)

Métro
Odéon

Suburban train station
Luxembourg (RER)

Buses
21, 27, 38, 84, 85, 89

Times of opening
Daily 9 a.m. until dusk

Palais du Luxembourg (Musée du Luxembourg)

The Palais du Luxembourg is the seat of the French Senate (Upper House) which together with the Assemblée Nationale

Location
19 Rue de Vaugirard (6th arr.)

Church of the Madeleine

Métro
Odéon, Luxembourg

Suburban station
Luxembourg (RER)

Buses
5, 8, 84, 85

Times of opening
Museum: daily (except Mon.)
11 a.m.–6 p.m.,
Fri. until 10 p.m.

Entrance fee

(see Palais Bourbon) makes up the French Parliament. Only parts of it are open to the public, and then only on Sundays (apart from the exhibition rooms of the "Musée du Luxembourg"). Groups must apply in writing to the Secrétariat général de la questure du Sénat, 15 Rue de Vaugirard, 75006 Paris. Marie de Médicis, the wife of Henri IV, acquired the property in 1612 from Duke Francis of Luxembourg in order to have her dowager's residence built there – in the Florentine style of her homeland in accordance with her wishes. However, the architects of the palace, built between 1615 and 1631 according to the plans of Salomon de Brosse, closely followed the traditional French style: the principal and side wings, bounded by pavilions (domed structures with high-pitched roofs), form a courtyard (Cour d'Honneur); the living quarters in the "classical" sequence of garderobe, cabinet, anti-chambre, chambre (bedroom) each make up one unit. Two huge galleries were intended for series of paintings but Peter Paul Rubens' famous "Medici" series showing the Countess at various ages, is now in the Louvre (see entry) and its counterpart for Henri IV was never painted. The remarkable paintings on the walls of the library are by Eugène Delacroix (1845–7).

Marie de Médicis never used the palace, as shortly after it was finished she had to flee the country – she had lost the game of political intrigue against her adversary Cardinal Richelieu. She died in exile in Cologne in 1642.

The palace changed hands several times before Napoleon decided it should be used for the Senate and had it altered by J. F. Chalgrin (garden wing).

*Madeleine G4

The church of Saint Mary Magdalen, generally known as La Madeleine, is a pseudo-Grecian building (54 Corinthian columns) of considerable size (108 m (354 ft) long, 43 m (141 ft) wide, height of columns: 15 m – 49 ft). Although of minor significance from the art-historical point of view, it is always of interest to foreign visitors and affords a chance of glimpsing a spectacular wedding.

The story of the building of the Madeleine reflects the confused state of French history from the end of the Ancien Régime until the time of the Citizen-King: the foundation stone was laid in 1763 in the reign of Louis XV for a cruciform Baroque church with a dome. Under Louis XVI it was planned to remodel it on the Classical lines of the Panthéon (see entry), then under construction, with more emphasis on the dome. During the Revolutionary period building came to a complete standstill. Various plans for a completely different use (as a stock exchange, Parliament or bank) were advanced and rejected. In 1806 Napoleon decided on a Hall of Fame for the army in the style of the Parthenon in Athens but shortly before his abdication he reverted to the idea of a church. Louis XVIII, protagonist of the Restoration, wanted a church of expiation to atone for the Revolution. It was not until the reign of Louis-Philippe, the Citizen King, that the church dedicated to Saint Mary Magdalen was completed as a "Greek temple" (1842).

The gable frieze on the façade (1833, Philippe-Henri Lemaire) is of the Last Judgment. The reliefs on the bronze door relate to the Ten Commandments.

Light enters the interior (vestibule, nave, semicircular choir) through three huge domes. The spandrels are decorated with reliefs of the 12 Apostles and the main altar with a group of figures in marble (1837), Ascension of Mary Magdalen. Above the altar is a vast fresco showing Constantine the Great, Frederick Barbarossa, Joan of Arc, Saint Louis, Michelangelo, Raphael, Dante, Cardinal Richelieu, Napoleon and other historical figures. Famous Cavaillé-Coll organ (recitals).

Location
Place de la Madeleine (8th arr.)

Métro
Madeleine

Buses
24, 42, 52, 84, 94

Maisons-Laffitte

This impressive château was built between 1642 and 1651 by François Mansart for the president of the Royal Court of Justice (Parliament), René de Longueil. It is the most important example of the early period of Classical French château-architecture in the 17th c. The whole of the interior dates from that time. Especially worthy of note are the many double pilasters with their fine detail.

This is where Mansart first used the high gable windows that later entered the French language as "mansardes".

Location
Maisons-Laffitte (western suburb)

Rail
from Gare Saint-Lazare

Times of opening
Mon.–Sat. 9 a.m.–noon and 2–6 p.m.;
Sun. 2–6 p.m.

*Malmaison

This château, situated in the western suburb of Rueil-Malmaison, contains many mementoes of the Emperor Napoleon I and the Empress Joséphine. It has been a French national museum since 1906. The château of Malmaison was built in 1620 in the

Location
Rueil-Malmaison (suburb 16 km (10 miles) W on the N13)

Marais

Late-medieval Hôtel de Sens

Suburban station
Défense (RER)

Bus
158A (from Défense)

Times of opening
Mon., Wed.–Sun.
10 a.m.–12.30 p.m.,
1.30–5 p.m.; last admission
noon or 4.30 p.m.
Closed: Tues. and public
holidays

Guided tours

Entrance fee

early Baroque style and bought in 1799 by Joséphine de Beauharnais, the wife of Napoleon Bonaparte. After their divorce the Empress lived here withdrawn and alone. She died here in 1814, ten months before Napoleon – after the failure of the "100 days" – took his leave of family and country here to go into final exile on the island of St Helena.

The interior furnishings date back to the time of the Empire. Most of the objects were originally in the château but some come from the palaces of Saint-Cloud and Fontainebleau and from the Tuileries Palace.

The ground floor houses the billiard room, Golden Drawing Room (Sèvres porcelain), Music Room (complete 1812 décor), Dining-room (the gilded dinner service was a coronation gift from the city of Paris in 1804), council chamber, study (military décor) and library (in its original state).

The rooms on the first floor: Emperor's drawing-room and bedroom, Marengo drawing-room (after the wall painting of the victory of Marengo), Empress's rooms, exhibition rooms.

*Marais   J/K5/6

Location
4th arrondissement

Métro
Saint-Paul, Rambuteau

Buses
29, 75, 96

The Marais quarter covers more or less the same area as the 4th arrondissement. In the last 20 years costly restoration work has saved a chapter in the history of the city of Paris from ruin and demolition.

The Marais is the "birthplace" of the "hôtel", the magnificent Paris town houses of the French landed gentry. A "hôtel" is always laid out with a courtyard (Cour d'Honneur) opening on to the street, main section with lateral wings, terrace and gardens at the back.

At the end of the 17th c. the Marais, whose showpiece in town-planning terms is the Place des Vosges (see entry), lost its attraction for the nobility and rich bourgeoisie who moved out to Versailles or the Faubourg Saint-Germain. Craftsmen and small tradesmen moved into the district. The Revolution left terrible scars, the hôtels fell into decay or were demolished by the people to make way for new housing and subsequent attempts at restoration in the 19th c. were fruitless. Not until 1962 did the French Ministry of Culture under André Malraux tackle the pressing task of conserving the heart of the city of Paris, valuable both in town-planning and in historical terms, thereby rediscovering the almost forgotten hôtels of the Marais.

The restoration and development of the quarter may have brought the speculators on to the scene, but the Marais has managed to retain its charm which can be experienced by sampling its lively combination of medieval settings and modern everyday living or by visiting the "Festival du Marais" (see Practical Information, Calendar of Events).

The hôtels most worth seeing are:

Built 1475–1507 by the Archbishops of Sens; 1 Rue du Figuier, tel. 42 78 40 24; métro: Pont-Marie, Saint-Paul.

Hôtel de Sens

The Forney Library contains documents on fine art and industrial technology.

Forney Library

Built 1630–50 by Louis Le Vau, altered by François Mansart 1656; 7 Rue de Jouy; métro: Saint-Paul.

Hôtel d'Aumont

1658–60, Antoine Lepautre; 68 Rue François-Miron, tel. 48 87 74 31; métro: Saint-Paul.

Hôtel de Beauvais

Hôtel des Ambassadeurs de Hollande; 1657–60; 47 Rue Vieille-du-Temple; métro: Rambuteau.

Hôtel Amelot de Bisseuil

1705–9, Pierre Alexis Delamaire; 60 Rue des Francs-Bourgeois, métro: Rambuteau.

Hôtel de Rohan-Soubise/
Archives Nationales

The French National Archives housed here are among the largest in the world. This fine patrician mansion was built by Delamaire for the Princess of Soubis and given its present name in 1808. It contains several million documents on the history of France from the 7th c. to the Second World War, which are collected in the Musée de l'Histoire de France (open: daily except Tue. 2–5 p.m.). The Rococo rooms, especially the "Salon ovale" (1735–8), are well worth seeing.

Built 1648–51 by François Mansard; 60 Rue des Archives, tel. 2 72 86 43; métro: Rambuteau.

Hôtel Guénégaud/Musée de la Chasse et de la Nature

Museum of Hunting and Nature with an interesting collection of old shot guns and hunting knives as well as works by 18th c. French painters of animals (open: Wed.–Mon. 10 a.m.–12.30 p.m., 1.30–5.30 p.m.).

1594–8, Jean Baptiste Androuet du Cerceau; 24 Rue Pavée, métro: Saint-Paul.

Hôtel Lamoignon

This contains the Library of the City of Paris (Bibliothèque Historique de la Ville de Paris); open: daily except Sundays and holidays, 9.30 a.m.–6 p.m. (with reading-room).

Marché aux Puces

Hôtel de Sully de Béthune	1625, Jean Androuet du Cerceau; 62 Rue Saint-Antoine, métro: Saint-Paul.
Musée Carnavalet	See entry.
Musée Picasso	See entry.

Marché aux Puces (fleamarket)   H1

Location
Northern outskirts

Métro
Porte de Clignancourt

Buses
50, 254, PC

Times of opening
Sat., Sun., Mon. 6 a.m.–
5 p.m.

This great kingdom of "bric à brac" lies between the Porte de Clignancourt and the Porte de Saint-Ouen (outside the Boulevard Périphérique) on the northern outskirts of Paris. Walking towards the fleamarket from the Métro at the Porte de Clignancourt the visitor's heart may well sink at first on seeing the stalls selling cheap plastic wares that line the pavement, but the fleamarket proper does not begin until you pass under the motorway.

Here, too, the goods on offer are rather mixed: brand new jeans jostle with worthless junk and genuine (?) antiques: pictures, furniture, books, china – when buying anything here you need to know what you are about! The visitor who goes simply to browse can happily immerse himself in this welter of junk, skilful reproductions and valuable antiques.

It's worth knowing which parts of the market specialise in particular items, viz. Malik – spectacles, records; Jules-Vallès – country furniture; Paul Bert – china; Cambo – household articles, pictures; Biron – valuable antiques; Vernaison – period furniture, trinkets.

Monnaie   H5

Location
Quai de Conti (6th arr.)

Métro
Pont-Neuf, Odéon

Buses
24, 27

Times of Opening:
Workshops: Mon. Wed. 2.15–
3 p.m.

Coin museum: temporarily
closed.

The former royal, now State, Mint is one of Paris's few monuments (1771–7) in the early Louis XVI style.

It was begun towards the end of Louis XV's reign (plans by Jacques Denis Antoine), and the notable feature of its architecture is that it lacks the ornamentation usually found to a large degree in Rococo and Baroque. On the portal of the 117 m (384 ft) long façade there are allegories of Trade and Agriculture.

Besides the ordinary one-franc coins special gold and silver coins are also minted here. Visits to the workshops can be arranged.

Montmartre   G/H3

Location
the northern part of the city
(18th arr.)

Métro
Place Clichy, Blanche, Pigalle,
Anvers, Abbesses

Buses
30, 54, 80, 85

There are two common explanations for the name Montmartre. One is that it is derived from "Mont de Mercure" (mount of Mercury) after one of the Roman temples dedicated to Mercury which is supposed to have stood here. The other is connected with the legend of Saint Denis (or Dionysius), the first bishop of Paris, who is supposed to have been beheaded here along with his companions Rusticus and Eleutherius (see Saint-Denis), hence "Mont des Martyrs" (Mount of the Martyrs).

Today Montmartre stands for three things: "La Butte Montmartre" is the hill of Montmartre (129 m (423 ft) above sea level) with the Sacré-Cœur and the Place du Tertre (see entries); Montmartre also means the residential quarter of Montmartre, and, finally, also stands for the entertainment quarter of Montmartre (see entries) on the Boulevard de Clichy.

La Butte Montmartre

The "Butte Montmartre" is not only a place where legends were created but also where history was made. From the 12th c. the hill was the site of a powerful Benedictine convent run by abbesses (see Saint-Pierre-Montmartre) which was razed to the ground during the French Revolution (1794) (hence the name "Abbesses" for the métro station). At that time the hill was temporarily named "Mont-Marat" after the Revolutionary leader Jean-Paul Marat.

In 1871 Montmartre was the scene of the bloody beginning and even bloodier end of the Paris Commune, whose defenders made their last stand here (and on the Buttes Chaumont) against the troops of Thiers' bourgeois-reactionary government. Today Montmartre still proudly calls itself "commune libre" (free commune).

The former vine-growing village, which was only incorporated into the city in 1860, owed its international fame to the artists' colony that settled on the hill before the turn of the century and attracted from everywhere singers, writers and above all painters: Manet, Van Gogh, Toulouse-Lautrec, Utrillo, Apollinaire, Max Jacob, Picasso and many others. After the First World War the artistic and intellectual centre of Paris shifted to the quarter of Montparnasse (see entry).

But it is not only the memories that linger on. Although art and commerce may have become one and the same thing in the Place du Tertre and people may argue about the "wedding-cake" style of the "Sacré-Cœur", if one takes the time to explore the narrow alleys and steep steps of la Butte Montmartre, with their views of Paris, many of them quite unexpected, one gets the feeling of what Paris has to offer – her "infinite variety". Since autumn 1985 visitors must explore Montmartre on foot, for tourist buses have to off-load their passengers and return to the official parking places where passengers rejoin them.

As Montmartre is the highest "mountain" in Paris it has its only funicular railway which travels daily from 6.45 a.m. to 0.45 a.m. between the Place Saint-Pierre and the Sacré-Cœur.

See cemeteries.

. Cimetière de Montmartre

*Entertainment quarter

On the SW fringe of the Butte Montmartre lies one of the night-time centres of attraction of Paris with a lot to offer in a very small area: the Boulevard de Clichy between Place Pigalle and Place de Clichy. Here and in the adjoining side streets running into Place Pigalle, Place Blanche and Place de Clichy there is everything that commercialised sex can offer: sex shops, cinemas showing pornographic films, striptease shows, cabarets, bars and prostitution.

Location
Boulevard de Clichy
(between Place de Clichy and Place Pigalle; 18th arr.)

Métro
Place Clichy, Blanche, Pigalle

Montmartre: Moulin Rouge

Buses
30, 54, 74, 80, 95

Night-life begins with the illumination of the neon signs at dusk: at the entrances to the "establishments" the touts take up their positions as do the women and girls on the corners and in the doorways around the Place Pigalle.

Those who still have enough money left and feel like eating are well catered for in the Place Clichy and several restaurants also stay open after midnight (with full menu).

Montparnasse   G6

Location
On the border between 6th and 14th arr.

Métro
Vavin, Montparnasse-Bienvenue

Buses
48, 58, 82, 89, 91, 94, 95, 96

The quarter of Montparnasse is today almost better known for its 59-storey "tower" than for its former artists' colonies, the last remnants of which still linger on in the southern part of the 14th arrondissement.

While Montmartre and Saint-Germain-des-Prés (see entry) may have served as the rendezvous for artists and intellectuals before the First World War and in the decade that followed the Second World War, it was Montparnasse that fulfilled this function in the twenties and thirties. Simone de Beauvoir and Jean-Paul Sartre, Ernest Hemingway, Henry Miller and James Joyce met in the cafés, bars and restaurants at the junction of Boulevard du Montparnasse and Boulevard Raspail (Dôme, Coupole, Select, Rotonde). The painters Henri Matisse, Wassily Kandinsky, Amedeo Modigliani and Marc Chagall worked in this quarter. The café-restaurant "Closerie des Lilas" was the domain of the poets Paul Fort and Guillaume Apollinaire, and Jean-Paul Sartre was a regular customer.

View of the Dôme des Invalides from the Tour Montparnasse

Today Montparnasse is dominated by a tower block ("Tour Montparnasse") from the restaurant (open noon–2 p.m.) and open terrace of which there is a view of Paris from 200 m (656 ft) up which can only be compared with the view from the Eiffel Tower. The "tower" rises up near the entrance to the railway station of Montparnasse, built in the seventies, from which trains leave for the W of France, especially Brittany.

On the level of the Cinq-Martyrs-du Lycée-Buffon Bridge the largest Paris railway station is being built for the high-speed trains (TGV) which from 1989 will run from Paris to the Atlantic coast. The future increase of traffic is estimated to reach about 60 million passengers a year. A length of 350 m (383 yards) will be roofed in over the tracks; this will have a garden layout and will also form a link between the districts of Vaugirard and Plaisance.

Since the 60s the city has been carrying out probably the most extensive and radical redevelopment programme in Paris behind Montparnasse Station. The area between the Rue Vercingetorix and the Rue Commandant René Mouchette, which was once popular for its ambience with artists such as the naïve painter Henri Rousseau, fell more and more into decay until an almost complete redevelopment became necessary over an area of some 80 ha (198 acres). The functional modern classicism which resulted, where the residential buildings often resemble theatrical scenery, continues to be the subject of controversy.

The most recent example, which has towered over the sea of houses since 1986, is the building containing offices and flats

Tour Montparnasse
33 Avenue du Maine

Times of opening
Daily 9.30 a.m.–11 p.m.

Entrance fee

Redevelopment
Montparnasse/Plaisance

Echelles du Baroque

77

Neo-classical "Echelles du Baroque" by Ricardo Bofill

Statue of Louis XIV in the courtyard of the Musée Carnavalet

known as the "Echelles du Baroque" (Baroque ladders) in the Place de Séoul. This eliptical building, which is faced with blue glass, and the associated "Amphithéâtre" house 270 apartments. The Catalan architect Ricardo Bofill was already well-known because of his building complexes in Marne-la-Vallée ("Les Espaces d'Abraxas") and in Saint-Quentin-en-Yvelines ("Viaduc", "Les Temples du Lac").

See Cemeteries

Cimetière de Montparnasse

*Mosquée (mosque)   J6

The Islamic house of prayer was built between 1922 and 1926. The building also houses the Islamic Institute for Religious Studies. Its minaret is 33 m (108 ft) high. The prayer room may be visited every day except Friday. Remember that the religious custom is to remove one's shoes before entering the prayer room.
A Turkish bath, a small Arab restaurant and a bazaar also form part of the complex of buildings.

Location
39 Rue Geoffroy-Saint-Hilaire (5th arr.)

Métro
Censier

Times of opening
Daily except Fri.

*Musée Carnavalet   K5

Carnavalet is a mocking distortion of the name of the former owner, the widow of the Breton Sire de Kernevenoy. The hôtel was built in the 16th c. (probably by Pierre Lescot, the architect of the Renaissance façade of the Louvre). The entrance with sculptures of lions (by Jean Goujon) and the section opposite date from that period. The other sections of the courtyard, in which stands a remarkable statue of Louis XIV by Antoine Coysevox (1698), were altered in the 17th c. by François Mansart. Madame de Sévigny lived in the Hôtel Carnavalet between 1677 and 1696. Her letters to her daughter (over 1500 of them) describing life in Paris and at the court in Versailles are an exceptionally valuable account of the period of Louis XIV. Around the turn of the century the hôtel was enlarged to its present size for the purposes of the museum.

The Musée de l'Histoire de Paris (history of the city of Paris) has been housed here since 1880. Since additional space became necesary for the continually increasing material, the museum was extended in 1989 around the neighbouring Hôtel Le Peletier de Saint-Fargeau. The sober style of this building, erected 1686–1690 under the supervision of the architect Pierre Bullet, reveals the influence of François Blondel.

The delightfully proportioned exhibition rooms of the Hôtel Carnavalet permit a comprehensive collection of paintings, sculptures, etchings, ceramics, funiture and household articles of the most varied kinds, and give the visitor a vivid survey of the history of the city from its Gallo-Roman beginnings through the Middle Ages up to the reign of Louis XVI, while the new sections in the Hôtel Le Peletier de Saint-Fargeau are devoted to the historical development of the city from the French Revolution to the present day. Notable features include the Galerie Sévigné, the Bouvier Collection, the workshop of the jeweller

Location
23 Rue de Sévigné (3rd arr.)

Métro
Saint-Paul, Chemin-Vert

Buses
29, 69, 76, 96

Times of opening
10 a.m.–5.40 p.m.; closed Mon.

Entrance fee

Hôtel Carnavalet

Hôtel Le Peletier de Saint-Fargeau

Musée de l'Histoire de Paris

Fouquet d'Alphonse Mucha (1900) and the ballroom of Madame de Wendel designed by José Maria Sert.

Musée Condé

Location
Chantilly, 40 km (25 miles) N
(autoroute de Lille; N16)

Rail
from Gare du Nord – RN16
(Survilliers)

Times of opening
10.30 a.m.–5 p.m. (except
Tues. and race days)

The Musée Condé, housed in the Château of Chantilly (see entry), stems from a donation by the Condé family to the Institut de France.

The art gallery contains paintings by Italian, Flemish, French and English masters (Raphael, Caracci, Van Dyck, Watteau, Delacroix, Ingres, Reynolds).

The splendid library, with 12,500 rare books and 1500 manuscripts, contains one of the world's finest illuminated manuscripts, the book of hours (prayer book) of the Duc de Berry ("Très riches Heures du Duc de Berry") with 15th c. hand painting.

In the Jewel Room (Cabinet des Gemmes) one can admire the "Grand Condé", the rose diamond belonging to the former owners of the château.

Musée d'Art Moderne de la Ville de Paris   E4

Location
Avenue du Président-Wilson
(16th arr.)

Métro
Iéna, Alma-Marceau

Buses
32, 42, 63, 72, 80, 82, 92

Times of opening
Daily (except Mon.)
10 a.m.–5.30 p.m.
Wed. 10 a.m.–8.30 p.m.

Entrance fee

Until the opening of the Musée d'Orsay (see entry) in 1986, a link between the art treasures of the Jeu de Paume (see entry; which will then be housed in the Musée d'Orsay) and those of the Centre Pompidou (see entry; modern works, principally from Cubism onwards), the civic museum of modern art, can be found in the west wing of the Palais d'Art Moderne (see Palais de Tokyo), which was built for the World Exhibition of 1937. This consists of a collection of important Post-Impressionists including Paul Cézanne, Georges Rouault, Raoul Dufy, André Dunoyer de Segonzac and Maurice Utrillo. Part of the collection, including Toulouse-Lautrec and Redon, will be taken over in 1986 from the Musée d'Orsay. Also represented are Pablo Picasso, Georges Bracque, Fernand Léger, Robert Delaunay; the Fauves: André Derain, Albert Marquet, Maurice de Vlaminck, Suzanne Valadon and Amedeo Modigliani. Among the sculptures on exhibition are works by Jacques Lipchitz, Chavigné and Ossip Zadkine.

Musée de la Marine   E5

Location
Place du Trocadéro (16th arr.)

Métro
Trocadéro

Buses
22, 30, 32, 63, 72, 82

Times of opening
Daily, except Tues. and public
holidays, 10 a.m.–6 p.m.

The collections of the Navy Museum in the Palais de Chaillot (see entry) recount the history of the French navy and merchant marine (from the galley to the steamer). Its 13 rooms of pictures and models of ships and port installations, nautical equipment, old charts and figureheads give one an excellent idea of its theme.

Especially interesting: Columbus' "Santa Maria" (room 1), the "Louis XV", one of the young king's toys (room 2), the "Valmy", a ship made of ebony, ivory and silver (room 5), one of the first steamers (room 5) and "La Gloire", the world's first iron-clad (room 6). Entrance fee.

*Musée de l'Armée (military museum)   F5

The various wings around the courtyard of the Hôtel des Invalides (see entry) house the military museum, which was founded as an artillery museum in 1794 and has since assembled a substantial collection of equipment and uniforms, weaponry, figures and curiosities from all ages and all countries (36,000 objects, 32,000 drawings and engravings). In addition to mementoes of Napoleon there are also memorabilia honouring famous generals or describing the plans of French campaigns. Some exhibits from the Late-Gothic and Renaissance periods are important from the art-historical point of view.

The entrances to the museum are in the middle of each side wing of the courtyard. Documentary films about the World Wars are shown from 2 p.m. on the ground floor.

The Museum of Relief Maps (Musée des Plans-Reliefs) formerly housed here is now in Lille.

Location
See Hôtel des Invalides
(7th arr.)

Métro
Latour-Maubourg, Invalides

Buses
28, 49, 69, 82, 87, 92

Times of opening
1 Oct.–31 Mar.: daily
10 a.m.–5 p.m.; 1 Apr.–
30 Sept. 10 a.m.–6 p.m.

Entrance fee

Musée des Plans-Reliefs

*Musée de l'Homme (Museum of Anthropology)   E5

One-third of the area (altogether 10,000 sq. m – 108,000 sq. ft) of the Museum of Anthropology in the Palais de Chaillot (see entry) is taken up with the prehistoric and anthropological collections of the museum proper. The other part is reserved for temporary exhibitions and the library (180,000 volumes) on the top floor. On the 1st floor: prehistoric finds relating to the development of Man; including Menton man, a cast of the Hottentot Venus and the famous "Venus of Lespugue" carved from a mammoth tusk.

The anthropological section on the 1st floor is devoted to Africa (inc. Ethiopian medieval frescoes, West African sculpture). On the 2nd floor: anthropological collections from the Arctic regions, Asia and America (esp. the art of the Mayas and Aztecs).

Location
Place du Trocadéro
(16th arr.)

Métro
Trocadéro

Buses
22, 30, 32, 63, 72, 82

Times of opening
9.45 a.m.–5.15 p.m.; closed
Tues. and Public Holidays

Entrance fee

**Musée de l'Hôtel de Cluny   H6

The former Hôtel de Cluny, today the Museum of Medieval Art and Culture, stands on part of the site of the former Roman baths (see Thermes) the ruins of which can be seen on the corner of the Boulevard Saint-Michel and the Boulevard Saint-Germain (see entries).

At the beginning of the 14th c. the Benedictine abbey of Cluny (in Burgundy) acquired the site to build accommodation in Paris for its abbots. The Hôtel de Cluny was built by Abbot Jacques d'Amboise between 1485 and 1500 and today it and the Hôtel de Sens (see Marais) are Paris's only large private residences dating from the late medieval period. After changing hands frequently, even in the Middle Ages, it fell into decay after the French Revolution but was acquired by the State in 1842 and has been a museum since 1844.

The Musée de Cluny houses an important collection of medieval art (showpieces: valuable tapestries) based on the private collection of the antiquarian Alexandre du Sommerard.

Location
6 Place Paul-Painlevé
(5th arr.)

Métro
Saint-Michel, Odéon

Buses
21, 27, 38, 86, 87

Times of opening
9.45 a.m.–12.30 p.m. and
2–5.15 p.m.; closed Tues. and
Public Holidays

Entrance fee

Roman Baths near the Musée Cluny

Especially noteworthy are:

Cour d'Honneur (courtyard): this reveals the charm of this Late-Gothic/early-Renaissance complex as a whole. The fine well, on the left, is 15th c.

Statues of the Apostles from Notre-Dame and Sainte-Chapelle (room IX).

Stone sarcophagi of the 7th c., capitals (room X).

High-Gothic and Late-Gothic sculpture (room VIII).

Gold and enamelled artefacts, 7th–13th c. (room XIII).

Stained glass (room XVI).

French, Italian and Spanish faïence and ceramics (room XVII).

Treasure items such as the gold altar frontal from Basle cathedral (11th c.) (room XIX), which was presented by the Emperor Henry II.

Tapestries, the finest example being the famous series of the "Lady with the Unicorn" (15th c.) from the Loire valley (rooms XI, II).

The Late-Gothic chapel, formerly the abbot's oratory. The priceless Auxerre tapestries (15th c.) depict 23 scenes from the "Legend of Saint Stephen" (Saint Etienne) (room XX).

*Musée des Monuments Français (Museum of French Monuments)   E5

Location
Place du Trocadéro
(16th arr.)

Métro
Trocadéro

The E wing of the Palais de Chaillot (see entry) houses a museum with full-size reproductions and models of important French works of art.

The museum was set up in 1880 at the suggestion of the architect Viollet-le-Duc. It gives a vivid idea of the history of styles (sculpture, painting, architecture) in chronological order covering 12 centuries of the development of art in France from early Romanesque to Classicism.

The wall paintings are on the right of the entrance hall (on all three floors) and the sculpture department (in the E wing of the palace) is on the left.

Wallpaintings

Ground floor: early Romanesque works (c. 800–1000) inc. crypt paintings from Auxerre, "Life of Saint Stephen" (c. 850). 1st floor: Romanesque art (c. 1000–1200), inc. the impressive representation of biblical history (from Genesis to Revelations) from the abbey church of Saint-Savin-sur-Gartempe in Vienne (southern France).

2nd floor: Early and High Gothic (c. 1200–1400).

3rd floor: Late-Gothic art (c. 1400–1550).

Sculptures

In chronological order:

Early Romanesque: sarcophagi (6th–7th c.), first tomb with three-dimensional portrait (11th c., room 1).

Romanesque: 11th c. tympana (sculptures and reliefs), and church doorways (rooms 2–6).

Crusader architecture in Palestine: (12th–13th c., room 7).

Early Gothic: reproductions of reliefs and statues from the cathedrals of Chartres, Reims, Paris and Strasbourg (12th–13th c., room 8).

High Gothic: burial chapel of the Dukes of Burgundy (14th c., rooms 14 and 15).

High and Late Gothic: (14th–15th c., rooms 16–18).

Late Gothic and early Renaissance: (15th–16th c., rooms 19–21).

Renaissance (16th–17th c.): works by Jean Goujon (1510–68), Ligier Richier (1500–66), Germain Pilon (1536–90, rooms 22–4).

French Classical (Baroque, 17th–18th c.); works by François Girardon (1628–1715), Antoine Coysevox (1640–1720), the Nicolas brothers (1658–1733) and Guillaume Coustou (1677–1746, room 25).

Rococo (18th c.): represented by Maurice-Etienne Falconet (1716–91), Edme Bouchardon (1698–1762), Jean Antoine Houdon (1741–1828) and Jean Baptiste Pigalle (1714–85).

Busts of Voltaire, Mirabeau, Rousseau (rooms 26 and 27).

Early 19th c. Classicism, inc. the "Marseillaise" of the Arc de Triomphe (room 28).

Buses
22, 30, 32, 63, 72, 82

Times of opening
9 a.m.–6 p.m.

Entrance fee

Musée d'Orsay G5

Built for the World Exhibition from plans by Victor Laloux, the Quai d'Orsay Station is a gigantic glass and iron construction, surmounted by a glass dome. On three sides it is surrounded by the palace-like façades of the Hôtel d'Orsay, extending along the bank of the Seine opposite the Tuileries gardens. From the broad entrance hall the platforms serving trains to the southwest of France could not be seen, as might have been expected; they were located several metres lower down. As engines became more powerful and were able to haul more carriages, the platforms of the Quai d'Orsay Station were too short. In 1939 long-distance trains ceased to be handled, the imposing station was now only used for local trains, and eventually these, too, were withdrawn and replaced by the "express métro" RER. In 1973 the station and the hotel were made a protected monument and plans materialised to convert

Location
62 Rue de Lille (7th arr.)
Main entrance: 1 Rue de Bellechasse

Métro
Solférino

Buses
24, 63, 68, 69, 73, 83, 84, 94

Times of opening
Daily (except Mon.) 10 a.m.–6 p.m. (Thur. till 9.45 p.m.), Sun 9 a.m.–6 p.m.

Entrance fee

Musée d'Orsay: Sculpture corridor in the Central Hall

Jacquemarts „Rhinoceros"

the buildings into a museum. The conversion was directed by the architects Pierre Colboc, Renaud Marden and Jean-Paul Philippon; designs for the internal layout were the responsibility of the lady architect Gae Aulenti.

In 1986 the Musée d'Orsay opened its doors. The museum, with 17,000 sq. m (185,140 sq. ft) of exhibition space, is devoted to the 1848–1916 era. The tour of the museum is arranged chronologically, following great themes and artistic techniques, including music and literature. As far as possible works belonging to the various artistic genres are presented according to individual artists (e.g. rooms for Daumier, Courbet, Van Gogh; an open space for Carpeaux, a terrace for Rodin.

Only in the ballroom was the arrangement of sculpture and paintings chosen predominantly for the way in which it fitted into the 1900 Rococo décor.

Contemporary events and intellectual movements affecting the works are shown in separate rooms (initiation into history; date gallery, press gallery).

Going in through the entrance of the former hotel on the west side we come into the reception hall with bookstalls and a café. The original location of the platforms on the lower level is now a sculpture alley, flanked right and left on the ground-floor level by exhibition rooms for paintings, photography and architectural exhibits. The glass dome, 138 m (151 yards) long, 40 m (44 yards) broad and 32 m (105 ft) high, towers above the central hall; the floors of the former hotel as well as the station concourse have been converted into exhibition rooms.

Second Empire

Admirers of the Second Empire will find on the ground floor sculptures by the "Florentines", such as the "Comédie

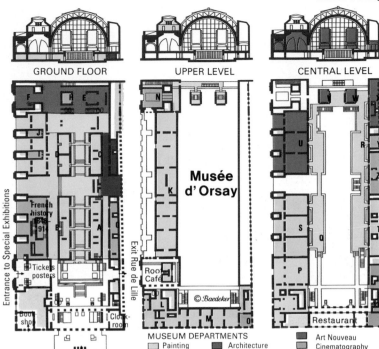

GROUND FLOOR   UPPER LEVEL   CENTRAL LEVEL

Entrance to Special Exhibitions

French history 1848–1914

Tickets posters

Book shop   Cloak-room

Main Entrance

Exit Rue de Lille

Musée d'Orsay

Room Café

© Baedeker

Restaurant

MUSEUM DEPARTMENTS

☐ Painting ■ Architecture
☐ Sculpture ■ Crafts

■ Art Nouveau
■ Cinematography
☐ Special Exhibitions

A Ingres and Ingrism, Delacroix, Chassériau, historical and portrait painting 1850–1880

B Daumier, Chauchard collection, Millet, E. Rousseau, Corot, Realism Courbet

C Puvis de Chavannes, Gustave Moreau, Degas before 1870

D Manet, Monet, Bazille and Renoir before 1870, Fantin-Latour, Whistler, open-air painting, Moreau-Nélaton and Eduardo-Mollard collections, Realism, Orientalism

E Opera Hall

F Upper Pavilion: architecture 1850–1900; Viollet-le-Duc, Pugin, Maurice Webb, Mackmurdo, Jeckyll, Godwin, Sullivan, Dossier 3

G Dossier 1

H Dossier 2

I Photography and graphic art 1

J Photography and graphic art 2

K Impressionism: Monet, Renoir, Pissarro and Sisley before 1880, Degas and Manet after 1870 Personnaz and Gachet collections: Guillaumin, Monet, Pissarro, Sisley Van Gogh, Cézanne, Degas (pastels)

L Post-Impressionism: Seurat, Signac Cross, Luce, Redon, pastel painting Toulouse-Lautrec

M Henri Rousseau, school of Pont-Aven: Gaugin, E. Bernard, Sérusier Nabis; Bonnard, Vuillard, Denis, Vallotton; Max and Rosy Kaganovitch

N Dossier 4
Way down to central level; Dossier 5

O Photography and graphic art 3

P Art and decor of the Third Republic

Q Barrias, Coutan, Fremiet, Gérôme, Rodin

R Desbois, Rosso, Bartholomé, Bourdelle, Maillol, J. Bernard

S "Salon" painting 1880–1900; Naturalism, foreign schools, Symbolism

T Painting after 1900: Bonnard, Denis, Vallotton, Vuillard, Roussel; transition to the 20th c.

U Art-Nouveau in France and Belgium: Guimard; school of Nancy: Gallé, Carabin, Charpentier, Dampt

V Guimard

W International Art-Nouveau

X Vienna, Glasgow, Chicago

Y Dossier 6

Z Dossier 7

"L'Estaque" by Paul Cézanne

Sculptures on the theme of "La Baigneuse" by Joseph Bernard Maillol

Humaine" by Ernest Christophe which inspired Baudelaire in the 20th lyric (Le Masque) of his "Fleurs du Mal". The introduction of polychromatic sculpture and the "oriental fashion", which was popular in Europe at this time, can be seen, for example, in Charles Cordier's "Nègre du Soudain".

When the Musée d'Orsay was opened the famous collection of Impressionist paintings was transferred here from the Jeu de Paume. All the greatest painters of that genre, which between 1870 and 1900 began the modern art movement, are represented in the upper gallery: Edouard Manet and his renowned "Le Déjeuner sur l'Herbe", the historic chef-d'œuvre of the collection; Claude Monet, Camille Pessaro, Alfred Sisley, Auguste Renoir and Edgar Degas, as well as the Post-impressionists – Vincent Van Gogh, Paul Gaugin and Paul Cézanne – and the Pointillists, Georges Seurat and Paul Signac and the unclassifiable work of Henri de Toulouse-Lautrec. The art of the "salon" painters is illustrated, for example, by Cabanel and Bouguereau on the ground floor; Naturalistic painting is on view on the central level where the Symbolists (including Sir Edward Burne-Jones) are also represented. Works by Octave Tassaert and Gustave Courbet are typical of the "plastic" Realist style. The visitor then sees sculptures by Maillol and Rodin and visits the towers, where international Art-Nouveau includes furniture by Hector Guirnard and Henry van der Velde, as well as glass and enamel work by Emile Gallé. The visit ends at the "Sources of the Twentieth Century" and the beginning of films.

Photography is represented by some 10,000 examples from Daguerreotype (1839) until the end of the First World War (for example by Félix Nadar, Clarence White and Gustave Le Gray).

Impressionist collection

Henry Van Der Velde (art nouveau)

Musée du Jeu de Paume

See Jeu de Paume

Musée du Louvre

See Louvre

*Musée Guimet   E5

The Musée National Guimet houses the most important collection of Indian, Indonesia, Japanese, Nepalese and Tibetan art in France.

The foundations for the collection of Far-Eastern treasures to be seen here were laid by the Lyon industrialist and explorer Emile Guimet at the end of the last century when he made a donation of his collection to the city of Paris. The collection has since been continuously expanded in close cooperation with the affiliated Research Institute for East-Asian Culture.

Especially noteworthy are the art treasures on display from the following countries:

India: Buddhist and Brahmin works of art, including "Shiva's cosmic dance" (ground floor).

Location
6 Place d'Iéna (16th arr.)

Métro
Iéna

Buses
32, 63, 82

Times of opening
9.45 a.m.–noon and
1.30–5.15 p.m.;
closed Tues.

Entrance fee

Female head in the sculpture garden

Large still-life, with tables

Bullfight: the death of the toreador

Cambodia: Khmer art (ground floor).
Indonesia: bronzes from Java (ground floor).
Tibet: ritual weapons, jewellery, articles connected with
Lamaism. Pièce de résistance: dancing Dakini in gilded bronze
(ground floor).
China: lacquered furniture, jade and porcelain (1st floor), paint-
ings (2nd floor), frescoes (rotunda).
Japan: theatrical masks, jewellery, paintings (2nd floor).

Musée National d'Art Moderne

See Centre Pompidou

**Musée Picasso K5

The undoubted creator of the Picasso Museum is André Malraux. While he was Minister of Culture a law was enacted, on
his initiative, whereby important works of art could be set
against estate duty. Thus after the death of Pablo Picasso
(1881–1973) the French state inherited over 200 paintings,
150 sculptures, 30 reliefs, up to 100 ceramics, more than
3000 drawings and graphics, as well as manuscripts and
correspondence.

The collection is on view in an hotel which Aubert de Fontenay
had had built by Jean Boulier and lavishly decorated by Martin
Desjardin and the Marsy brothers. As it was Fontenay's job to
collect salt tax on behalf of the state, his residence soon
acquired the appropriate name of "Hotel Sale" (the "Salted
House").

In the richly stuccoed interior (carefully restored according to
the design of Roland Simounet) the visit begins with Picasso's
"Man with a Lamb". In harmony with the fine carving, the
original figured décor and furniture by Diego Giacometto,
twenty rooms are devoted to the development of the artist from
his "Blue Period" to the most recent works, for example
"Seated Old Man" (1970/71). Room 1: early years, Blue Period
(1895–1903); Room 2: from the Pink Period to the "Demoiselles
d'Avignon" (1904–1905); Room 3: from the "Demoiselles
d'Avignon" to the beginning of Cubism (1907–1909); Room 4:
Cubism (1910–1917); Room 5: Picasso's private collection
(bequeathed), exhibited in the Louvre from 1978–1985 under
the title "Gift of Picasso"; Room 6: Classical Period (1918–
1924); Room 7: on the borders of Realism – periods of change
(1925–1929); Room 8: Picasso as graphic artist; Room 9:
Women Bathing (1928–1931); Room 10: Boisgeloup (1830–
1835); Room 11: Bullfighting, Crucifixion, Minotauromachie
(1930s); Room 12: "Women at their Toilet" (1938); Sculpture
Garden: sculptures (1929–1950); Room 13: the Muses (1930s);
Room 14: ceramics; Room 15: from "Guernica" until the war
(1935–1939); Room 16: War and Liberation (1940–1947); Room
17: Picasso and Literature; Room 18: Vallauris (1948–1954);
Room 19: Cannes, Vauvenargues (1955–1961); Room 20: Last
Period (1961–1973).

In selecting the exhibits, in which Dominique Bozo the present
director of the museum took overall control, the principle

Location
Hotel Sale
5 Rue de Thorigny
(3rd arr.)

Métro
St Sebastien-Froissart

Times of opening
Daily (except Tues.)
9.15 a.m.–5.15 p.m.,
(Wed. until 10 p.m.)

Entrance fee

*Woman sitting at the
window*

Musée Rodin

Porte d'Enfer . . .   *. . . in the Musée Rodin*

adopted was to present the whole spectrum of Picasso's creative work and at the same time to reveal all the different styles which the artist initiated and influenced during his lifetime. In no other museum in the world can be found such an abundance of art forms and nowhere else is the line of work presented in such a complete and balanced manner. The Picasso collection is rounded off and complemented with works by artists who were influenced by his artistic creativity: Cézanne, Renoir, Matisse, Derain, Braque, Miró and Rousseau.

*Musée Rodin   G5

Location
77 Rue de Varenne
(7th arr.)

Métro
Varenne

Buses
69, 82, 92

Times of opening
Daily (except Mon.):
1 Oct.–31 Mar.
10 a.m.–5 p.m.,
1 Apr.–30 Sept. 10 a.m.–
5.45 p.m.

Entrance fee

The sculptor Auguste Rodin lived in the former Hôtel Biron (constructed 1728–31) until his death in 1917. Having been given some of his works and his personal collections, the State was able that same year to open the museum and its lovely gardens to the public.

Full-size copies of his monumental world-famous statues: "Le Penseur" (The Thinker), "Les Bourgeois de Calais" (The Burghers of Calais), "Ugolino", "L'homme qui marche" (The Walker) – are all displayed in the garden; smaller works and studies of models are inside the museum, including "Le Baiser" (The Kiss), the bust of Clemenceau, "Eve", "L'Age d'Airain" (The Age of Brass), "Saint-Jean-Baptiste" (John the Baptist), studies of "Balzac" and "Victor Hugo".

Rodin's private collection (furniture, paintings and sculptures) complement the exhibition of his works.

For a long time two other internationally famed artists lived in

Notre-Dame, South Front

what was then the Hôtel de Biron without getting to know each other: a young man, who had lodgings in one of the wings, by the name of Jean Cocteau, and a German who worked as Rodin's secretary by the name of Rainer Marie Rilke.

**Notre-Dame   J5/6

The Cathedral of Notre-Dame de Paris was begun in 1163. Louis IX (Saint Louis) and Canon Maurice de Sully wanted to build a church on the Ile-de-la-Cité (see entry) similar in style and beauty to that built by the Abbot of Saint-Denis (see entry), where the first Gothic church had been begun in 1135. In the 150 years it took to build, all the various stages of Gothic architecture (partly borrowed from the other great cathedrals of Chartres, Reims and Amiens) were used in the design of the Cathedral of Notre-Dame. (For the history of the Gothic style, see Saint-Denis.) The Choir was constructed in 1163–82 and the Nave in 1180–1200 in the Early-Gothic style. The transition to High Gothic is shown on the W Front (main façade; 1200–20). The Nave was later reworked in the High-Gothic style (1230–50). The transepts are pure High Gothic (1250–60). Finally the Choir was also reworked in High Gothic (1265–1320).

Here, as later in Saint-Denis, the great 19th c. restorer Viollet-le-Duc made a marvellous job, from 1841 to 1864, of restoring the almost dilapidated cathedral.

Location
Ile-de-la-Cité (4th arr.)

Métro
Cité

Buses
24, 27

Notre-Dame

Crypte archéologique du
Parvis de Notre-Dame
(cathedral square)

**Visits to the archaeological
crypt**
10 a.m.–5 p.m. daily
(in summer 6 p.m.)

Entrance fee

It is possible to get an unobstructed view of the W Front (main
façade), even when there are hordes of tourists, from the broad
Parvis (square) of Notre-Dame, which itself conceals interesting treasures of the past under its paving. Since 1980 the 117 m
(384 ft) long "crypte archéologique" (archaeological crypt)
under the Parvis has been open to the public. The remains of
16th and 18th c. houses (see Cité), of the Merovingian church of
Saint-Etienne and of Gallo-Roman buildings were discovered
when an underground car park was being built. The entrance to
this historical dig, which is clearly laid out with explanatory
notes and is unique in size, is by the staircase leading to the
underground car park.

The bronze plaque in the centre of the Parvis denotes the
"administrative geographical centre" of Paris from which all
distances are measured.

Exterior

The W Front: the monumental overall view of the main façade
of Notre Dame reveals on closer inspection the sequence of
the stages of construction and hence the development into
the High-Gothic style. The doorway (c. 1200), the windows
(c. 1200), the tracery balustrade above the rose window and the
unfinished towers (1225–50) illustrate the progressive refine-
ment of the Gothic language of form. The three vertical divisions are to be regarded as corresponding to the three aisles of
the Nave. The five horizontal divisions (doors, king's gallery,
windows, tracery gallery, towers) also correspond to the interior: the portal corresponds to the arcades, the kings' gallery to
the balcony and the window area to the windows inside the
cathedral.

The Kings' Gallery: the identities of the figures of the kings
seem to be as yet unresolved. For a long time they were considered to represent the kings of Judah but there is also reason
to think that they are statues of the French kings from Childeb-
ert I (511–588) to Philippe Augustus (1180–1223). The fact that
they had their heads chopped off during the French Revolution
has not helped to solve the problem.

Sides: The richness of High-Gothic form is illustrated on both
sides.

On the N front (1250–60) Jean de Chelles completed the transept in 1250 with the Portail du Cloître which led to the former
cloister (cloître). The door of the S transept, Porte de Saint-
Etienne (St Stephen's door) was the work of Pierre de Montreuil. The pointed false gable of the portal, rising up almost to
the rose window, and the upper half of the end wall of the
transept broken up into glass and rosette arches, together with
the bold sweep of the flying buttresses, give this front the
typical appearance and vibrant forcefulness of the High-Gothic
cathedral.

Times of opening
10 a.m.–4.30 p.m. (in summer
6 p.m.)

Entrance fee

Tower: The view over the city centre from 70 m (230 ft) up is one
of the finest in Paris: unlike the views from the Eiffel Tower,
Sacré-Cœur (see entries) or the "tower" of Montparnasse, here
the historical heart of the city seems to be within tangible reach
(Hôtel de Ville, Louvre, Sorbonne, Panthéon, Ile Saint-Louis).

Portals

Portail du Cloître (cloister doorway, 1250): tympanum: childhood of Jesus (below), Deacon Theophilus' pact with the Devil,
Redemption through Mary (centre), the Bishop shows the people the pact (top). Pier: original statue of Mary (13th c.). The
rose window (1270) shows Mary encircled by figures from the
Old Testament.

Notre-Dame: view of the choir . . .   *. . . and of the rose window in the north transept*

Porte Rouge (red door, by Pierre de Montreuil): tympanum:
Mary, Louis IX and his wife Marguerite de Provence.
Portail Saint-Etienne (St Stephen's door): tympanum: sermon,
capture of St Stephen (bottom), stoning and entombment (centre), ascension (top). Centre pillar: St Stephen.
Portail de Sainte-Anne (St Anne's door, 1210–20): tympanum:
story of Mary's parents, Anne and Joachim, before the Temple,
in the desert, the Annunciation of Mary's birth, at the wedding
(bottom); Mary in the Temple, Mary's Annunciation, the birth of
Jesus, Herod and the Three Kings (centre); Mary and Jesus, left
and right next to the angels the founders of the cathedral,
Maurice de Sully and Louis IX, kneeling (top). The sculptures in
the top and centre sections are the oldest in the cathedral and
were made between 1165 and 1175 for another doorway but
then installed here. Intrados: the heavenly choir. Pier: St Mar-
cellus (Bishop of Paris, 19th c. copy). Splays: kings, queens and
saints.
The four figures in the recesses between the flying buttresses
represent (from left to right): St Stephen, the "Church triumphant", the "vanquished Synagogue", St Denis (see Saint-
Denis).
Portail du Jugement Dernier (Door of the Last Judgment, 1220–
30): tympanum: Resurrection (bottom); the Archangel Michael
sending the Good to Heaven and the Wicked to Hell (centre);
Christ the Supreme Judge. This tympanum was destroyed in
the 18th c. and restored by Viollet-le-Duc but the figure of Christ
the Supreme Judge is the original Gothic. Intrados: Choir of the
Blessed being received by Abraham (left), Hell with Demons
(right). Pier: Christ (19th c.). Jambs: the wise (left) and foolish
(right) virgins. Splays: the 12 Apostles (19th c.). Medallions:

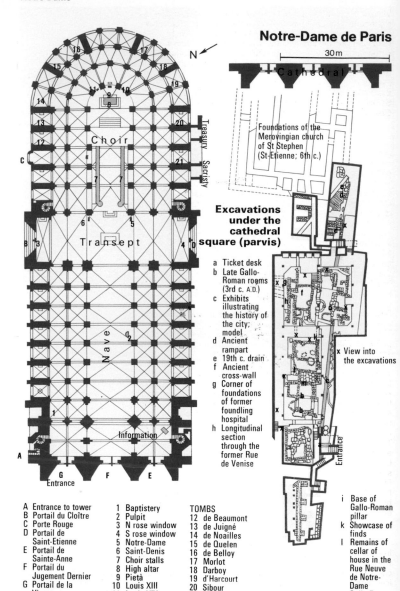

Notre-Dame de Paris

30 m

Cathedral

Foundations of the Merovingian church of St Stephen (St-Etienne; 6th c.)

Excavations under the cathedral square (parvis)

- a Ticket desk
- b Late Gallo-Roman rooms (3rd c. A.D.)
- c Exhibits illustrating the history of the city; model
- d Ancient rampart
- e 19th c. drain
- f Ancient cross-wall
- g Corner of foundations of former foundling hospital
- h Longitudinal section through the former Rue de Venise

x View into the excavations

- i Base of Gallo-Roman pillar
- k Showcase of finds
- l Remains of cellar of house in the Rue Neuve de Notre-Dame
- m Gallo-Roman tiled room

Choir — Transept — Nave

Treasury — Sacristy

Information

Entrance

A	Entrance to tower	1	Baptistery
B	Portail du Cloître	2	Pulpit
C	Porte Rouge	3	N rose window
D	Portail de Saint-Etienne	4	S rose window
E	Portail de Sainte-Anne	5	Notre-Dame
F	Portail du Jugement Dernier	6	Saint-Denis
G	Portail de la Vierge	7	Choir stalls
		8	High altar
		9	Pietà
		10	Louis XIII
		11	Louis XIV

TOMBS
12 de Beaumont
13 de Juigné
14 de Noailles
15 de Quelen
16 de Belloy
17 Morlot
18 Darboy
19 d'Harcourt
20 Sibour
21 Affre

Excavations under the cathedral square (parvis) see right

Virtues (top row) and Vices (bottom row); the figures on the right-hand side are original. Portail de la Vierge (Door of the Virgin, 1210–20): tympanum: bottom section: Ark of the Covenant with Old Testament kings and prophets; middle section: entombment of Mary, surrounded by Christ and the Apostles; top section: Mary's Assumption, Intrados: angels with censers and candlesticks, patriarchs, prophets and Christ's forefathers. Pier: 19th c. statue of Mary by Viollet-le-Duc, with symbols of the months on both sides. Jambs: signs of the Zodiac. Splays: St Denis (see Saint-Denis), kings (left); John the Baptist, St Stephen, St Genevieve, figure of a pope (right).

A special feature of the architecture of the interior is the reworking of the Early-Gothic side walls of the nave which already had galleries built into them. Those were retained and not replaced with a triforium, the narrow arcade usually found with High-Gothic side aisles and transepts. The windows modelled on Chartres (double windows with pointed arches and round windows above) were incorporated above the galleries. In the first span of the nave Viollet-le-Duc, while carrying out his work of restoration, began to convert the High-Gothic (tripartite) arrangement back to the Early-Gothic (four-part) arrangement. Fortunately he gave up this plan, so that we can acknowledge the greater elegance in comparison of the High-Gothic solution.

Interior

The cathedral is 130 m (426 ft) long, 48 m (157 ft) wide, and 35 m (115 ft) high and can hold 9000 people (1500 of them in the galleries).

Besides the many important tombs and statues, the pulpit and altar, the following are of particular interest:

The interior as a whole, with its 75 round pillars, effectively picked out by indirect lighting.

The large rose window in the N transept with 80 illustrations from the Old Testament (c. 1270).

The large rose window in the S transept (1257).

Statue of Mary "Notre-Dame de Paris" (c. 1330), the best-known miraculous image of the Patron Saint of the cathedral (in front of the pillar to the right of the entrance to the choir). 23 stone reliefs of the life of Christ (1319–51) by Jehan Ravy and his nephew Jehan de Bouteiller, painted and partly gilded (choir screen).

Tomb of the Count d'Harcourt (d. 1718) by Pigalle (second apsidal chapel on the left of the entrance to the sacristy).

Cavaillé-Coll organ, recently restored, with 8500 pipes; its 110 stops make it the largest in France.

Free and therefore well-attended organ recitals take place in Notre-Dame every Sunday evening at 5.45. High Mass is celebrated every day at 10 a.m. (There is an information desk at the entrance.)

In addition to the Holy Relics, for which Louis IX originally built the Sainte-Chapelle (see entry), the displays here include precious ecclesiastical treasures (monstrances, crucifixes, chalices) and Napoleon's coronation robe.

Trésor (treasury)

Times of opening
Wed., Sat., Sun.
2.30–6 p.m.
(except Easter).

Grand Staircase in the Paris Opera

Obelisk of Luxor

See Place de la Concorde

*Opéra   H4

Location
Place de l'Opéra (9th arr.)

Métro
Opéra

Buses
20, 21, 22, 27, 29, 42, 52, 53, 66, 68, 81, 95

Visits
11 a.m.–4.30 p.m. daily
(auditorium only 1–2 p.m.)

The construction of the Paris Opera House saw the creation of a "style Napoleon III" and resulted in a splendid neo-Baroque building.

Charles Garnier (1825–98), hitherto unknown, won the competition for its design, and the biggest opera house in the world (over 11,000 sq. m (118,000 sq. ft) of floor space but "only" 2200 seats) was built according to his plans between 1862 and 1875. The façade is horizontally divided into three. The seven arches on the ground floor are flanked by allegorical figures (from the left): Poetry (by Jouffroy), Music (Guillaume), Idyll (Aizelin), Recital (Chapu), Song (Dubois), Drama (Faguière), Dance (Carpeaux, the most important sculpture; the original is in the Louvre), Lyric Drama (Perraud). Over the statues there are medallions with portraits of Cimarosa, Haydn, Pergolesi and Bach.

The loggia (with 16 large and 14 small Corinthian columns) is decorated with the busts of Halévy, Meyerbeer, Rossini, Auber, Spontini, Beethoven and Mozart.

On the attic storey there are four gilded groups glorifying Poetry and Fame.

On the Rue Scribe side is the Pavillon d'Honneur which used to give the President direct access to his box from the approach

Palais de Chaillot

road. Today this houses a small library and a museum of opera props (Monday–Friday 11 a.m.–5 p.m.).

The interior of the building can be visited only at certain times but the magnificent grand staircase (Escalier d'Honneur) in multi-coloured marble can be admired at any time. The large foyer is decorated with an allegorical ceiling painting and wall paintings by Paul Baudry (1828–86). In the auditorium, which is decorated entirely in red and gold, the painting in the cupola is by Marc Chagall (1964).

Following the opening of the new opera house in the Place de la Bastille in 1989 the Palais Garnier is now used only for celebrity concerts and ballet.

* Palais-Bourbon   G5

The former Palais-Bourbon is directly in line with the Madeleine and the obelisk in the Place de la Concorde (see entries). It is the seat of the French National Assembly (Assemblée Nationale), the lower house of the French Parliament (the upper house is the Senate, see Palais du Luxembourg). Until 1946 this legislative body (which corresponds to the British House of Commons) was called the Chambre des Députés (Chamber of Deputies).

The Palais was built in 1722–8 for the Duchess Louise-Françoise de Bourbon, legitimised daughter of Louis XIV and Madame de Montespan. It was seized during the Revolution, later converted into the parliamentary building, and since 1827 has been the meeting place of the French Parliament.

The imposing design of the side facing the Seine with its

Location
Quai d'Orsay (7th arr.)

Métro
Chambre des Députés

Buses
24, 63, 83, 84, 94

Palais de Chaillot

Palais de Justice

Visits
On written application only to:
Questure de l'Assemblée
Nationale,
126 Rue de l'Université,
75007 Paris.
Application may also be made
to sit in on a session.

portico dating from the time of Napoleon (1806) is reminiscent of the façade of the Madeleine (see entry) which also drew on the Classical model (columns and triangular gables). One gets a good view of this example of 18th and 19th c. urban architecture (Madeleine, see Rue Royale, see Place de la Concorde, Palais-Bourbon) from the Pont de la Concorde (see entry).

The monumental statues in front of the portico represent ministers of the kings of France (from left): Sully (Henri IV), l'Hospital (François I and Henri II), d'Agnesseau (Louis XV) and Colbert (Louis XIV). The allegories on the tympanum (Liberty, France, Order) were done by the sculptor Cortot between 1839 and 1841. Left and right of the open staircase: Minerva (Wisdom) and Themis (Justice).

The Place du Palais-Bourbon at the rear of the building provides a very good idea of what a square in the elegant quarter of the Faubourg Saint-Germain (see entry) was like in the 18th c. The façade of the Palais-Bourbon facing on to this square has been retained from the 18th c. and contains the entrance used by the Deputies.

The French Ministry for Foreign Affairs (Ministère des Affairs Etrangères) adjoins the W of the Palais.

The former Hôtel de Salm at No. 64 Rue de Lille is the Palais of the French Legion of Honour.

Palais de Chaillot E5

Location
Place du Trocadéro
(16th arr.)

The two wings of the Palais de Chaillot were built in 1937 on a small elevation overlooking the Seine, on the site of an earlier palace (Palais du Trocadéro). The austere but imposing building was designed by the architects Jacques Carlu, Louis-Auguste Boileau and Léon Azème. The broad terrace (with gleaming bronze statues on both sides) between the two wings was the entrance to the 1937 World Fair.

Under the terrace is the Théâtre de Chaillot with two stages. The palace also houses three museums: the Museum of Anthropology (see Musée de l'Homme), the Navy Museum (see Musée de la Marine) and the Museum of French Architecture (see Musée des Monuments Français). The E wing houses a cinémathèque and the Musée du Cinéma (see Practical Information).

Métro
Trocadéro

Buses
22, 30, 82

---

*Palais de Justice (Law Courts)   J5

On the site of the present Law Courts, on the Ile-de-la-Cité (see entry), the Celtic Gauls, followed by the Romans and later the Frankish Merovingians, built fortified squares, fortresses and royal castles. This was the birthplace of French royal power. Under Louis IX (Saint Louis, 1226–70) the royal palace here, with its newly constructed chapel (see Sainte-Chapelle), reached the peak of its magnificence, but soon after the French kings moved to the Louvre (see entry). (In 1358 the palace was stormed by the rebellious merchants led by Etienne Marcel, see Hôtel de Ville.)

From the 16th c. onwards the palace was the seat of the "parlement" (law court) whose approval was required before royal decrees acquired the force of law. This purely formal privilege was removed, after the "parlement" had made a half-hearted stand against the power of the king (war of the "Fronde", 1648–52), by Louis XIV when he was a young ruler on the way to becoming an absolute monarch.

The French Revolution in its turn removed both the king and the "parlement" (all its members were sent to the scaffold). The new (citizens') courts moved into the building which is now known as the Palais de Justice.

The palace has been damaged and destroyed by fire several times. The present building dates from the turn of the century; the S wing was not added until 1911–14.

Especially worth seeing are:

The entrance with the fine wrought-iron gate from the time of Louis XVI and the forecourt, the Cour de Mai (where the maypole used to be set up). Steps leading up into the interior.

Galérie Marchande (Merchants' Hall): at the time of Louis IX this was the passage joining the royal palace to the Sainte-Chapelle. Until the Revolution merchants offered their wares for sale here.

Galérie Duc (named after the architect and great restorer of many important monuments, Eugène Emmanuel Viollet-le-Duc – 1814–79): view of the Sainte-Chapelle and, at the other end, of the Cour des Femmes of the Conciergerie (see entry).

Vestibule de Harlay with statues of Charlemagne, Philippe Augustus, Louis IX and Napoleon (rulers who have been especially concerned with law-making).

Première Chambre Civile (1st Civil Chamber): formerly the bedroom of Louis IX; later the meeting place of the "parlement"; in 1793 "Salle de la Liberté" where the Revolutionary tribunal condemned over 2500 people to death. Salle des Pas Perdus (Hall of the lost steps, a poetic reference to the lost causes of those waiting to be tried here): this room is situated

Location
Boulevard du Palais
(1st arr.)

Métro
Cité

Buses
21, 24, 27, 38, 81, 85, 96

Visits
Mon.–Fri. 9 a.m.–6 p.m.

Palais Royal: seat of the Conseil d'Etat

above the Salle des Gens d'Armes of the Conciergerie (see entry). This was the pièce de résistance of the royal palace, the famous Palace Hall. The present neo-Classical décor dates from the time of the restoration work carried out after the great fire of 1871.

Musée de la Préfecture de la Police. See Practical Information – Museums.

*Palais de la Découverte   F4

Location
Avenue Franklin-D.-Roosevelt
(8th arr.)

Métro
Champs-Elysées-Clemenceau,
Franklin-D.-Roosevelt

The Palais de la Découverte (Palace of Discovery) is housed in the W wing of the Grand Palais (see entry). It is an exceptionally interesting museum which seeks to impart to the visitor the history of the natural sciences and their practical results.

There are guided tours (in French only), a new room devoted to the solar system, experiments which visitors can do themselves, a planetarium (11.30 a.m., 2.30 and 3.45 p.m.; closed Mon.) and film shows (2.30 and 4 p.m.; closed Mon.).

Times of opening: daily (except Mon.) 10 a.m.–6 p.m. Entrance fee.

Palais de Tokyo   E4

Location
13 Avenue du Président-
Wilson (16th arr.)

The Palais de Tokyo, the E wing of the Palais de l'Art Moderne, was the home of the Musée National d'Art Moderne until the Centre Pompidou (see entries) was opened. Besides a permanent museum (Musée d'Art et d'Essai) housing educational exhibitions with art objects from the Louvre, there are now plans for temporary exhibitions illustrating trends in avant-garde art. Non-European modern art is also displayed in the Palais de Tokyo. The palace also contains the National Photographic Centre and a media library.

The whole Palais d'Art Moderne, today split into the Musée d'Art Moderne de la Ville de Paris (see entry) and the Palais de Tokyo, was constructed for the 1937 World Fair. The architects (Aubert, Dastugne, Dondel and Viard) created a functional building in the Bauhaus tradition which is also apparent in the nearby Palais de Chaillot (see entry). Traces of the Classical style are evident in both buildings. The allegories of "Strength" and "Victory" in the peristyle and the allegory of "France" (1927) in the pool are the work of Antoine Bourdelle (1861–1929).

Métro
Iéna, Alma-Marceau

Buses
32, 63, 82, 92

Times of opening
9.45 a.m.–5.15 p.m.; closed Tues.

Entrance fee

Palais du Luxembourg

See Luxembourg

Palais-Royal   H4/5

The Palais-Royal is today the official seat of the Council of State (Conseil d'Etat) and the Directorate of Fine Arts (Secrétariat de la Culture et de la Communication).

Between 1634 and 1639 Cardinal Richelieu (1585–1642) had the Palais built for himself near the Louvre (see entry) and later left it to the king in his will. After the death of Louis XIII his widow Anne of Austria moved into the Palais which was thenceforward known as the Palais-Royal (Royal Palace).

Her son, Louis XIV, moved back into the Louvre in 1652. Later, after a period spent in the Château de Vincennes (see entry), he moved his court to Versailles (see entry). The king then granted the palace to his aunt, Henrietta Maria, widow of England's King Charles I and it subsequently came into the hands of the House of Orléans, Louis-Philippe of Orléans, called Philippe-Egalité (because although a nobleman he sided with the Revolutionaries – which did not save him from the guillotine), had the palace altered to its present form (late 18th c.) and laid out the small park with colonnades, shops and apartments.

It was under these colonnades that on 13 July 1789 the advocate and journalist Camille Desmoulins led a revolutionary assembly which next day stormed the Bastille. Before and during the Revolution and during the First Empire the Palace was a social meeting place with restaurants, cafés, gambling halls and brothels. (The gaming halls and the brothels were closed in 1830.) Since the mid-1890s controversial sculptures, the "Colonnes" by Buren, have stood in Place du Palais Royal.

Location
Place du Palais-Royal
(1st arr.)

Métro
Palais-Royal

Buses
21, 27, 39, 48, 67, 69, 72, 74, 81, 85, 95

*Panthéon   J6

The Panthéon, originally built as a church, is the national monument and burial place of France's "famous men".
In 1756 Louis XV commissioned the architect Jacques-Germain

Location
Place du Panthéon
(5th arr.)

Panthéon

Panthéon

Suburban station
Luxembourg (RER)

Buses
84, 89

Times of opening
10 a.m.–noon, 2–5 p.m.

Soufflot (1713–80) to start building what was planned to be a magnificent church on the site of the dilapidated abbey church of Saint Genevieve (the patron saint of Paris, see church of Saint-Etienne). The church was finished in 1790, ten years after Soufflot's death, with the completion of the cupola, and during the Revolution, in 1791, the National Assembly voted for it to be turned into a "Panthéon français" (in classical Greece a "pantheon" was a temple dedicated to all a country's gods). 42 windows of the former church were walled up; this gave the building the cold outer aspect and the gloomy inner aspect of a mausoleum which characterise it today.

The architecture of the Panthéon is a clear indication of the break with the ornate Rococo style (Louis XV style, see Marais, Hôtel de Soubise) which in turn had been a reaction against the distinct "classic" French Baroque style under Louis XIV. The Panthéon is the first monumental building in Paris in the Classicist style which attempted to revive the simplicity and monumentality of the architecture of Classical times. It set the standard for the period before and after Napoleon (see Arc de Triomphe, see Madeleine, see Bourse).

In his design Soufflot wanted to distinguish himself from Sir Christopher Wren (Saint Paul's Cathedral) on whom he modelled himself. This is why the portico projects right out in front of the façade, preventing the observer looking at it from the front from seeing the cupola. This was supposed to make the cupola appear to be hovering above the lower part of the building.

The triangular pediment on 18 Corinthian columns bears the inscription "To great men, their grateful country" and a relief by David d'Angers of the history of the French Nation: left, among others, Mirabeau, Voltaire and Rousseau; right, Napoleon and his generals. Victor Hugo, Emile Zola and the resistance fighter Jean Moulin are interred here.

The interior was designed by Soufflot to give the idea of transmitted light and clarity, an effect that was to be attained by having a great many windows and using slender columns, even when it came to supporting the cupola. However, faults in construction meant that massive pillars had to be used and most of the windows were sacrificed when the church became a mausoleum.

The cupola was decorated with a fresco "Ascension of Saint Genevieve" (1811) on the orders of Napoleon, in whose time the Panthéon was a church for a while. Several frescoes on the side walls by Puvis de Chavannes depict the life of the Saint. (Others show Charlemagne, Louis IX and Joan of Arc.)

*Pavillon de l'Arsenal   K6

Designed in 1878 as a private museum for watercolours, the Pavillon de l'Arsenal was opened in December 1988 as a documentation and information centre of the history of Paris. In an area of 16,000 sq. m (17,222 sq. ft) an exhibition is presented concerning the development of the city and its architecture. The highlight of the permanent exhibition "Paris, the City and its Projects" (covering 800 sq. m/8611 sq. ft) is a large model of the city to a scale of 1:2000, covering 40 sq. m (430 sq. ft). Complementary temporary exhibitions every three months illustrate a theme concerning the history of the city, and include comparisons with other European capitals.

Another exhibition illustrates current projects which are being realised in Paris.

The documentation centre and a photographic display provide information about the history of French architecture.

Location
21 Boulevard Morland
(4th arr.)

Métro
Sully-Moreland

Times of opening
Tues.–Sat. 10.30 a.m.–
6.30 p.m.; Sat. 11 a.m.–
7 p.m.

Documentation centre and Fototheque
Tues.–Sat. 2–6 p.m.

Père-Lachaise

See Cemeteries

*Petit Palais   F4

Apart from interesting temporary exhibitions (mostly relating to the history of civilisation) the Petit Palais has since 1902 housed the valuable art collections of the city of Paris (Musée des Beaux-Arts de la Ville de Paris): paintings, furniture, books and tableware.

The collections are partly based on endowments such as those of the Dutuit brothers (ancient, medieval and Renaissance works of art together with paintings, icons, drawings, books and ceramics) and the Tuck collection (18th c. furniture and sculpture). The city has mainly bought 19th c. art, including paintings by Géricault, Ingres and Delacroix.

Its architecture is similar to that of the Grand Palais (see entry) which was also built for the 1900 World Fair. It has a magnificent main entrance, crowned by a cupola, and a wealth of sculptural decoration.

Location
Avenue W.-Churchill
(8th arr.)

Métro
Champs-Elysées-Clemenceau

Buses
28, 49, 72, 73, 83

Times of opening
10 a.m.–5.40 p.m.; closed
Mon.

Entrance fee

Place de la Concorde

Place Charles-de-Gaulle

See Etoile

Place de l'Etoile

See Etoile

**Place de la Concorde   G4

Location
8th arrondissement

Métro
Concorde

Buses
24, 42, 52, 72, 73, 84, 94

The Place de la Concorde, at the intersection of the roads between the Louvre and the Arc de Triomphe and the Madeleine and the Palais Bourbon, is said to be one of the most beautiful squares in the world. It was chosen by the Senate as the site for an equestrian statue of Louis XV and laid out as the Place Louis XV by the architect Jacques Gabriel who had two magnificent buildings erected on the N side (1755–75), on either side of the Rue Royale: the present Ministry of Naval Affairs (until 1792 the royal furniture repository) on the right and what is today the Hôtel Crillon on the left (see illustration). During the French Revolution the statue of the king was destroyed, the name of the square changed to the Place de la Révolution and the guillotine set up here. Among the thousands executed in this square were Louis XVI, Marie-Antoinette, Madame du Barry, Charlotte Corday, Danton and in the end even Robespierre and his supporters.

Place des Vosges

In 1795, during the rule of the Directoire, the square was finally given its present name: Place de la Concorde.

In 1833 an obelisk 22 m (72 ft) high and weighing 220 tons, from Luxor, the Thebes of Ancient Egypt, was erected in the centre of the square. It dates from the reign of Ramses II (13th c. B.C.) and was a gift from the Egyptian Viceroy, Mehmed Ali. Between 1836 and 1854 Jacob Ignaz Hittorf completed the square by adding the fountains (N: allegories of Agriculture and Industry, see illustration; S: Seafaring and Fishing) and the eight statues of women symbolising (clockwise) France's eight largest cities: Marseilles, Bordeaux, Nantes, Brest, Rouen, Lille, Strasbourg, Lyons. (The small shelters in the plinths of the statues used to be occupied by "gardiens", city employees.) The statues have recently been restored.

Obelisk

*Place des Vosges

K5

In the eastern part of the Marais (see entry), the spacious and uniformly planned Place des Vosges is the oldest public square in Paris and served as a model for the design of others (Place Dauphine, Place Vendôme, Place de la Concorde).
The completion of the square – or "Place Royale" as it was then called – in 1612 confirmed the Marais as the heart of the aristocratic part of the city. At the instigation of Henry IV an unknown architect laid out a magnificent setting, its symmetry reflecting the architectural concepts of the Renaissance, for tournaments, royal receptions, weddings and – despite a ban

Location
Centre E (4th arr.)

Métro
Saint-Paul, Bastille

Buses
29, 69, 76, 96

Colonne de la Grande Armée in the Place Vendôme

by Cardinal Richelieu – for duelling when this was a fashionable activity.

The middle of the square forms a little garden with an equestrian statue of Louis XIII.

Incorporated into the façades of this "royal square" are royal residences, and their arches, with the "Pavillon de la Reine" on N side and the "Pavillon du Roi", bearing Henry IV's initials, on S side. The remaining houses were privately owned.

In 1800 the square was renamed Place des Vosges in honour of the first Département to pay its taxes to the French Republic. Today the square, with its trees and fountains, is a children's playground and a place for the people of the Marais, old and young, to meet and relax in. In the south-eastern corner stands the house that Victor Hugo lived in from 1833 to 1848 (see Practical Information, Museums, Maison Victor Hugo).

Place du Tertre   H2

Location
Montmartre (18th arr.)

Métro
Abbesses

Buses
80, 85

The former village square on the Butte, Montmartre (see entry) is, together with Sacré-Cœur (see entry), one of the most popular tourist attractions on the "highest mountain" in Paris. Painters, portrait artists and caricaturists display their wares and offer their services.

The 18th c. houses (No. 3, built in 1790, was formerly the mayor's office) still form a picturesque backdrop for the tourist traffic that dominates the square. Certainly the paintings on display have less to do with art than with the souvenir trade. Near the square is the little Musée de Montmartre (see Practical Information, Museums).

Bouquinistes on the Quai de Montebello

*Place Vendôme   G/H4

This unique square on the N side of the Tuileries Gardens (see entry) dates from the late 17th and early 18th c. when Jules Hardouin-Mansart, one of the outstanding architects of the 17th c. – the "Grand Siècle" – drew up the plans for the square as it is today. The façades and houses around the square – originally to be called "Place Louis-le-Grand" – were built between 1686 and 1720 and were intended to house the Royal Academies (see Institut de France), the Mint (see Monnaie), the Royal Library and the Palace for Ambassadors Extraordinary. The city, granted the land when the king ran into financial difficulties, sold users' rights to aristocrats and wealthy citizens who, behind the façades, constructed an adjoining garden and palaces modelled on those of the nobility (see Marais).

During the Revolution, in 1792, the equestrian statue of Louis XIV was pulled down and replaced, in Napoleon's reign, by a column "in honour of the army". This 44 m (144 ft) high column, an imitation of Trajan's Column in Rome, was topped by a statue of Napoleon in the garb of a Roman Emperor which was destroyed during the Paris Commune (1871) but later replaced by a copy of the original.

Encircling the Column is a spiral bronze relief depicting the glorious deeds of the French army. An internal staircase leads to the top but is not open to the public.

One of the finest examples of harmony in urban architecture in Europe, the charm of the Place Vendôme is that it has retained, unspoilt, the consistency of the overall design, successfully blending royal opulence with civic simplicity.

Location
Centre W (1st arr.)

Métro
Madeleine, Tuileries, Concorde

Buses
29, 72

Famous jewellers – Boucheron, Van Cleef et Arpels, Cartier – are to be found on the Place Vendôme and in the Rue de la Paix leading from the N side of the square to the Opéra. Ernest Hemingway, Scott Fitzgerald and Gertrude Stein frequented the "Bar Américain" of the Ritz Hotel.

Ponts de Paris

See Seine Bridges

Quais (quays)   H–K5/6

Location
Centre (bank of the Seine between Pont Sully and Pont Royal)

Métro
Cité, Saint-Michel

It used to be possible to walk along the "Quais de la Seine" on two levels but the lower level along the right bank and part of the left is now completely given over to traffic. However, a walk along the upper level (next to the surging traffic) offers ample compensation in a beautiful panorama, with the Iles de-la-Cité and Saint-Louis, of the heart of Paris and the displays of the "bouquinistes" (bouquin=book, novel) whose wooden box-type stalls selling new and secondhand books, postcards, posters, prints and the like, often also specialise in postcards, detective novels, exhibition posters, etc., affording many a pleasant surprise for the collector.

The finest walks along the quays are undoubtedly on the Ile Saint-Louis and Ile-de-la-Cité (see entries).

Quartier Latin   H/J6/7

Location
Centre (5th arr.)

Métro
Saint-Michel, Cardinal Lemoine, Monge

Buses
63, 84, 86, 89

The Quartier Latin (or Latin Quarter) is bordered by the Seine on the N, the Boulevard de Port-Royal on the S and the Boulevards Saint-Marcel and de l'Hôpital on the E, while demarcation on the W from the quarter of Saint-Germain (see entry) is less well defined (roughly on a level with the Odéon métro station). In addition to the University of the Sorbonne (see entry) (Université de Paris IV), the Latin Quarter houses most of the "Grandes Ecoles" (exclusive colleges that do not belong to the University system, e.g. Ecole Polytechnique, Ecole Normale Supérieure) as well as Censier University (Paris III) and Jussieu Universities (Paris VI and VII). A number of grammar schools, with a wealth of tradition – Lycée Henri IV (next to the Panthéon – see entry), Lycée Louis-le-Grand (behind the Sorbonne) and Lycée Saint-Louis (Boulevard Saint Michel) – together with the Collège de France (see entry) complete this panorama of scholarship.

Towards the end of the Middle Ages lack of space forced the Schools of Latin and Theology to move from the Cité around Notre-Dame to the left bank of the Seine, thus establishing the "Latin" Quarter as it was popularly known, because Latin was the official language in everyday use there.

Nowadays the student quarter is also a great tourist attraction. The lower part of the quarter is packed with cinemas, discos and restaurants (mostly Arab, some Greek and Indochinese). The 80-seater Théâtre de la Huchette (23 Rue de la Huchette) has staged the same programme (to full houses!) every night for over 20 years – Eugène Ionesco's two famous one-act plays

South façade of the . . .   *Institut du Monde Arabe*

"La Cantatrice Chauve" (The Bald Primadonna) and "La Leçon" (The Lesson).
Chinese and Vietnamese restaurants are to be found around the Montagne Sainte-Geneviève (between the Rue des Ecoles and the Panthéon).
In the Rue Mouffetard it is Greek cooking that takes pride of place in the many eating places. Several students' bistros have old cellars where, after a meal upstairs, one can hear poetry, music and drama.

On the bank of the Seine opposite the Pont de Sully the imposing high building of the Institute du Monde Arabe was opened in 1988. The Arab culture centre (architect Jean Nouvel) consists of two parallel slim glass discs with book tower, library, lecture rooms and a museum, on 9 floors. A curiosity is the square glass discs of the south façade, several storeys high which combined with ornamental pierced metal shades project daylight into the rooms.

Institute du Monde Arabe

Rambouillet

Although the summer residence of the President of the Republic, the Château is open to visitors.
In 1706 the Château, which had been built on the site of an old manor-house, was bought by the Count of Toulouse, a legitimised son of Louis XIV. Sections dating back to the Gothic, Renaissance and Baroque eras testify to the fact that it has undergone constant extension and renovation. When Louis XVI acquired Rambouillet in 1783 it was, like his predecessors

Location
Rambouillet, 56 km (35 miles) SW (N10 and N306)

Rail
from Gare Montparnasse

109

Times of opening
Mon., Wed., Fri.–Sun.
10 a.m.–noon, 2–4 p.m.
(in summer to 6 p.m.)

Entrance fee

and those that came after him, to use it mainly as a hunting lodge. He had a "Laiterie" (dairy) built there for Marie-Antoinette in the form of a Greek temple and set up a sheep farm where today about 800 sheep are reared.

Napoleon I made the Château his residence and since 1959 it has been the summer residence of the President and is also occasionally used for cabinet meetings.

The elegant interior is sumptuously decorated and furnished (Delft tiles, period furniture).

*Rue de Rivoli   G–J4/5

Location
Between Place de la Concorde and Place de la Bastille (1st and 4th arr.)

Métro
Concorde, Palais-Royal, Châtelet

Buses
21, 67, 69, 74, 75, 81, 85

The Rue de Rivoli on the right bank (rive droite) of the Seine runs between the Place de la Concorde and the Place de la Bastille. The oldest and most interesting section is between the Place de la Concorde (see entry) and the Place du Louvre (Métro station: Louvre), running the whole length of the Tuileries and the N wing of the Louvre.

This section was designed in Napoleon's time and he named the street after Rivoli, near Verona, which was the scene of his victory over Austria in the Italian campaign (1797). It took a long time to plan (1802–11) and to build, and it was not until 1833, 12 years after Napoleon's death, that work on the street – a blend of the traditional (uniform façades, round-arched arcades) and the contemporary (multi-storeyed buildings, metal roof structures) – was finished, only to be resumed in 1853 when Baron Haussmann, the architect who transformed Paris into a modern city, extended the Rue de Rivoli (together with the Rue Saint-Antoine) as far as the Place de la Bastille. At the time of the French Revolution, when what is now the street was a maze of houses and alleyways, between the Place de Pyramides and the Rue Castiglione there stood the Royal Riding School, whose main building in 1789 was made the chamber of the Revolutionary Parliament and it was here that the Republic was proclaimed in 1792, a fact recalled by a commemorative plaque opposite No. 230.

In 1862 Ivan Turgenev, the Russian writer, wrote his celebrated novel "Fathers and Sons" at No. 210, and the French author and diplomat René de Chateaubriand lived at No. 194 from 1812 to 1814.

A stroll through the arcades of the Napoleonic section, with their jewellers, art galleries, antique shops and tearooms, is today as inviting a prospect for the window-shopper as ever it was.

Three of Paris's largest department stores (Samaritaine, Belle Jardinière, Bazar de l'Hôtel de Ville – BHV) are situated between the Louvre and Hôtel de Ville (see entries).

Rue Royale   G4

Location
N of the Place de la Concorde (8th arr.)

Métro
Concorde, Madeleine

The Rue Royale linking the Place de la Concorde with the Madeleine (see entry) is one of the most elegant streets in Paris. Its luxury establishments such as Villeroy et Boch, Christofle (tableware), Fauchon (delicatessen) and Cerutti (clothing) are not quite as expensive as those in the nearby Faubourg Saint-Honoré (see entry) but are nevertheless in the top price bracket. Maxim's, the restaurant at No. 3, whose Art Nouveau décor

Statue of Joan of Arc in the Place des Pyramides

Sacré-Cœur

Buses
24, 42, 52, 84, 94

dates from the Belle Epoque, is famous throughout the world. The Rue Royale dates from the 18th c. and some houses from that period are listed monuments.

Sacré-Cœur   H2

Location
35 Rue du Chevalier de la
Barre (18th arr.)

Métro
Anvers, Abbesses

Buses
30, 54, 80, 85

Times of opening
Daily 6 a.m.–11 p.m.

The "Basilica of the Sacred Heart" (Sacré-Cœur) is one of the landmarks of Paris and its gleaming domes seem to shine out from the hill of Montmartre (see entry) far over the city.

After France's defeat by the Prussians and the suppression of the Paris Commune (1871), the Catholics of France vowed to build a church on the hill of Montmartre as a symbol of contrition and hope. The National Assembly of 1873 declared the project to be "of public utility" and building work began under the supervision of Paul Abadie in 1876. This proved extremely difficult and protracted because of the porous sandstone base and the Basilica was not consecrated until 1919.

Its architectural style, which to some resembles a wedding cake, is reminiscent of Byzantine-Romanesque. Although the exterior is not particularly interesting, architecturally speaking, its oppressively ornate interior is impressive if only on grounds of the scale of its dimensions – 100 m (330 ft) long and 50 m (165 ft) wide. The huge mosaic of the vault of the choir depicts Christ and the Sacred Heart, with the Archangel Michael and the Maid of Orleans to the left and Louis XVI and family to the right.

For a magnificent panoramic view over Paris it is well worth going up to the top of the dome (entrance on the left of the main doorway). You also have one of the finest views of the city from the broad flight of steps, thronged on summer evenings with youthful musicians, in front of the church (Notre-Dame, with the Centre Pompidou just in front of it, almost straight ahead; the Opéra, and behind it the Dôme des Invalides, slightly to the right).

**Saint-Denis

Location
Saint-Denis
4·5 km (3 miles) N (A1)

Métro
Saint-Denis-Basilique

Bus
156 (from Porte de la
Chapelle)

Times of opening
1 Oct.–31 Mar.: daily
10 a.m.–4 p.m.; 1 Apr.–
30 Sept.: daily 10 a.m.–
6 p.m.

The building of the façade and the choir of the Basilica of Saint-Denis, the necropolis of the kings and queens of France, marked the beginning of Gothic architecture.

The northern and central European Gothic style of architecture, painting and sculpture was born in France, in the French province of Ile-de-France centred on Paris. It comes between Romanesque and Renaissance and covers the period from the 12th c. to the onset of the 16th. The concept stems from the Italian art historian, Giorgio Vasari (1511–74), who, from the standpoint of the Italian Renaissance, considered it to be a barbarian (northern) art form and associated it with the Goths! Eventually objectively reassessed because of the 19th c. Romantic movement's enthusiasm for history, Gothic has come to be regarded as medieval architecture at its zenith.

Since early Christian times Saint-Denis has been an important place of pilgrimage. Legend has it that St Dionysius (or St Denis), missionary, martyr and first bishop of Paris, walked from Montmartre after he had been beheaded, carrying his head in his hands, to the place where he wished to be buried. A church was built on this site as early as the 5th c. and an

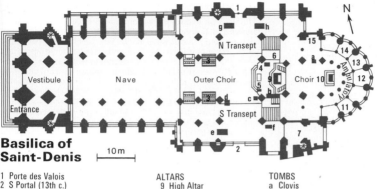

Basilica of Saint-Denis

|— 10 m —|

1 Porte des Valois
2 S Portal (13th c.)
3 Choir stalls
  (by Gaillon)
4 Bishop's throne
5 Mary with Infant Jesus
6 Entrance to crypt
7 Treasury
8 Cavaillé-Coll organ

ALTARS
9 High Altar
10 St Denis
11 Crucifixion
12 Childhood of Jesus
13 St Pérégrin
14 St Eustache
15 Evangelists
  (mosaics)

TOMBS
a Clovis
b Dagobert I/Nantilde
c Pépin le Bref (Pippin)
d Charles Martel
e François I/Claude de France
f Charles V
g Louis XII/Anne de Bretagne
h Henri II/Catherine de Médicis

abbey was added in the 7th c. The work on transforming the basilica from Romanesque to Gothic was begun in the 12th c. under Abbot Suger (1081–1151) with the Early-Gothic façade and porch (1137–40) and choir (1140–3). The middle section of the church was not demolished until a century later when Pierre de Montreuil (d. 1267), the architect of Louis IX (see Sainte-Chapelle), built the High-Gothic outer choir, transept and nave.

Over the centuries the basilica fell into decay but in the early 19th c. restoration began on an amateur basis and was finally completed between 1858 and 1879, in accordance with the historical records, by Viollet-le-Duc who left the church as we see it today.

Exterior

The early Gothic W façade brings together for the first time the characteristic features of Gothic architecture: simple, clear-cut structure (the narrative additions date from the 19th c.), symmetrical arrangement of the towers (the N tower was demolished in 1837 after being stuck by lightning), the transition from round to pointed arches, the insertion of a rose window (a feature found on a larger scale in the later High-Gothic cathedrals) and three portals (symbolic of the Holy Trinity) serving as focal points for the art of the ecclesiastical Gothic sculptor.

None of the original portal sculpture remains apart from the robed figures (central doorway: the wise and foolish virgins; right: the months; left: the signs of the Zodiac). The spandrel of the central doorway (restored) represents the Last Judgment; that on the right (recarved) the Last Communion of St Denis and that on the left (also recarved) the torture of the Saint and his companions Rusticus and Eleutherius.

With its crenellations and massive buttresses the exterior of the basilica has retained something of the "fortified" air that characterised Romanesque churches built as "God's fortresses".

Sainte-Chapelle

Interior

The interior of the church is 108 m (355 ft) long and almost 30 m (100 ft) high and makes an impressive effect with its soaring pillars and 37 windows, each 10 m (33 ft) high. It is divided into the vestibule, nave, outer choir, intersection, transepts and choir. Here one finds the final and possibly most important element of the Gothic style, perfected in High Gothic, namely, the "architecture of light", by which is meant light not only in its literal sense but as an integral part of the structure and spatial disposition of the building: the way the light falls (depending on the angle of incidence and how much light) breathes life into the spatial dimensions. Walls as load-bearing elements can be dispensed with and replaced with a great sweep of windows. The load-bearing function is performed by the ribbed vaulting which distributes the loading on to the underpinning arrangements of buttresses and pillars (the external buttresses provide stability). The use of the pointed Gothic arch makes for higher vaulting and greater spatial freedom.

Besides bringing together Early and High Gothic, the basilica also enjoys the special feature of having windows in the triforium which runs between the arcades and high windows of the aisles and transepts.

Royal tombs

Royal tombs: almost all of France's kings and queens, their children and certain great servants of the crown were buried in the basilica of Saint-Denis. Their tombs were plundered during the Revolution but since 1817 their mortal remains have again reposed in the church.

There are two communal tombs in the crypt, one for the royal house of Bourbon (including Louis XVI) and the other for about 800 members of the Merovingian, Capetian, Orléans and Valois royal families. The most notable of the many tombs are those of Louis XII (d. 1515) and his wife Anne de Bretagne (d. 1514), erected between 1517 and 1531 (in the N transept); Henri II (d. 1559) and his wife Catherine de Médicis (d. 1589), completed in 1573 (in the N transept); and Dagobert I (13th c.) with a statue of Queen Nantilde (on the right of the High Altar).

 ## **Sainte-Chapelle** J5

Location
4 Boulevard du Palais
(1st arr.)

Métro
Cité

Buses
21, 24, 27, 38, 81, 85, 96

Times of opening
1 Oct.–31 Mar.: daily
10 a.m.–4.20 p.m.; 1 Apr.–
30 Sept.: daily 10 a.m.–
5.20 p.m.

Entrance fee

A palace chapel on two levels, the Sainte-Chapelle (Holy Chapel) is the brightest of all the Gothic jewels of Paris. Mass is celebrated only on special occasions but concerts are given here frequently.

This magnificent High-Gothic masterpiece – probably the work of Pierre de Montreuil – was built in under 33 months by St Louis (Louis IX) to house the holy Christian relics obtained from the Emperor of Constantinople (at a cost 2½ times as much as the actual building).

At that time what was then the palace chapel stood in the great courtyard of the royal palace on the site of the present Palais de Justice (see entry). (The entrance to the Sainte-Chapelle is on the left inside the great ironwork railing at the main entrance to the Palais de Justice.) In the 18th c. a wing of the Palais de Justice was linked to the side of the chapel. Until its restoration (1841–67) the chapel served for a 30-year period as the legal archives.

Today the Sainte-Chapelle stands in an inner courtyard on the left of the Palais de Justice's main entrance. It is 33 m (110 ft)

Upper chapel . . .   *. . . of the Sainte-Chapelle*

long, 17 m (55 ft) wide, 76 m (250 ft) high and 42 m (140 ft) to the gable.

The lower chapel (chapelle basse) was originally for the servants. Its vault, which is only 6·6 m (22 ft) high, is not load-bearing but is supported by 14 pillars at intervals along the walls.

Lower chapel

The upper chapel is the actual Sainte-Chapelle. It was dedicated to the Holy Relics and reserved for the king, his family and high officials. (The relics – fragments of the Holy Cross and the Crown of Thorns, and a nail from the Cross – are today kept in the Treasury of Notre-Dame – see entry.)

Upper chapel

On entering the upper chapel one is immediately struck by the breathtaking beauty of the light filtering through the stained-glass windows that act as its walls, seemingly transcending earthly gravity. Apart from a low blind arcade around its base, decorated with scenes of martyrdom, the chapel has no walls as such and no supporting pillars or columns other than the fourteen 22 m (70 ft) high pillars that provide the framework for the great 4×15 m (13×50 ft) windows and buttress the superb vaulting.

The chapel is famous for its stained glass depicting over 1000 scenes from the Bible and flooding the interior with all the colours of the rainbow. About two-thirds is the original 13th c. glass and the rest has been restored to its original state. The Late-Gothic rose window, with scenes from Revelations, dates from the reign of Charles VIII (1493–8).

Each pillar in the nave has the statue of an Apostle at its foot but only half of these are originals (3, 4, 6, 11, 12, 13). In the 3rd bay

Sainte-Chapelle

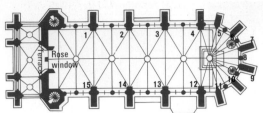

10m

N

CHAPELLE HAUTE
UPPER CHAPEL

SEQUENCE OF SCENES IN STAINED-GLASS WINDOWS (Total area c. 618 sq. m (6672 sq. ft) – partially restored)

1 Creation, Adam and Eve, Noah, Jacob
2 Flight from Egypt, Joseph
3 Pentateuch, Leviticus, Laws of Moses
4 Deuteronomy, Joshua, Ruth and Boas
5 Judges: Gideon, Samson

6 Isaiah, Root of Jesse
7 John the Evangelist, Life of Mary, Childhood of Jesus
8 Christ's Passion
9 John the Baptist, Daniel
10 Prophecies of Ezekiel
11 Jeremiah, Tobias
12 Judith, Job

13 Esther
14 Kings: Samuel, David, Solomon
15 Legend of the Holy Cross, Discovery of Christ's Cross, Acquisition of the Relics by Louis IX and their Deposition, Consecration of the Sainte-Chapelle

(on the left) there are two recesses that were reserved for the royal family, and St Louis was able to hear mass without being seen from his oratory in the 12th bay (on the right).

There is a small dais under a wooden baldachin in the apse where the reliquary for which the chapel was built used to stand; it is reached by two wooden staircases (the one on the left is original). The French kings were the only keyholders to the reliquary, the contents of which were displayed to the royal household on Good Friday.

*Saint-Etienne-du-Mont

J6

Location
Place Sainte-Geneviève
(5th arr.)

Métro
Cardinal Lemoine, Maubert-Mutualité, Luxembourg (RER)

Buses
84, 89

The present church dates from 1492 and was built for the servants of the Benedictine Abbey which used to be on this site. It is dedicated to St Stephen (Etienne) but St Genevieve, the patron saint of Paris and its supposed saviour from destruction by the Huns in the 5th c., is also venerated here. The quarter in which the church is situated (Montagne Sainte-Geneviève) is named after her.

The period and style of the building range from Late Gothic to early Renaissance. The choir and transept were completed in 1540 and the nave in 1610. Despite the Gothic ground plan and the Flamboyant vaulting above the intersection with a 5½ m (18 ft) pendant keystone ("Agnus Dei"), the most prominent feature was already the plain round pillars of the Renaissance. The richly decorated façade (1610–18) is pure Renaissance, the work of Claude Guérin. The small tower on the right probably survives from an earlier 13th c. building.

The triforium around the central nave constitutes a special architectural feature for a Renaissance church of this kind, since it is usually only to be found in Gothic churches.

The church is famous for its rood screen (1530–41, marble centrepiece) with spiral staircases on both sides, the only one left in Paris.

To the right of this, at the entrance to the Chapel of the Virgin, are the memorials of the philosopher Blaise Pascal (1623–62) and the playwright Jean-Baptiste Racine (1639–99) who are

Saint-Eustache

buried in the church. The second side chapel on the left contains a sarcophagus supposed to hold a stone from the grave of St Genevieve.

Stained glass in the N transept ("Revelations", 1614) and the S aisle ("Parable of the feast", 1586) dates from the church's construction.

Saint-Eustache   J5

The church of Saint-Eustache, dedicated to the early Christian martyr Eustachius, is generally considered the finest Renaissance church building in Paris. It is the parish church of the quarter of Les Halles (see entry).

Its foundation stone was laid in 1532 under François I but it was not completed until 1640. Modelled on Notre-Dame, it is Gothic in its ground plan, five-span nave, triforium (gallery under the windows) and fan vaulting. Its unique blending of Gothic and Renaissance forms is seen most clearly in the columns which, though built on the Gothic model, are Renaissance in outward appearance, and the church as a whole is as impressive as befitted the size and importance of its parish. It measures 100 m (330 ft) in length, 44 m (145 ft) in width and 34 m (110 ft) to the ceiling. The choir windows date from 1631 (Philippe de Champaigne) and show St Eustache surrounded by the Apostles and Fathers of the Church. The Martyrdom of St Eustache is depicted on the left spandrel of the portal (Simon Vouet, c. 1635). A note-worthy tomb is that of Colbert, Minister of Finance to Louis XIV, sculpted by Coysevox, designed by Lebrun and situated in the side aisle of the choir on the left of the apse.

Location
Rue Rambuteau (1st arr.)

Métro
Les Halles

Suburban station
Châtelet-Les Halles

Buses
29, 67, 74, 75, 85

Saint-Eustache is famous for its concerts (at 11 a.m. on public holidays), and works by Berlioz ("Te Deum", 1855) and Liszt (Mass, 1866) were heard here for the first time. Large Ducroquet/Gonzalès organ.

*Saint-Germain-des-Prés   H5/6

The Quarter

Location
6th arr.

Métro
Saint-Germain-des-Prés,
Odéon

Buses
39, 48, 63, 95, 96

The quarter of Saint-Germain-des-Prés, celebrated for the Existentialist circle around Jean-Paul Sartre and for the writers and artists of the forties and fifties, adjoins the western section of the Quartier Latin (see entry). Its borders are broadly the Seine (N), the Rue des Saints-Pères (W), the Rue de Vaugirard (S) and the Odéon métro station (E).

The artistic and intellectual atmosphere lingers on in the numerous art galleries, the Paris Academy of Art (Rue Bonaparte) and a number of cafés (Aux Deux Magots, Café de Flore) and restaurants, Saint-Germain-des-Prés is also famous for its sophisticated jazz bars.

As in the neighbouring Quartier Latin, the cinemas of Saint-Germain screen excellent programmes throughout the year (almost all foreign films are show in the original version, i.e. sub-titled, not dubbed).

The Church   H5

Location
Place Saint-Germain-des-Prés
(6th arr.)

Métro
Saint-Germain-des-Prés

Buses
39, 48, 63, 70, 86, 87, 95, 96

The church of Saint-Germain-des-Prés was part of the Benedictine Abbey established here in the 8th c. and destroyed during the French Revolution. It has borne the name of St Germain, Bishop of Paris, since his canonisation in 754.

The church which already stood here on the meadows (prés) of the Seine in the 6th c. was the burial place of the Merovingian kings Childerich I, Chlothar II and Childerich II (tombs plundered during the Revolution). Destroyed several times by the Normans, the church was rebuilt between 990 and 1021. Parts of it are late Romanesque (nave) and Early Gothic (choir completed in 1163).

The tombs of John Casimir, king of Poland (d. 1672) and a statue of St Francis-Xavier by Nicolas Coustou can be found in the right transept. In the second side chapel on the right of the choir are the headstones of the philosopher Descartes (d. 1650) and the two scholar monks Mabillon (d. 1707) and Montfaucon (d. 1719).

*Saint-Germain-en-Laye

Palace

Location
Saint-Germain-en-Laye
(suburb 20 km (12 miles)
W of Paris)

Métro
Saint-Germain-en-Laye (RER)

Saint-Germain-en-Laye, birthplace of the French composer Claude Debussy, has one of the Ile-de-France's many royal palaces.

In the 12th c. Louis VI built a castle on the ridge above the Seine which François I had demolished retaining only the keep and the Sainte-Chapelle (the predecessor of its namesake in Paris).

The château that he built in its place was the home of Mary Stuart between the ages of 6 and 16 and James II of England ended his days here after being deposed. Louis XIV was born in the château in 1638. The Renaissance château fell into decay in the 18th c. but was restored, together with the chapel, by Napoleon III in 1862–7.

Entrance fee

**Times of opening
(castle and museum):**
Daily, except Tues., 9.45 a.m.
–noon and 1.30–5.15 p.m.

National Museum of Antiquities

The chapel, probably the work of Pierre de Montreuil who built the Sainte-Chapelle on the Ile-de-la-Cité (see entries), was begun in 1245 and is one of the great works of early High Gothic in the Ile-de-France.
Saint-Germain is also famous for the château's terraces which afford superb views of Paris and the Seine.
Since 1867 the rooms of the former royal palace have housed the "Musée des Antiquités Nationales (Musée de la Préhistoire)", an outstanding and ever-growing collection of archaeological finds from all over France.

*Saint-Germain-l'Auxerrois   H5

The former royal parish church of Saint-Germain-l'Auxerrois is situated on the square at the E entrance to the Louvre (see entry: Place du Louvre) opposite the town hall (Mairie Annexe) of the 1st arrondissement. It is dedicated to St Germanus, bishop of Auxerre.
The present church is a mixture of styles (Romanesque belfry, Gothic chancel, Late-Gothic porch and nave and a Renaissance side porch). The front porch (1435–9) is an outstanding example of Late Gothic and the very fine royal pew (1684) in the nave is well worth seeing.
Many artists who served the French kings are buried in the church: the architects Le Vau and Robert de Cotte, the painters François Boucher and Jean-Marc Nattier, the sculptor Coysevox and the brothers Nicolas and Guillaume Coustou.

Location
Place du Louvre (1st arr.)

Metro
Louvre

Buses
21, 67, 69, 72, 74, 76, 81, 85

*Saint-Julien-le-Pauvre   J5

This little church on the Quai-Saint-Michel behind the Square Réne-Viviani is today the church of the Greek Orthodox community.
It was built in the High-Gothic style between the middle of the 12th and 13th c. The elections of the Chancellors (Recteurs) of the Sorbonne (see entry) were held here in the 15th and 16th c. and its bell summoned the students to lectures. Today its interior is dominated by an iconostasis (a screen of icons) dating from 1901.

Location
Quai-Saint-Michel (5th arr.)

Métro
Saint-Michel

Bus
24

*Saint-Pierre-de-Montmartre   H2

Four black marble pillars (two in the choir and two against the inner wall of the façade) date from the Merovingian church erected here in the 7th c. on the site of a Roman temple. The

Location
Rue du Mont-Cenis
(18th arr.)

Saint-Séverin

Saint-Germain-des-Prés   Saint-Séverin

Métro
Anvers, Abbesses

Bus
80

present church is Early Gothic (choir, apse, transept) and was consecrated in 1147.

The Church of Saint-Pierre is all that remains of the large 12th c. Benedictine Abbey of Montmartre the last Abbess of which was guillotined in 1794.

*Saint-Séverin   J6

Location
1 Rue des Prêtres-Saint-
Séverin (5th arr.)

Métro
Saint-Michel

Buses
21, 24, 27, 38, 67, 81, 85, 96

The Church of Saint-Séverin (named after the hermit who lived on this spot in the 6th c.) is in the lower part of the Quartier Latin (see entry) and is one of the finest examples of "style flamboyant", the Late-Gothic form of Flamboyant art.

This was at one time the site of an oratory (destroyed by the Normans), a chapel and then a church. The present building was begun in the first half of the 13th c. Parts of it were probably destroyed by fire in the 15th c. and it was completed in the Late-Gothic style about 1520.

The first three sections of the nave are in the simple style of the 13th c. but from the 4th span onwards one finds richly decorated pillars and imaginatively worked keystones. The choir has a double ambulatory of great beauty and with its wonderfully intricate fan vaulting is a masterpiece of Late-Gothic art. The 14th c. stained-glass windows depicting the Apostles in the first three sections come from the choir of Saint-Germain-des-Prés (see entry), whereas the other windows in the nave are 15th c. and contrast sharply with the modern windows (1966, Jean Bazaine) in the chancel. The side door on the right leads into a small garden covering the old cemetery and surrounded by ossuaries.

*Saint-Sulpice   H6

The Abbey of Saint-Germain-des-Prés (see entry) commissioned the plans for this new parish church in 1634 but building was not finished until the façade was completed in 1766. Six architects were involved in the work.

The Place Saint-Sulpice in front of the church was originally intended by the Florentine architect Jean-Nicolas Servandoni (1695–1766) to be a half-circle fronted by uniformly designed houses but this project was abandoned. The square in its present form dates from 1808 while the fountain (1844) with the four bishops (Bossuet, Fénelon, Massillon, Fléchier) is by Louis Visconti.

The façade, modelled on Sir Christopher Wren's St Paul's Cathedral, is the work of Servandoni and with its two tiers of columns (Ionic above, Doric below) is a rare example of simple, unadorned Classicism.

The N tower (73 m – 240 ft) was built (1777) by Jean François Chalgrin, while the S tower is incomplete (68 m – 220 ft).

The nave was begun by Christophe Gamard in 1646 and continued by Louis Le Vau from 1655 onwards. The barrel-vaulted interior is impressively spacious and is evenly lit by high side windows.

Two stoups near the entrance, the gift of the Venetian Republic to François I, bequeathed to the church by Louis XV.

Frescoes by Eugène Delacroix (in the first side chapel on the right): St Michael and the dragon, Heliodorus driven out of the temple, Jacob and the angel (completed in 1861).

Statues near the choir pillars by Bouchardon of Christ, Mary and eight Apostles (from 1734).

In the chapel of the Virgin: four paintings by Carle van Loo (1705–65), a fresco in the cupola by François Lemoyne (1688–1737) and a marble statue of the "Queen of Heaven" by Jean-Baptiste Pigalle (1714–85).

In the right and the left transepts: a copper plate and a marble obelisk that together form a sundial (1744). Victor Hugo and Adèle Foucher were married in the church in 1822. – Enormous Cliquot organ, rebuilt and enlarged by Cavaillé-Coll in 1860 (recitals).

Location
Place Saint-Sulpice
(6th arr.)

Métro
Saint-Sulpice

Buses
63, 70, 84, 86, 87, 96

Items of special interest

Saint-Vincent-de-Paul   J3

This church – completed in 1844 and the most important church to be built in the reign of Louis-Philippe (1830–48) – was designed by Jacob Ignaz Hittorf (1792–1867) who hailed from Cologne. Hittorf combined the Christian architectural form of a five-sectioned basilica with elements of Roman (triumphal arch) and Greek (Ionic and Corinthian columns). Outstanding features of the magnificent interior are the fresco "Procession of the Saints" (1849–53) by Hippolyte Flandrin and the altar sculpture by François Rude (1784–1855).

Location
Place La Fayette (10th arr.)

Métro
Poissonnière

Buses
32, 42, 43, 49

Seine Bridges

The actual city of Paris itself has 33 bridges across the Seine. It takes 13 of them alone to connect the two Seine islands, Ile-de-

Pont du Caroussel

la-Cité, Ile Saint-Louis (see entries), with one another and the rest of the centre. These are among the oldest of Paris's bridges, most of the others upstream and downstream from the centre having been built in the 19th c. The cast-iron Pont des Arts, called "Passerelle" (gangway) by the Parisians and restricted to pedestrians, joins the Louvre (see entry) with the Institut de France (see entry) on the opposite bank.

The bridges of medieval Paris served as promenades and meeting places for people to gossip and do business. Merchants built shops on them, with their living quarters above, but as modern times dawned these vanished to make room for roads and their traffic.

In 1991 the newest bridge, the Pont Genty near the Pont d'Austerlitz, will link the Gare de Lyon with the Gare d'Austerlitz.

*Pont Alexandre III
F4/5

Between the Grand Palais and the Petit Palais the Avenue Alexandre III leads S to the 170·5 m (117 yards) long Pont Alexandre III, built for the world exhibition 1896–1900. The bridge is richly decorated with allegorical statues (regilded in 1989) and provides a splendid view especially of the Dôme des Invalides.

Pont au Change J5

Métro Châtelet

Buses
21, 24, 27, 38, 81, 85, 96

During the reign of Louis XIII the two 14th c. wooden bridges between Châtelet and Conciergerie (see entries) were replaced by the Pont au Change, and the occupants of the old bridges (merchants, hawkers, dealers and moneychangers, i.e. "changeurs") moved to the new bridge. During the Revolution those condemned to death passed over the Pont au Change on their way to be guillotined in the Place de la Concorde (see entry).

Pont Neuf, the oldest bridge in Paris

In 1859–60 the bridge was aligned with the present Boulevard du Palais.

On a level with the Palais Bourbon (see entry; National Assembly), the Pont de la Concorde connects the square of the same name with the left bank of the Seine. Stone from the demolished Bastille was used in the building of the bridge (1787–91).
The view on the right bank from the bridge is of the Place de la Concorde, the Obelisk and the Madeleine beyond (see entries). Looking upstream you can see the Tuileries Gardens and the Louvre, with the Ile-de-la-Cité and the towers of Notre-Dame rising above the Seine in the distance (see entries). On the left bank there is a very good view of the Eiffel Tower (see Tour Eiffel) and the Hôtel (see entry), and Dôme des Invalides. An excellent spot to get your bearings – and take photographs!

Pont de la Concorde
G4/5

Métro
Chambre-des-Députés

Buses
24, 73, 83, 84

The five-arched bridge linking the Ile Saint-Louis (see entry) with the right bank of the Seine was built between 1614 and 1635 at the behest of Louis XIII by its architect, Christophe Marie, whose name it bears.
121 people were killed when part of the bridge broke away during a major flood disaster in 1658, and all its occupants were evacuated when, in 1740, Paris was again hit by flooding. A year later it was made illegal to build new houses on the Seine bridges and the old ones were gradually demolished. The Pont Marie's "hump" was straightened out in the 19th c.

Pont Marie
J5/6

Métro
Pont Marie

Bus
67

A popular catch question on the history of Paris is "Which bridge is the oldest?" The answer is "the New Bridge" – the

Pont Neuf
H5

Sorbonne

Métro
Pont Neuf

Buses
21, 24, 27, 58, 67, 70, 75, 85

Pont Neuf – which, though restored in the 19th c., was begun in 1578 and completed in 1607. It is one of the most beautiful and also, at 330 m (1080 ft), the longest of the old Seine bridges and spans both channels of the river at the western end of the Cité (see entry). (The "Square du Vert-Galant" was added subsequently.)
It was built like a modern road bridge, without houses and with pavements.
For two weeks in 1985 the packaging artist Christo clothed the 12 arches of the bridge with 40,000 sq. m (48,000 sq. yd) of champagne-coloured material, thus making the bridge into a "sculpture".

Pont Royal
G/H5

Métro
Musée d'Orsay

Bus
681

After several failures to build a bridge that could withstand floods downstream from the Cité (level with the Tuileries – see entry), public money was used up and when the bridge was finally built in 1685–9 (as designed by Jules Hardouin-Mansart) it was paid for by Louis XIV from his own privy purse – hence its name, literally "bridge of the king". Its "hump" was flattened in 1850 to make way for a road.

Sorbonne   H/J6

Location
Rue des Ecoles, Place de la Sorbonne (5th arr.)

Métro
Odéon, Saint-Michel

Buses
21, 27, 38, 63, 81, 85, 86, 87

Times of opening
Mon.–Fri., 8 a.m.–8 p.m.

The influential cathedral canons (chanoines) of medieval Paris are often described as hungry for power and possessions but Robert de Sorbon, canon and father confessor to St Louis (IX), seems to have been an exception. With the king's help he established a college (la Sorbonne) in 1257 where poor theology students could live and study at his expense. The college soon became a leading school of theology and later a university, only to decline in importance towards the end of the Middle Ages. Cardinal Richelieu, when Rector of the University, stopped the buildings deteriorating and had them partly rebuilt by Jacques Lemercier (1624–42). Napoleon made the Sorbonne a State university and considerably extended it.
The present building, with 22 large lecture theatres, 38 smaller rooms, 37 academics' studies, 240 laboratories, a library, observatory and numerous offices, dates from between 1885 and 1901 (architect: Nenot).
The Sorbonne was one of the centres of the student unrest of May 1968 which spread to become a general strike throughout France. Subsequent reform of the university system split the Sorbonne into four universities. These still have their headquarters and some departments here but most facilities have been distributed throughout the city and its suburbs. (Greater Paris now has a total of 13 universities.) A new university law planned for 1987/8, including the introduction of "numerus clausus", was temporarily dropped in 1986 because of violent student unrest.
The main façade on the Rue des Ecoles bears allegorical representations of the sciences. Arrangements can be made in the office on the right of the main entrance to visit the largest of the lecture theatres, the Grand Amphithéâtre, which seats 2700 and contains Puvis de Chavannes' famous classical mural "the Sacred Grove".

Sorbonne

Église de la Sorbonne

The church in the courtyard of the Sorbonne was built between 1635 and 1648. The tomb of Cardinal Richelieu (1694) which stands in the S transept was designed by Charles Lebrun (1619–90) and executed by François Girardon (1628–1715).

The Théâtre Français, the home of the Comédie Française

(Entrance to the church in the courtyard; if closed, apply to the concierge at 1 Rue de la Sorbonne under the arch.)

Théâtre Français H5

The Théâtre Français is the home of France's national theatre company, the Comédie-Française.

Founded by Louis XIV in 1680, the Comédie-Française was originally the troupe headed by Molière until his death in 1673. In 1812 Napoleon enacted a decree giving the company its official status, with a Director appointed (as today) by the government. The original building into which the Comédie-Française moved in 1792 burnt down in 1799 and was rebuilt in 1807. The present façade dates from 1867 and the interior from the turn of the century (restored and extended after a second fire in 1900).

In the foyer visitors can see the chair in which Molière suffered a haemorrhage, and the famous bust of Voltaire by Jean-Antoine Houdon (1781). The Comédie-Française only performs the classics: plays by Corneille, Racine, Molière, Marivaux and Beaumarchais, as well as "modern" classics by Claudel, Giraudoux and Anouilh.

Location
Place Malraux (1st arr.)

Métro
Palais-Royal

Buses
21, 27, 39, 48, 67, 69, 72, 74, 81, 85, 95

Times of opening
Advance bookings (a week ahead); 11–6 p.m.

Thermes (Roman baths) H6

The remains of these Roman baths are on land next to the Musée de Cluny (see entry). It is not known exactly when they

Location
6 Place Paul-Painlevé (5th arr.)

Tour Eiffel

The Eiffel Tower

The Tuilleries in autumn

Métro
Saint-Michel, Odéon

Buses
21, 27, 38, 86, 87

Times of opening
9.45 a,m,–12.30 p.m. and
2–5.15 p.m.; closed Tues.

Entrance fee

were built but their destruction is put at about A.D.380. It is not possible to enter the ruins (on the corner of Boulevard Saint-Michel and Boulevard Saint-Germain) but they can be seen from the outside.

The Frigidarium is the only room still intact and this was due to the building of the Hôtel de Cluny (entrance).

The ruins are of the following:

Caldarium (hot bath): farthest W of the three main rooms, visible from Rue du Sommerard. Tepidarium (warm bath): visible from Boulevard Saint-Michel. Two Gymnasiums: visible from Boulevard Saint-Germain.

Swimming pool, 10 m (33 ft) long.

Frigidarium (cold bath) with the "Autel des Nautes": the best preserved of the baths, 20 m (66 ft) long, 12 m (39 ft) wide and 16 m (52½ ft) high. The capitals of the pillars supporting the cross vaulting on the N side look like ships' prows, hence the supposition that the baths were financed by the "Nautes", the rich corporation of Paris boatmen. The "Autel des Nautes" (altar of the Nautes) is from the excavations of the temple of Jupiter located beneath the choir of Notre-Dame (see entry). Bearing a dedication by the "Nautes", its sculpture of Gallic and Roman deities is the oldest found in Paris to date (1st c. B.C.).

****Tour Eiffel**   E5

Location
Quai Branly (7th arr.)

Despite oft-repeated doubts as to its stability, the Eiffel Tower celebrated its centenary in 1989. Over 60 years ago it lost its title as the world's highest building to New York's Empire State

Building and later to the Sears Tower in Chicago, but still has 5000 visitors a day (average over the year). The Eiffel Tower continues to be the symbol of Paris. The steel tower was thoroughly overhauled between 1981 and 1989.

The designs and calculations for the tower were the work of Gustave Eiffel (1832–1923), an engineer from Dijon, and it was built for the World Fair in 1889. The tower is 307 m (1000 ft) high (320·75 m (1050 ft) to the top of the mast) and consists of 15,000 steel components held together by 2·5 million rivets. Its method of construction distributes the total weight of 7500 tonnes in such a way that the pressure it exerts on the ground is only 4 kg per sq. cm (60 lb per sq. in), the equivalent of an average-sized adult on the seat of a chair. However, since no individual component is exchanged but always replaced by a new concrete section, the weight has increased to 11,000 tonnes. As renovation proceeds 1500 concrete parts will be removed and replaced by steel plates.

People protested vigorously when it was being built and the construction cómpany was obliged to give an undertaking to meet any claims for damages in the event of the tower collaps-ing on to surrounding buildings. Fortunately this has never happened, and the "purification" treatment (removal of rust, etc.) which it undergoes has increased its safety and has modernised its construction.

The top platform (with orienteering table) is reached by a lift. Although in fine weather the panorama from here stretches up to 70 km (44 miles), nevertheless the first platform has the advantage that the surrounding buildings and areas of the town can be seen in more detail. Here (and also on the second platform) there are restaurants, a post office (with special "Tour Eiffel" franking) and a cinema where an audio-visual pro-gramme is shown giving information about the history of the structure. After dark the tower is impressively illuminated.

Métro
Ecole Militaire, Bir Hakeim, Trocadéro

Buses
42, 69, 80, 82, 87

Times of opening
1st and 2nd platforms:
Mon.–Sat. 10 a.m.–
11 p.m.; Fri., Sat. and Sun. in summer until midnight
3rd platform 10 a.m.–
10.30 p.m. (closed in winter)

Entrance fee

Tour Saint-Jacques (St James' tower)　　　　J5

On the N corner of the Place du Châtelet stands the Tour Saint-Jacques, the Late-Gothic steeple of what was the parish church of the butchers' guild, Saint-Jacques-la-Boucherie, built 1508–22 by Jean de Félin under François I.

In the Middle Ages the church was the assembly point for pilgrims setting out for Santiago de Compostela (NW Spain), the reputed tomb of St James the Apostle and the most impor-tant pilgrim shrine of medieval Christendom.

Pilgrims proceeding from the N by the Rue Saint-Martin passed along the Rue Saint-Jacques on their way S. On top of the 52 m (170 ft) high tower stands a statue of St James (in French, Saint Jacques; in Spanish, Santiago).

The pilgrims' symbol was the scallop shell or "coquille Saint-Jacques", which has subsequently also become famous as a culinary delicacy.

Location
Rue de Rivoli (4th arr.)

Métro
Châtelet

Buses
38, 47, 58, 69, 70, 75, 76, 96

---

*Tuileries　　　　G/H4/5

One of the largest and best-known parks in Paris is the Tuileries Gardens. When Catherine de Médicis had a palace built in 1563 on what is today the whole length of the Avenue du Général

Lemonnier, close to the Palace of the Louvre (see entry), she named it the "Tuileries" after the tile-kilns that had stood on that site. In 1664 Colbert, Louis XIV's Minister of Finance, commissioned André Le Nôtre, later to be responsible for the park at Versailles (see entry), to design the Tuileries Gardens. The palace burnt down during the Paris Commune in 1871 and was never rebuilt.

Coysevox's Baroque statues of winged horses guard the entrance on the Place de la Concorde (see entry) through which, by way of terraces and ramps, one reaches the large octagonal fountain surrounded by 18th c. busts and statues by the sculptors Coustou and Coysevox (copy of a bust of Le Nôtre on the terrace of the Jeu du Paume (see entry)). From the central avenue one has a unique view of the obelisk in the Place de la Concorde, the Champs-Elysées and the Arc de Triomphe (see entries) in one direction and the "Parterres" (formal lawns) of the Louvre Museum and the small triumphal arch "du Carrousel" in the other. To the left and right of the rather dusty "Grande Allée" you can rest on benches in the shade or watch the games of "boules" on the terraces by the Rue de Rivoli.

In this northern section there is also a Punch and Judy show as well as donkey rides for the children. Many children sail their model boats on the yacht pond at the other end of the central avenue (boats can be hired in the summer months).

*UNESCO   F6

This building is the headquarters of UNESCO, the United Nations Educational, Scientific and Cultural Organisation.

Jointly created in 1955–8 by its architects Marcel Breuer (USA), Pier Luigi Nervi (Italy) and Bernard Zehrfuss (France), it embodies a piece of modern architectural history.

Picasso's mural "Victory of Light and Peace over Darkness and Death" adorns the walls of the trapezoidal hall of the conference building. Outside it has a recumbent figure by Henry Moore (GB) and a black steel mobile by Alexander Calder (USA) and the two walls of the Moon and the Sun are decorated with ceramics by Joan Miró. Inside there are bronze reliefs by Hans Arp and tapestries by Le Corbusier.

Val-de-Grâce   H/J7

The imposing Baroque church of Val-de-Grâce is part of a well-preserved 17th c. convent (nowadays a military hospital). Anne of Austria, wife of Louis XIII, bought the convent for the Benedictine nuns and vowed to endow it with a church if she gave birth to an heir to the throne (her marriage had been childless for 23 years). She kept her promise in 1645 after the birth of her son, the future Louis XIV, in 1638 and commissioned Jacques Lemercier to build the church, which was completed by Gabriel le Duc in 1667.

Val-de-Grâce is the only Baroque church in Paris the architecture of which bears the stamp of Rome, the capital of 17th c. Baroque. Its architect Lemercier modelled the main façade, with its double row of columns, on that of St Susanna in Rome. The dome recalls the dome of St Peter's but is more ornate, with sculptured vases, windows and a frieze of fleurs-de-lys, and the initials "A" and "L", while its tambour is markedly three-dimensional with prominent pilasters and cornices and deep-set windows.

The interior of the church is also marked by the three-dimensional approach that governs the church's architecture and décor as a whole. The barrel-vaulted nave is divided into three sections, each with side-chapels. On the round arches there are reliefs representing the virtues (medallions: Christ's forefathers). At the intersection of the nave and chapels there is a stepped dais and a canopy supported by columns (reminiscent of Bernini's baldachin over the High Altar of St Peter's – another echo of Rome).

In the cupola (40 m (130 ft) high, 17 m (55 ft) in diameter) the great fresco of God the Father surrounded by the Saints and Martyrs is the work of Pierre Mignard (1665). Anne of Austria's portrait can be seen in the fresco in the cupola of the chapel on the left of the choir. The chapel on the right is dedicated to St Louis and is the former Benedictine choir.

*Vaux-le-Vicomte

The Château of Vaux-le-Vicomte, 6 km (4 miles) NE of Melun (on the D215) is one of the finest of the 17th c. nobles' châteaux and served as the model for the palace and park at Versailles (see entry).

Nicholas Fouquet, Finance Minister of Louis XIV, called in the three greatest architects of that time to work on his project: Louis Le Vau (château), Charles Lebrun (interior) and André Le Nôtre (park). The magnificent château and park were completed in a relatively short time (1656–61) and cost Fouquet the enormous sum of 10 million "livres" (French pounds).

Fouquet's enjoyment of his property was short-lived. Accused of profiteering while in office, he was arrested at the instigation of his successor Colbert soon afterwards (he died in prison) and Vaux-le-Vicomte was confiscated. This château prompted Louis XIV to resolve to build for himself the finest palace in France, and with this in mind he seized part of the confiscated treasure (vases, statues, even trees and plants) and engaged Le Vau, Lebrun and Le Nôtre to create for him the palace to end all palaces, the focal point of power and splendour for all France – Versailles.

Location
55 km (34 miles) SE
(A4, A6)

Rail
From Gare de Lyon to Melun

Times of opening
1 April–31 Oct. 10 a.m.–
6 p.m.; 1 Nov.–31 March
(except Jan.).
Sat., Sun. 2–5 p.m.

Fountains
1 April–31 Oct. every 2nd and
last Sat. in month
3–6 p.m.

Entrance fee

**Versailles

Versailles, once the magnificent residence of the French kings and now the chief town of the département Yvelines and see of a bishop, is situated to the SW of Paris on a sandy plain.

**Château de Versailles

The Palace of Versailles with its parks and gardens is among the most beautiful, famous and historical sights in Europe. The architecture, interior, park and, in fact, the entire court of the French kings at Versailles in the 17th and 18th c. served as the

Location
Versailles, Département of
Yvelines (78), 20 km
(12 miles) SW, A13/12 or N10

Versailles

Château de Versailles

Rail
from Montparnasse, Saint-Lazare and Invalides

Times of opening
9.45 a.m.–5.30 p.m.; closed Mon. and public holidays

Guided tours
in French and English, Tues.–Sun., 9.45 a.m.–3.30 p.m.; Appartement du Roi et Opéra. Tues.–Fri. 2 and 3.30 p.m.; App. de Mme de Pompadour and Mme du Barry, Cabinets intérieurs de la Reine, Appartement de Mme de Maintenon (subsequently visit continued without commentary)

Entrance fee

Exterior

model for many European royal and princely courts of that time. What was originally a small hunting lodge, built in 1631–4 by Philibert Le Roy for Louis XIII, was extended and rebuilt from 1661 to 1710 to become the royal seat of Louis XIV, the "Roi Soleil" (sun king). The architecture of Versailles is the work of Louis Le Vau, Jules Hardouin-Mansart and Robert de Cotte. Charles Lebrun was responsible for the interior and the gardens were landscaped by André Le Nôtre. Louis XIV's successors made little or no alterations apart from minor additions (Rococo apartments and the classicist Petit Trianon: Louis XV; garden extensions: Louis XV and Louis XVI).

Versailles was the residence of the French kings for over a century (1682–1789). The principles of absolute monarchy required the nobles of high rank to be in constant attendance at the court of the king. Thus Versailles was made the centre of power of absolutist France where the king, aloof from strong princes and growing unrest in Paris, was able to rule as an autocrat. Consequently Louis XIV's extravagant claim "l'Etat, c'est moi!" (I personify the State) can also be regarded as confirming the true state of affairs. The palace and park of Versailles provided the fitting setting for this abundance of power.

Seen from the outside the palace is already impressive. Three broad avenues converge in the square in front of the palace (Place d'Armes). The former royal stables (Mansart, 1679–85) can be seen on both sides of the central avenue. Entering the forecourt through the palace gates the visitor is faced by the equestrian statue of Louis XIV (1835) where the forecourt becomes the Cour Royale – the courtyard formerly reserved for

Château de Versailles: façade facing the park

the royal family. This narrows to become the Cour de Marbre – the "marble courtyard" – which until 1830 was slightly higher and paved with coloured marble. The entrance to the palace and to the park is on the right side of the Cour Royale.

The oldest buildings are those fronting the Cour de Marbre. These were part of Louis XIII's hunting lodge, and contain the royal private apartments (1st floor). Le Vau enlarged the original building by adding on wings to house the State Apartments (Grands Appartements) on the 1st floor and the suites of the heirs to the throne on the ground floor. Mansart joined Le Vau's wings by building the Hall of Mirrors on the 1st floor overlooking the park and extended the palace by adding the N and S wings. The palace chapel (Mansart/Cotte) and opera house (Jacques-Ange Gabriel) completed the palace in its present form. The overall length of the park façade amounts to 680 m (2230 ft).

Today's visitor can still fully appreciate how the splendour revealed inside the palace must have impressed even royal contemporaries. Of the many rooms the following are particularly well worth seeing:

Interior

Galerie des Batailles: in this gallery, which is 120 m (390 ft) long and 13 m (40 ft) wide and extends for almost the entire length of the S wing, the paintings of battles cover 14 centuries of French history. 82 busts of famous military leaders line the walls and the Corinthian columns in the middle section of the gallery.

Gallery of Battles

Salle du Sacre: the room gets its name from the painting by Jacques Louis David (1748–1825) of the coronation of

Coronation Room

Napoleon I and Empress Josephine. In the time of Louis XI it was a chapel.

Queen's Apartments
Queen's staircase

Escalier de la Reine: the magnificent staircase with multi-coloured marble and gilded bronze reliefs on the ceiling fillet and over the doors leads to the state and private apartments of the queen. A recess in the centre of the 1st floor landing contains the king's coat of arms.

Hall of the Queen's Guards

Salle des Gardes de la Reine: the ceiling paintings and marble walls date from the time of Louis XIV. The paintings (1676–81) are by Noël Coypel (1628–1707). The central octagonal painting shows Jupiter in a silver chariot drawn by two eagles. The four pictures in the arches are classical representations of divine virtues.

Queen's ante-chamber

Antichambre de la Reine: visitors used to wait here before an audience with the queen in her drawing-room or bedchamber. The ceiling paintings (dating from Louis XIV) show famous women of antiquity (1673, Claude Vignon). The four Gobelins are of the same period.

Queen's audience chamber

Salon de la Reine: the ceiling paintings (allegories of the arts and sciences, 1671, Michel Corneille) are all that remain from the time of Maria Theresa of Austria since in 1785 Marie-Antoinette transformed this room into its present form. The large Gobelin portrait of Louis XV (by P. F. Cozette from a design by Michel van Loos) dates from 1770.

Queen's bedchamber

Chambre de la Reine: 19 princes and princesses were born in this bedchamber which was created for Maria Theresa of Aus-

Château de Versailles: Hall of Mirrors

tria, wife of Louis XIV. Queens also gave private audiences in this room. The Rococo ceiling showing the four virtues of a queen (charity, fertility, wisdom, fidelity) is of a later date (1729–35) and its "grisaille" paintings are the work of François Boucher (1703–70). Marie-Antoinette was responsible for the addition of the Gobelin medallions depicting Empress Maria Theresa of Austria, Emperor Joseph II and her husband Louis XVI. The little jewellery chest (1787, Schwerdtfeger) on the left of the queen's bed was a gift to Marie-Antoinette from the city of Paris, two years before the Revolution.

Petits Appartements de la Reine: these can be reached from the Queen's bedchamber and are furnished as they would have been in Marie-Antoinette's time (1770–81).

Queen's Private Apartments

Salon de la Paix: in the "classical" symmetry of Versailles this "Salon" (1680–6) was built to offset the Salon of War on the other side of the Hall of Mirrors. The ceiling is by Lebrun and the portrait of Louis above the fireplace is by Lemoyne.

Salon of Peace

Galerie des Glaces: after the annexation of Lorraine Louis XIV also acquired the dukedom of Burgundy in the Peace of Nijmegen (1678), thus consolidating France's supremacy in Europe. In that year the king decided to build a gallery which, with the Salons of War and Peace, completed the principal part of the palace and paid tribute in allegorical form to Louis XIV as the lord of war and peace. This celebrated Hall of Mirrors, which is 75 m (246 ft) long, 10 m (33 ft) wide and 12 m (40 ft) high, was based on plans by Jules Hardouin-Mansart (1646–

Hall of Mirrors

133

1708) and the interior was designed by Charles Lebrun (1619–90), director of the State Gobelins workshops. As with all galleries in hotels, palaces and châteaux, the Hall of Mirrors served as a corridor (between the apartments of the king and queen) in which courtiers paid their respects. It was rarely used for solemn occasions. The Hall gets its name from the 17 arched panels of mirrors, each consisting of 18 mirror-panes (making 306 altogether), opposite the round-arched windows overlooking the park. It was in this historical hall that the new German Empire was proclaimed in 1871 and the Peace Treaty of Versailles was signed in 1919.

Since June 1980 the Hall has again been fitted out with (restored and reproduction) items of furniture, statuary and chandeliers (many in gilded plastic); the originals had been removed or destroyed before and during the Revolution. The paintings in the barrel-vaulted ceiling of the Hall of Mirrors are, taken as a whole, the most monumental ceiling paintings of their kind in France. They tell the story of Louis XIV's regency up till the Peace of Nijmegen.

Ox-eye drawing-room

Salon de l'Oeil de Bœuf: this drawing-room, named after its oval (ox-eye) window, dates from 1701 and originally contained paintings by the Italian painter Veronese. These were replaced by the portraits of the royal family. Worth noting is the frieze of children (53 m (174 ft)) which, like the group of cherubs in the park, expresses the ageing king's wish for "more youth and less seriousness".

King's bedchamber

Chambre du Roi: Louis XIV's bedchamber was constructed in 1701 in what had been the main hall of Louis XIII's hunting lodge. It was here that the king died on 1 September 1715, and that the famous ceremonies of the "Lever du Roi" and the "Coucher du Roi" took place when the king granted morning and evening audiences. After many years of costly work the furnishings were restored to their original state in 1980.

Council Chamber

Cabinet du Conseil: in the reigns of Louis XV and XVI all important decisions of state were taken in this room. The room's décor is a masterpiece of French Rococo (1755, based on designs by Jacques-Ange Gabriel).

King's Private Apartments

Petits Appartements du Roi: these can be reached from the council chamber. Dating from 1755, they were furnished in the Rococo style by Jacques-Ange Gabriel for Louis XV as somewhere to recover from the ceremonial etiquette of the court. Louis XV died in the first room (bedroom) on 10 May 1774.

Salon of War

Salon de la Guerre: this affords a unique view through the Hall of Mirrors to the Salon of Peace opposite on one side, and through the salons of the Grands Appartements on the other. The large oval stucco relief glorifying Louis XIV (between the corridors) is by Antoine Coysevox (1640–1720).

State Apartments
Salon of Apollo

Salon d'Appollon: "Apollo in the sun chariot accompanied by the seasons" (ceiling painting by Charles de la Fosse, a student of Lebrun) is the central allegorical theme from which Louis XIV derived his additional title of "le Roi Soleil" (the sun king). The walls are hung with priceless Gobelin tapestries and above the fireplace is the famous portrait of the king in the robe of ermine.

Salon of Mercury

Salon de Mercure: in the three salons of Apollo, Mercury and

Mars the magnificent ceiling paintings are all that remain of the original décor (1670–80) – the marble was replaced by wood and the walls covered with fabric. The Grands Appartements were the staterooms where the king held court from 6 till 10 a.m.

Salon de Mars: this salon, the former Guard Room with its ceiling painting by Audran, contains the famous picture of Marie-Antoinette with her three children (1787, Madame Vigée-Lebrun).

Salon of Mars

Salon de Diane (1675–80): the ceiling painting of Diana leading the hunt is by Gabriel Blanchard and the bust of Louis XIV is by Lorenzo Bernini (1665).

Salon of Diana

Salon de Venus: here, too, as in the Salon de Diane, one finds, in the "cold and severe" marble décor, the style of the 1670s that originally characterised all seven of the Grands Appartements. This style echoed Louis XIV's determination to be remembered for his power and glory by constant reference to the heroes of classical antiquity. This theme is taken up in the marble walls and pillars, the classical-type statues (Louis XIV as a Roman emperor) and the paintings on the ceiling of Titus and Berenice, Antony and Cleopatra, Jason and Medea, Theseus and Ariadne, Europa and Jupiter, Amphitrite and Poseidon.

Salon of Venus

Salon d'Abondance (c. 1680): the ceiling painting of the Goddess of Plenty, with her cornucopia, is by R. A. Houasse, a student of Lebrun. This room was used for the buffet at receptions.

Salon of Plenty

Salon d'Hercule: ceiling painting: Triumph of Hercules (1710–36; François Lemoyne); two paintings by Veronese, gifts from the Republic of Venice to Louis XIV (1664): "Elisha and Rebecca" (over the fireplace), "The Meal with Simon the Pharisee".

Salon of Hercules

La Chapelle (1699–1710, Jules Hardouin-Mansart, completed by his brother-in-law Robert de Cotte): the gallery with its Corinthian colonnade is on a level with the king's apartments (for the royal family only). Masses: 1st Sun. in month, Easter and Whit. Sun., 1st Nov. at 5.30 p.m.

Palace Chapel

Musée de l'Histoire de France: the history of France from the 17th to 19th c. in paintings and sculpture. Because of restoration work some rooms will be temporarily closed during 1986.

Museum of the History of France

Times of opening
see Château

Opéra (guided tours only): the plans for an opera-house at Versailles were drawn up by Jacques-Ange Gabriel (1698–1782) for Louis XV. It took only two years to build (1768–70) and was completed for the wedding of the future Louis XVI to Marie-Antoinette. Like the palace chapel and the east façade of the Louvre (see entry) it has a colonnade of Ionic columns. With its gilded, marble and mirror décor it is tastefully furnished to fit in with the rest of the palace.

Opera House

**The Park of Versailles

Palace and park together form one unit: without the palace the vast park would lack a focal point and lose its function as an imposing context for the Royal Court while without the park the

Times of opening
from sunrise to sunset

135

Versailles

Note:
It is possible to visit the Bosquets – (de la Salle de Balle, la Colonnade, des Dômes, des Bains d'Apollon) – during the main fountain displays (3 May–4 Oct.; 1st, 3rd, 4th Sun. in month at 11.15 a.m. and 3.30 p.m.). Otherwise enquiries should be made at the Office de Tourisme, 7 Rue des Réservoirs.

palace would seem little more than an enormous building complex, a pent-up power source, lacking an appropriate setting. This is borne out by the history of the park since the plans for it were completed before the final plans (the Hall of Mirrors and the wings) for the palace took shape. On the other hand the way the park is laid out (with raised lawns, for example) conforms to the requirement to extend the imposing bulk of the palace out into the park.

The Park of Versailles is the perfect example of French landscape gardening in the 17th c. Its creator, André Le Nôtre (1613–1700), was the son of a gardener in the royal Jardins des Tuileries (see entry) in Paris and in this, his great masterpiece, he drew on his earlier landscape gardening for the Tuileries and for Vaux-le-Vicomte (see entry) in particular.

The main features of the "French gardens" (symmetry, geometrical topiary) which can rightly be described as unnatural, correspond to the ideals of French Classicism which saw these as expressing man's mastery over nature. The relationship between the palace and the park is of profound significance in so far as the palace symbolises the power of the monarch over his people in its domination of the park which, by its mastery over nature, reflects the Sun King's own mastery over nature. This is at its most apparent in the "Bassins" and the "Grand Canal" where artificial means are used to ensure that the water is always still.

The "English Gardens" near the Petit Trianon were added to Le Nôtre's French Gardens in the 18th c. and the contrast in the two styles is obvious. The English landscape garden copies nature by artificial means, with the possibility of acting out "genuine" rural life in its little "hamlet".

Versailles: Bassin d'Apollon, Allée Royale/Tapis Vert, Palace

The Trianons (small châteaux) were the king's only private domain at Versailles. Elsewhere they were subject to the same rules of etiquette and ceremonial as all the other members of the royal court.

Bassin de Neptune (1679–84, designed by Le Nôtre): sculptuary (1740 by Adam, Bouchardon and Lemoyne): Neptune, with trident, and his wife Amphitrite, with sceptre, in the centre; Oceanus, on a unicorn, and Proteus, with sea creatures, at the sides.

Tour
Neptune's Basin

Parterres: on the stone terrace, with steps leading down to the parterres (open terraces), there are four bronze statues (Bacchus, Apollo, Antony, a silenus) and two fine marble vases with reliefs by Antoine Coysevox (Turkish War and Peace Treaties of Aix-la-Chapelle and Nijmegen).
Parterre du Nord: the cosmic forces are represented by 24 statues in groups of four – the seasons and times of day, elements, continents, temperaments and literature.
Parterre d'Eau (centre): two pools with 24 bronzes, allegorical representations of the French rivers.
Parterre du Midi and Orangerie: the southern section of the terraces, with sumptuous flower ornamentation. Especially impressive is the Orangerie (1684–6) below the Parterres, the

Parterres

Park of Versailles: Grand Trianon . . . ⁣ ⁣ ⁣ ⁣ *. . . and English Garden*

central gallery of which is 155 m (170 yd) long. Behind it extends the lake (Pièces d'Eau des Suisses), constructed by the Royal Swiss Guard.

Parterre de Latone: Latona is the Latin name for Leto, wife of Zeus, who is portrayed in this pool with her children Diana and Apollo fleeing from the wicked Lycians whom Zeus punishes by turning them into frogs.

Salle de Bal

Bosquet de la Salle de Bal (Bosquet des Rocailles): an amphitheatre made out of natural stone for games and dancing (can only be visited during the fountains display).

Royal Avenue

Allée Royale (Tapis Vert): also designated the "green carpet", runs between the pools of Latona and Apollo in the long axis of the park.

Colonnade

Colonnade (1685): Jules Hardouin-Mansart created this circular arcade (Ionic marble columns) as a particularly elegant setting for festivities (guided tours only).

Apollo's Basin

Bassin d'Apollon: the figure of Apollo in the sun chariot (1670, Jean-Baptiste Tuby) is an allegory of the "Sun King", Louis XIV.

Canal

Canal: in Louis XIV's time golden gondolas, presented to him by the Republic of Venice, floated on the waters of the "Grand Canal" and the "Petit Canal".

Grand Trianon

Grand Trianon (1678–88): this little château, built for Louis XIV by Jules Hardouin-Mansart and Robert de Cotte, served as his own private domain, free from the etiquette of the court, where he and his favourite, Madame de Maintenon, each had their own wings. Napoleon was responsible for its subsequent restoration which is why its décor is partly Baroque and partly Empire (furniture).

Petit Trianon (1763–7, architect: Jacques-Ange Gabriel): Louis XV had this little château built for his mistresses, Louis XVI gave it to his queen, Marie-Antoinette.

Petit Trianon

English garden: this was laid out on the site of Louis XV's botanical gardens for Marie-Antoinette and contains a little hamlet with a farm, dairy, mill and dove-cot. Also worth seeing: Temple d'Amour (temple of love, 1778), Belvedere (octagonal pavilion, 1777), the Queen's Theatre (1780), French Pavilion (Gabriel, 1750).

English garden

Bosquet des Dômes: all that remains of the fine pavilion are its base, statues and reliefs. In the middle of the grove stands the group of Titans by Gaspard Marsy.

Bosquet des Dômes

Bosquet des Bains d'Apollon: the Romantic-style trimmings were added to the famous Apollo group at a later date.
Ile des Enfants: on the NW edge of this grove there is a group of cherubs (*putti*) as playing children (1710) which dates from the time when the ageing Louis XIV wanted to see representations of "more youth".

Bosquet des Bains d'Apollon

Vidéothèque de Paris   J5

The Vidéothèque de Paris, opened in 1988 and covering an area of 4000 sq. m (4784 sq. yd), is the most modern audio-visual archive in the country. At present 3000 films on the most varied themes from cinema, television and video sources are shown here. In the foreseeable future the collection is expected to increase to 20,000 cassettes.
Fifty television screens are controlled by the "Magnus" computer system, which is named after Gaston Leroux's legendary three-armed figure, and at each screen the visitor can select the film he wishes to see. There are also three other rooms where larger scale screenings can be put on for groups of 20 to 300 people.

Location
Forum des Halles
(1st arr.) Porte Saint-Eustache

Métro
Les Halles

Times of opening
Tues.–Fri., Sun. 12.30–11 p.m.; Sat. 10 a.m.–11 p.m.

*La Villette   M2

On a site in the NE of Paris, covering 55 ha (136 acres), an area which until now has had no attractions for tourists, there is being established the Parc de la Villette, a new recreation park with a cultural aim. Two factors influenced the choice of the site; one was that in the 1960s a central abbatoir was built here but never used; the other was that here there was a market hall, which was built of cast iron in the 19th c. and which it was intended to preserve.
Reconstruction work lasted six years before the Cité des Sciences et de l'Industrie was opened in 1986. This building is 270 m (295 yd) long and 47 m (154 ft) high with a glass-hung façade and four huge metal roof bearers.

The south front is reflected in a small lake and in "La Géode" cinema which appears to be floating in the water.

Location
In NE (19 arr.)

Métro
Porte de Pantin
Porte de la Villette

Buses
75, 150, 151, 152, 251

Boulevard Périphérique
Porte de Pantin (in W)
Porte de la Villette (in N)

Géode

La Villette

The Géode spherical cinema, outside the new Museum of Technology

Performances Tues. and Thurs. hourly 10 a.m.–6 p.m.; Wed. and Fri.–Sun. hourly 10 a.m.–9 p.m.

La Géode is a futuristic building 36 m (118 ft) in diameter, made of polished chrome-nickel steel. At night the metal sphere is illuminated from below, creating its own starlit firmament. Inside, the audience reclines comfortably in bucket chairs, surrounded by the hollow dome of wafer-thin aluminium sheet, now transformed into a screen. On to this screen, which is 1000 sq. m (10,764 sq. ft) in area, documentary films are projected at an angle of 172° with 12-channel stereo sound and 12,000 watts. These films were made for La Géode using a special camera developed for the Canadian "Omnimax" system. Up to the present time there are in the world only half a dozen of these extra wide films and cinemas which can show them. The huge computer-controlled projector works with a 15 kW lamp (normal projectors operate with a 1½ kW lamp), and the 70 mm film produces pictures which are ten times as large as those of normal format. Since demand for tickets for performances is considerable visitors are recommended to book in good time. (Information: tel. 40 05 06 07).

Cité des Sciences et de l'Industrie

Times of opening
Tues., Thurs. and Fri. 10 a.m.–6 p.m.; Wed. noon–9 p.m.; Sat., Sun and public holidays noon–8 p.m.

Explora

According to its director, Maurice Levy, this project (opened in 1986) is more a great communications tool rather than a museum. Its object is to make technology and science accessible to everyone and to explain to the visitor national development, the state of research and tendencies for the future. At the same time it is to provide a forum for the exchange of ideas for all French undertakings which are active in this field. Above the central concourse of the technical museum, where each visit begins, the sunlight shines in on to domes and is directed by a system of movable mirrors. The interior presents a full-scale replica of an American space station. From here escalators convey visitors to the permanent "Explora" exhibition

la Villette

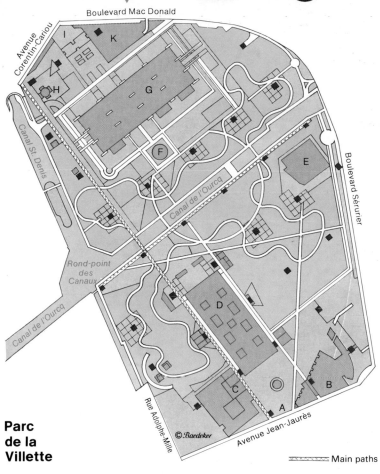

Boulevard Mac Donald

Avenue Corentin-Cariou

Canal St-Denis

Canal de l'Ourcq

Boulevard Sérurier

Rond-point des Canaux

Canal de l'Ourcq

Rue Adolphe-Mille

© Baedeker

Avenue Jean-Jaurès

Parc de la Villette

〰〰〰 Main paths

A Porte de Pantin
B Cité de la Musique
C Théâtre Paris-Villette
D Grande Halle
E Zénith

F Géode
G Cité des Sciences et de l'Industrie
H Maison de la Villette
I Porte de la Villette
K Logements

141

Zénith and Folie

which in an area of 30,000 sq. m (36,000 sq. yd) comprises four themes: "Language and Communication" (language; information studies; mathematics; sound; light; mental activity; art and technology): "From the Earth to the Universe" (astronomy; space and space travel): "The Adventure of Life" (biosphere; building and construction; transport; technology; natural science; archaeology) and "Materials and the Work of Man" (the earth and its resources; energy, construction of materials; manufacture of basic materials and products). In addition there are 10,000 sq. m (107,640 sq. ft) of space available for special exhibitions (including artificial materials, telecommunication, transport technology, fashion, nutrition) and for conferences. Other facilities are a photographic library, a cinematographic library, a video library and a sound library. Visitors can watch video films, carry out experiments or work together with computers. Everywhere the aim is to motivate and intensify the learning process by taking part in pleasurable activity. Visitors can also relax with a cup of coffee or a snack while looking at hydro and maristem cultures or the Ariane rocket.

Inventorium

To awaken in the very young an enthusiasm for science and technology, the "Inventorium" was set up. This has two sections, one for children from 3 to 6 years of age and one for the 6 to 12 year-olds. By actually "building" on a "site", for example, training is provided in team work and leadership, while at the computer terminals logical reasoning is taught. Finally, for adults, the "Minitel" serves as an introduction into the age of information technology.

La Villette: Grande Halle

The Media Library was provided for a broad spectrum of the public. It houses some 300,000 volumes, 5,000 periodicals and 1000 educational programmes from 1988 as well as a collection of international documentary films on video cassettes.
Finally visits can be made to the "Maison de l'Industrie", to "L'Espace Entreprise", the "Louis Lumière" cinema or the "Planetarium" (demonstrations: Wed. to Sun. 2.30 p.m.; Fri. also 10.30 a.m.).

Mediathèque

In the old rotunda at the Porte de la Villette entrance to the park, where the veterinary staff was once quartered, information on local history has been available since 1987.

Maison de la Villette

At the east end of the park stands the "Zénith" concert hall, the architects of which were Philippe Chaix and Jean-Paul Morel; it can seat 6,400 and is used primarily for rock concerts and variety presentations.

Zénith

The "Great Hall", formerly called the "Halle aux Bœufs" is impressive for the elegance of its wrought iron work of 1867. Conservation and restoration of the building were achieved within two years by the architect Bernard Reichen and Philippe Robert for 250 million francs and it was dedicated by President Mitterand in 1985.
An area of 20,000 sq. m (23,920 sq. yd) is used for exhibitions, concerts, theatrical productions and other events of every kind. On the surrounding spacious lawns there are little buildings called "Folies" where visitors can obtain refreshments.

Grande Halle

Times of opening
Tues., Fri., Sat. 10 a.m.–10 p.m.; Mon., Thurs., Sun. 10 a.m.–7 p.m.

143

Vincennes

Théâtre-Paris-Villette

Bernard Gillaumot was the architect responsible for the design of the nearby "Théâtre-Paris-Villette" (300 seats). Here most of the productions are by contemporary playwrights.

Cité de la Musique

The "Cité de la Musique" was inaugurated in the south of the park in 1989 (architect: Christian de Portzamparc). The western part houses the teaching rooms of the new conservatory of music, while the eastern section will consist of a concert hall, holding 1200 and is due to open in 1990, together with other rooms for public performances. In addition the "Musée de la Musique" has been moved here from the Rue Madrid; the exhibits include more than 4000 instruments. A sound studio and the Institut de Pédagogie are also housed here.

---

*Vincennes N/O7/8

*Bois de Vincennes

Location
SE outskirts (12th arr.)

Métro
Porte Dorée, Château de Vincennes

Buses
46, 86

Times of opening
Summer: 9.30 a.m.–8 p.m.
Winter: 9.30 a.m.–5 p.m.

The Bois de Vincennes on the SE edge of the city is the counterpart of the Bois de Boulogne (see entry) in the W and is roughly the same size. It lies on the Boulevard Périphérique and is bordered on the S and E by the Marne.
The forest here was enclosed for hunting by Philippe II Auguste in the 13th c. and in the 17th c. it was already becoming popular for outings. Louis XV restocked it with trees. Napoleon III gave it to the city of Paris for a park and nowadays its paths, tracks and man-made lakes make the Bois de Vincennes an attraction in its own right, apart from all else that it has to offer, such as the Zoo de Paris (see entry), the Château de Vincennes (see entry) and the Lac de Saint-Mandé. Here, too, are situated the Cartoucherie with the Théâtre de Soleil (see Practical Information – Theatres) and the Hippodrome de Vincennes (see Practical Information – Sport).

Lac Daumesnil

Lac Daumesnil: it is possible to walk around the lake and on the two islands (café-restaurant) reached by a small bridge. Boats can be hired for rowing on the lake.

Parc Floral

Parc Floral (gardens): the Parc Floral was established here following on from the Flower Show in 1969 and is a venue for art exhibitions as well as annual flower displays. It has an aquarium with exotic fish and reptiles as well as a sculpture garden, lake, children's playground and restaurant (open daily 9.30 a.m.–5 p.m.).
Lac des Minimes: rowing boats for hire, café-restaurant (on the small peninsula).

*Château de Vincennes

Location
Vincennes, Avenue de Paris, E outskirts

Métro
Château de Vincennes

Bus
56

Looking at the Château of Vincennes as it is today, a combination of medieval fortifications and Baroque castle, it is relatively easy to trace its history in architectural terms. The walls and nine towers of the fortification with the finest donjon (keep) in France enclose a spacious inner courtyard with four pavilions (living quarters) dating from the 17th c.
From the 11th c. the Forest of Vincennes (see Bois de Vincennes) belonged to kings of France who built a hunting lodge here (12th–13th c.) which became a castle (14th c.) and was

finally one of their favourite residences (15th c.). With the defeat of the Fronde the castle became the prison for those opposed to absolutist monarchy in particular (the Prince de Condé, Cardinal Retz) and a century later for those opposed to the monarchy in general (Diderot, Mirabeau: the Marquis de Sade was also a prisoner here for several years). Cardinal Mazarin ordered the building of the Pavillon du Roi and the Pavillon de la Reine in the 17th c. and the young King Louis XIV spent his honeymoon here in 1661.

Used as an arsenal by Napoleon, the castle was restored in the reign of Napoleon III by Viollet-le-Duc. Further restoration was required after 1944 because of the serious damage inflicted by German troops during their retreat.

Worth seeing:

Donjon (c. 1330): this impressive keep served both as watchtower and living quarters. It is five storeys high (52 m – 170 ft) with walls 3 m (10 ft) thick. The keep has four round towers at the corners and is surrounded by walls and a moat. (The tower-rooms were prison cells; museum since 1934.)

Keep

Ground floor: kitchen and stores; 1st floor: hall for receptions, study; 2nd floor: royal bedchamber (where Henry V of England died of dysentery in 1422) and chapel; 3rd floor: royal suite of rooms and treasury; 4th floor: servants' quarters; 5th floor: armoury. (Fine view from the roof terrace.)

Premises

Sainte-Chapelle (1379–1552): modelled on the Sainte-Chapelle (see entry) of the royal palace on the Ile-de-la-Cité, the architecture of this palace chapel is still Gothic (Flamboyant façade, etc.) despite its not being complete until the Renaissance (beautiful Renaissance windows in the choir).

In the N oratory is the tomb of the Duc d'Enghien, the last Prince de Condé, shot on Napoleon's orders in 1814. (A column outside the walls at the foot of the Tour de la Reine marks the spot where he died.)

Sainte-Chapelle

Pavillon de la Reine, Pavillon du Roi (1654–61): these are the last of the castle buildings and the work of Louis Le Vau. The Pavillon de la Reine was the home of Anne of Austria, the mother of Louis XIV. Cardinal Mazarin died in the Pavillon du Roi in 1661.

Pavilions

Times of opening
10 a.m.–5 p.m. (summer to 6 p.m.)

Entrance fee

---

*Zoo de Paris (zoological gardens; also: Zoo de Vincennes)   O7

The zoo has a great many large open-air enclosures and fits well into the recreation area of the Bois de Vincennes (see entry).

The large number of native and foreign species (c. 600 mammals and 1200 birds) take up 17 ha (40 acres) of land and there is heated accommodation for the animals in the winter months.

From the 72 m (235 ft) high concrete "Rocks" one has a view over the Bois de Vincennes and its castle and, with good visibility, the eastern part of Paris.

Location
W section of the Bois de Vincennes (12th arr.)

Métro
Porte Dorée

Times of opening
9 a.m.–5 p.m. daily (summer to 6 p.m.)

Practical Information A–Z

Advance Booking (Location)

Advance booking (location) of tickets for theatre, opera, ballet, etc. is usually done over the phone (if one speaks French).

Tickets can also be bought in advance at several theatres and concert halls. The exact details are given in "L'Officiel", "Pariscope" and "7 à Paris" (see Programmes of Events).

There are also ticket agencies, especially around the Opéra and Champs-Elysées.

Reduced price tickets (see Theatres).   Note

Airports (Aéroports)

The smallest of Paris's airports, 40 km (25 miles N of Paris.   Le Bourget
Information: tel. 48 34 93 90.
Connections with Paris:
Car: Autoroute A1, 40–70 min. (City centre).
Bus: RATP 350 (Gare du Nord, Gare de l'Est; 10th arr.)
        30 min., RATP 152 (Porte de la Villette; 19th arr.)
        25 min.

23 km (14 miles) N. Information: tel. 48 62 22 80.   Roissy/Charles de Gaulle
Connections with Paris:
Car: Autoroute A1, 50–90 min. (City centre).
Bus: RATP 350 (Gare du Nord, Gare de l'Est and Porte de la
        Chapelle, 10th arr.) 50 min., RATP 351 (Place de la
        Nation; 12th arr.) 40 min. Cars Air France to and from
        Maillot air terminal (Aérogare Centre Internationale,
        Porte Maillot, 16th arr.) 30 min. Departures every 15
        min. from 6 a.m. to 11 p.m.
Rail: SNCF "Roissy Rail" (Gare du Nord; 10th arr.) 30 min.
        Departures every 15 min.

14 km (9 miles) S. Information: tel. 48 84 32 10.   Orly (Sud/Ouest)
Connections with Paris:
Car: Autoroute A6, 40–60 min. (City centre).
Bus: RATP 215 (Place Denfert-Rochereau; 14th arr.)
        25 min., RATP 183A (Porte de Choisy; 13th arr.)
        50 min. Cars Air France to and from Invalides air
        terminal (Aérogare des Invalides; 7th arr.) 40 min.
        Departures from Orly Sud every 15 min. from 6 a.m.
        o 11 p.m.; Orly Ouest every 20 min. from 6 a.m. to
        11 p.m.
Rail: RER line C, also called "Orly-Rail". Departures every 15
        mins.

◀ *Obelisk in the Place de la Concorde*

Antique Shops (Antiquités)

Shops	Le Village Suisse 78 Avenue de Suffren (15th arr.); tel. 43 06 69 90 Métro: La Motte-Piquet Open: 11 a.m.–7 p.m.; closed Tues. and Wed. About 100 first-class shops.
	La "Nouvelle" Cour aux Antiquaires 54 Faubourg St-Honoré (8th arr.); tel. 40 73 43 99 Métro: Concorde Open: 10.30 a.m.–9 p.m.; closed Sun. and Mon. In eighteen small boutiques there is everything from designer fashions to etchings and Chinese porcelain.
	Le Louvre des Antiquaires 2 Place du Palais-Royal (1st arr.); tel. 42 97 27 00 Métro: Palais-Royal Open: Tues.–Sun. 11 a.m.–7 p.m. 250 antique dealers on three floors offer furniture and objets d'art of all periods.
Quarter	Village Saint-Paul Many shops in the Rues St-Paul, des Jardins St-Paul, de l'Ave-Maria and the Quai des Celestins Métro: Sully-Morland Open: 11 a.m.–7 p.m.; closed Tues. and Wed.
	Carré Rive Gauche Rue du Bac, Rue de Beaune, Rue de Lille, Rue de l'Université, Rue des St-Pères, Quai Voltaire Métro: Bac Open: 10 a.m.–noon, 2–7 p.m.; closed Sun. and Mon. morning.
Auctions	Vente aux Enchères au Nouveau Drouot Salle Drouot 9 Rue Drouot (9th arr.); tel. 42 46 17 11 Métro: Richelieu-Drouot Open: Mon.–Sat. 11 a.m.–6 p.m. Viewing and auctions in 21 rooms.

Banks/Exchange Bureaux (Banques/Change)

Banks	Times of opening: 9 a.m.–12 noon and 2–4.30 p.m. (closed at weekends).
Exchange Bureaux	At Orly and Roissy/Charles de Gaulle airports exchange bureaux are open from 6 a.m. to 11.30 p.m.
Counters open late	The following stations have counters that stay open late: Gare de Lyon: daily 6.30 a.m.–11 p.m. Gare de l'Est: Mon.–Fri. 7 a.m.–9 p.m. Gare d'Austerlitz: daily 7 a.m.–9 p.m. Gare St-Lazare: Mon.–Fri. 7.30 a.m.–9 p.m. Gare du Nord, daily 6.30 a.m.–10 p.m. Porte Maillot (Société Générale): Mon.–Fri. 9.30 a.m.–12.20 p.m. and 2.15–4.20 p.m.

Boulevard de Clichy

Banks with counters open late:
U.B.P., 154 Champs-Elysées (8th arr.)
Open: Mon.–Fri. 9 a.m.–5 p.m., Sat., Sun. 10.30 a.m.–1 p.m.,
2–6 p.m.

C.C.F., 117 Champs-Elysées/Rue Galilée (8th arr.)
Open: Mon.–Sat. 8.30 a.m.–8 p.m.

Boat Trips (Excursions en bateau)

Pont de l'Alma (8th arr.); tel. 42 25 96 10
Métro: Alma Marceau
Daily: 10 a.m.–11 p.m. (every 30 min.; departures at 10.30,
11.30 a.m., 1.30, 5.30–8 p.m. and 10–11 p.m. may be cancelled)
Lunch daily 1 p.m., afternoon coffee with music 3.45 p.m.,
dinner 8.30 p.m.

Bateaux-Mouches (rive droite)

Pont d'Iéna (8th arr.); tel. 47 05 50 00
Métro: Bir Hakeim/Iéna
Daily in the high season 9.30 a.m.–10.30 p.m. (every 20 min.),
low season 10 a.m.–5 p.m. (every 30 min.).

Bateaux Parisiens (Tour Eiffel, rive gauche)

Pont-Neuf (Square du Vert-Galant; 1st arr.); tel. 46 33 98 38
Métro: Pont-Neuf
10.30, 11 a.m., noon, 1.30–5 p.m. (every 30 min.).

Vedettes Pont-Neuf

Port de Suffren (7th arr.); tel. 47 05 71 29
Métro: Bir Hakeim
Daily: 10 a.m.–5.30 p.m. (every 30 min.).

Vedettes de Paris
Ile de France

149

Canauxrama	Trips exploring the Paris canals, tel. 46 07 13 13 Breakfast trip on the St Martin Canal 9.15 a.m. at the Bassin de la Villette (19th arr.), Quai de Loire Métro: Jaurès Arrival: Bassin de l'Arsenal (new Paris boat harbour) Métro: Bastille Afternoons in the opposite direction: 2 p.m.
Day trip	On the Canal de l'Ourcq, return by car. Mon., Tues. 8.45 a.m. from the Bassin de la Villette (19th arr.), Quai de Loire Métro: Jaurès La Villette Yesterday and Today: Reservations: tel. 46 24 86 16 Mon., Tues., Wed., 9.15, 10.45 a.m., 2, 3.20 p.m. at the Bassin de la Villette (19th arr.), Quai de Loire Métro: Jaurès Arrival: Parc ou Bassin de la Villette.
La Patac Eautobus (waterbus)	Trip along the Seine and through the canals of Paris, tel. 48 74 75 30 May–Nov. 9 a.m.–12.30 p.m. from Quai Anatole-France Métro: Solférino Arrival: Bassin de la Villette Métro: Porte de Pantin Afternoons in the opposite direction.
Water-bus	Since 1989 a water-bus has run to and from the Hôtel de Ville and the Eiffel Tower. From 10 a.m. to 8 p.m., ever 45 minutes (150 seats, journey time 20 minutes). An extension of the jour- ney is planned for next year.

Breakdown Service (Dépannage)

Automobile Clubs	The most important addresses for motorists are the French automobile clubs. Automobile Club de France (ACF) 6–8 Place de la Concorde (8th arr.); tel. 42 66 43 00
Breakdown Service	A 24-hour breakdown service is obtainable on the following telephone number: 42 36 10 00 Lost car keys: tel. 7 07 99 99
Emergency Service	Emergency Service Telephone Number: 17 (Police Secours)
Petrol Stations	The following petrol stations are open: Garage Saint-Honoré 58 Place du Marché Saint-Honoré (1st arr.) Antar; 42 Rue Beauborg (3rd arr.) Shell; 109 Rue de Rennes (6th arr.) Esso; 1 Avenue Matignon (8th arr.) Total; 53 Rue Marcadet (18th arr.)
Traffic Information	"Inter Service Route" gives information (in French) on traffic and road conditions, tel. (day and night) 48 58 33 33.

Confectionary in a Parisian pâtisserie

Cafés/Salons de Thé

French cafés are somewhat different from those in Great Britain and can best be described as places of refreshment which are open all day and often into the night serving drinks, ice cream and occasionally cakes and pastries. With their typical marble-topped tables and tub chairs the Paris cafés provide an opportunity for relaxation after walking round the town and for watching the bustling life in the streets of the capital.

Note

Cakes and pastries can be bought from a "patisserie" but are generally not eaten there.

When a visitor orders a "café" he will generally be served a small black Espresso. If he wants coffee with milk he must order "café crème", "grand crème" or "café au lait". Tea drinkers might care to try the popular herbal teas called "tisane" and "infusion".

Angelina
226 Rue de Rivoli (1st arr.),
tel. 42 60 82 00;
daily 10 a.m.–7 p.m.
Chairs are in Louis XV style.

Cafés (selection)

Costes
4 Rue Berger/Place des Innocents (1st arr.)
opposite Les Halles
daily 10 a.m.–2 a.m.

Café Costes: the modern interior, designed by Philippe Stark

The exclusive furnishings were made to the design of Philippe Starck.

La Coupole
102 Boulevard du Montparnasse (14th arr.),
tel. 43 20 14 20;
daily 8 a.m.–2 a.m.
The famous "holy halls" of the 30s in Art-Deco style were renovated 1988/89 and are still the meeting place of artists, politicians and businessmen.

Dalloyau
101 Rue du Faubourg Saint-Honoré (8th arr.),
tel. 43 59 18 10;
Mon.–Sat. 9.30 a.m.–7.15 p.m., Sun. 8.45 a.m.–1.45 p.m.
2 Place Edmond-Rostand (6th arr.),
tel. 43 29 31 10;
Mon.–Sat. 9.30 a.m.–7.15 p.m., Sun. 9 a.m.–7 p.m.
Finest pastries and exceptionally elegant customers.

Les Deux Magots
170 Boulevard Saint-Germain (6th arr.),
tel. 45 48 55 251;
daily 8 a.m.–2 a.m.
It was here that famous literary figures such as Jean-Paul Sartre and Simone de Beauvoir used to meet.

La Flore
172 Boulevard Saint-Germain (6th arr.),
tel. 45 48 55 26;

Daily 7.45 p.m.–1.45 a.m.
Rendezvous of the younger generation of writers.

Lipp
151 Boulevard Saint-Germain (6th arr.),
tel. 45 48 53 91;
Tues.–Sun. 8 a.m.–12.45 a.m. (closed July)
A favourite meeting place of politicians, the press and the art world; interesting furnishings.

Procope
16 Rue de l'Ancienne Lemidre (6th arr.),
tel. 43 26 99 20;
daily 12 noon–2 a.m.
Opened in 1685 and restored in 1989, this café was regularly frequented by literary folk, including Molière, Racine, Diderot, Alfred de Musset and Victor Hugo.

In the Salons de Thé, an up-market variant of the cafés, tasty sandwiches, salads and hot snacks such as quiches and omelettes are served.

Salons de Thé (selection)

Caramelle
6 Rue de l'Arbalète (5th arr.),
tel. 43 31 59 88;
Tues.–Sat. 10 a.m.–7.30 p.m., Sun. 10 a.m.–6.30 p.m., Fri. until midnight
Well-known for herbal teas and for Sunday brunch. On Fridays poetry readings and minor art exhibitions.

Carette
4 Place du Trocadéro (16th arr.),
tel. 47 27 88 56;
Mon., Wed.–Sun. 8 a.m.–7 p.m.; (closed August)
The "Jeunesse dorée" meets on the large terrace of the café.

A la Cour de Rohan
59–61 Rue Saint-André-des Arts (6th arr.),
tel. 43 25 79 67;
Wed.–Fri. noon–7 p.m., Sat., Sun. 3–7 p.m.
In addition to a good selection of teas, antiques are also on sale.

Aux Delices
39 Avenue de Villiers (17th arr.),
tel. 47 63 71 63;
Mon.–Sun. 9 a.m.–6.45 p.m.
Sarah Bernhardt and Mistinguette liked to visit the Café aux Delices. After a walk in the nearby Parc Monceau the visitor should try the Mousse au Chocolat which is named after the park.

l'Escale
25 Rue de Miromesnil (8th arr.),
tel. 42 65 30 98;
Sun.–Fri. 6.30 a.m.–8.30 p.m.
Probably serves the best sandwiches in Paris.

Olsson's
62 Rue Pierre Charron (8th arr.),
daily 10 a.m.–midnight
Favourite meeting place of the fashion world.

Military parade on the Champs-Elysées; Bastille Day, July 14th

Au Priori Thé
35–37 Galerie Vivienne (2nd arr.),
tel. 42 97 48 75;
Mon.–Sat. noon–8 p.m.
Only a stone's throw from the futuristic boutique of the celebrated fashion designer Jean-Paul Gaultier, this salon serves
American "brownies" and apple cakes.

Business Hours – see Times of Opening

Calendar of Events

January
Last Sunday: the Prix d'Amérique (horse-race), Hippodrome de
Vincennes (see Sport).

March
Palm Sunday: the Prix du Président de la République (horse-
race), Hippodrome d'Auteuil (see Sport).

Other events in March:

Festival International du Son.

Salon des Indépendants (Spring exhibition of visual arts) in the
Grand Palais.

Foire Internationale (Paris International Fair): Parc des Expositions, Porte de Versailles (lasts until May).

Festival de Poésie (end April–early May).

International tennis championships, Stade Roland-Garros (see
Sport).

Festival de l'Ile-de-France: concerts, guided visits (lasts until
July).

"Nuits de Sceaux" (music festival at Sceaux), see Excursions
(lasts until June).

Festival du Marais (music and drama in the Marais quarter)
(lasts until July).

International Competition for Rose-Growers in the Bagatelle
(see A–Z) Castle Park.

14th July (Quatorze Juillet): Fête Nationale (national holiday)
with military parade, dancing and fireworks.

Other events in July:

Festival Estival de Paris (Paris summer festival); classical and
contemporary music (lasts until September).

Final stages of the Tour de France with the finish in the Champs-
Elysées.

Salon d'Automne (autumn exhibition of visual arts) in the
Grand Palais.

Internationale des Antiquaires (biennial antique dealers' fair,
last held in 1980 in the Grand Palais; on until October).

Biennale de Paris
Exhibitions and happenings by young international avant-
garde artists, all sections of the visual arts (biennial, 1990, 1992,
etc. on until November).

Festival International de Danse (Ballet festival): important international ballet gathering (on until December).
Information: Main Tourist Office; tel. 47 23 61 72 (see Information).

Festival d'Automne (autumn festival): contemporary music,
jazz, theatre, folklore (on until December).
Information: Main Tourist Office; tel. 47 23 61 72 (see Information).

Festival de l'Ile-de-France (lasts until December).

Festival de Musique de Paris.

Salon de l'Automobile (International car show): Parc des Expositions, Porte de Versailles.

International Film Festival.

Festival de Jazz.

April

May

June

July

September

October

155

Vendanges de Montmartre (Montmartre's wine harvest and wine festival held in the last vineyard in Paris, located on the corner of the Rue des Saules and the Rue de l'Abreuvoir as a reminder of the past).

The Prix de l'Arc de Triomphe (horse-race), Hippodrome de Longchamp (see Sport).

November

11th November: Armistice Day ceremony at the Arc de Triomphe (Anniversary of the armistice of 1918).

Festival d'Art Sacré (lasts until December).

Camping

The green Michelin guide "Camping Caravaning France" is brought up-to-date annually.

Visitors who are spending more than six months camping in France must pay duty on both car and caravan on arrival.

The Tourist Office of Paris (see Information) has a complete list of all camping sites in the Région Ile-de-France. Brochures are published by the following organisation:

Fédération Française de Camping
78 Rue de Rivoli (4th arr.)
Métro: Châtelet.

Car Rental (Location de voitures)

Avis
Train + Auto

5 Rue Bixio (7th arr.); tel. 45 50 32 21
Métro: Ecole Militaire
Open: Mon.–Fri. 8.30 a.m.–7 p.m., Sat. 9 a.m.–3 p.m.

Budget France

Tel. 05 10 00 01
This firm has an office in each of the 6 SNCF stations.

Europcar

145 Avenue Malakoff (16th arr.); tel. 45 00 08 06
Métro: Porte Maillol
Open: daily 8 a.m.–8 p.m.

Hertz

27 Rue St-Ferdinand (17th arr.); tel. 45 74 97 39
Métro: Porte Maillol
Open: 24 hours a day.

Intertouring Service

117 Boulevard Auguste Blanqui (13th arr.)
Tel. 45 88 52 37
Métro: Glacière
Open: Mon.–Sat. 8.30 a.m.–6.15 p.m.
(vehicles for handicapped available).

Chauffeur driven

Executive Car Carey Limousine
25 Rue d'Astorg (8th arr.); tel. 42 65 54 20
Métro: St-Augustin
Open: daily 7.30 a.m.–9 p.m.

Cemeteries (Cimetières)

See A to Z.

Chemists (Pharmacies)

Pharmacie des Arts   Open at Night
106 Boulevard Montparnasse (14th arr.); tel. 43 26 56 20
Métro: Vavin
Open: Mon.–Sat. until midnight, Sun. 8 p.m. until midnight.

Pharmacie Mozart
14 Avenue Mozart (16th arr.); tel. 45 27 38 17
Métro: Muette
Open: Mon.–Sat. until 10 p.m.; closed Sun.

Pharmacie Dhéry, Galeries des Champs-Elysées
84 Avenue des Champs-Elysées (8th arr.); tel. 45 62 02 41
Métro: George V
Open: 24 hours a day.

Pharmacie Opéra
6 Boulevard des Capucines (2nd arr.); tel. 42 65 88 29
Métro: Opéra
Open: daily until 0.30 a.m.

Pharmacie d'Italie
61 Avenue d'Italie (13th arr.); tel. 43 31 19 72
Métro: Place Pigalle
Open: daily until midnight.

Church Services (Service, Cultes)

Information regarding all the churches, church services and   Information
religious communities in Paris is available from the following
address:
Centre d'Information et de Documentation Religieuse, 8 Rue
Massillon (4th arr.) tel. 46 30 01 01.

Catholic; 38 Rue Spontini (16th arr.); tel. 47 04 31 49
Métro: Porte Dauphine.

Protestant (Lutheran); 25 Rue Blanche (9th arr.);
tel. 47 26 79 43
Métro: Trinité.
Service on Sun. at 10.30 a.m.

Reformed; 4 Rue de l'Oratoire (1st arr.)
Métro: Louvre.

Jewish; 44 Rue de la Victoire (9th arr.)
Métro: Trinité.

British Embassy Church   Services in English
5 Rue d'Aguesseau
Métro: Madeleine/Concorde.

Christ Church
Boulevard Victor-Hugo
Métro: Neuilly-sur-Seine.

Saint-Georges
7 Rue Auguste-Vacquerie
Métro: Kleber.

Eglise Ecossaise
17 Rue Bayard
Métro: F. D. Roosevelt.

Cathédrale Américaine Sainte-Trinité
23 Avenue George-V
Métro: George V.

Eglise Américaine de Paris
Quai d'Orsay
Métro: Invalides/Chambre des Députés.

Paris A–Z, see Notre-Dame (10, 11.30 a.m.); see Saint-Eustache
(11 a.m.); see Saint-Sulpice (noon); see Madeleine (11 a.m.).
Russian Cathedral (10 a.m.); 12 Rue Daru (8th arr.).
Métro: Ternes.

Cinemas (Cinémas)

From 250 to 300 films are shown in Paris every week. Visitors
spending some time in the capital can see series of films on
particular themes which are screened by certain arts cinemas
and cinémathèques, for example on particular directors,
actors, countries or historical periods.
For the domed screen "La Géode"; see A to Z La Villette.

Programme

There are several hundred cinemas; the programmes change
on Wednesdays. A survey is given in the periodicals "Pariscope", "7 à Paris" and "L'Officiel des Spectacles". Many cinemas screen films 24 hours a day.

Tipping

Do not forget to tip the usherette 10%; it is the only pay she
receives.

Cinémathèques

Cinémathèque Chaillot
Palais de Chaillot, corner of Avenue Albert-de-Mun and Avenue
du Président Wilson (16th arr.); tel. 47 04 24 24
Métro:Trocadéro
(closed Mon.)
see Museums – Musée du Cinéma, Palais de Chaillot

Cinémathèque du Centre Pompidou
Rue Rambuteau (corner of Rue Saint-Merri) (4th arr.);
tel. 42 78 35 57
see A to Z; Centre Pompidou

Centre Pompidou
Salle Garence, tel. 42 78 37 29;
(closed Tues.)
Métro: Rambuteau
see A to Z; Centre Pompidou

Roundabout near Montparnasse

Vidéothèque de Paris
Forum des Halles,
Porte Saint-Eustache (1st arr.)
tel. 40 26 34 30; (closed Mon.)
Métro: Les Halles
see A to Z; Vidéothèque

Vidéothèque

In January 1989 the foundation stone of a European Film Centre was laid in the Place d'Italie. Supervised by the Japanese
architect Kenza Tange, it is to be opened in 1993. A giant screen
measuring 20×10 m (65×33 ft) will be installed in the large
auditorium which will seat 800. In addition there will be two
smaller cinemas, each with 150 seats, and other audio-visual
equipment.

European Film Centre

Circus (Cirque)

Cirque Gruss
106 Rue Brancion (15th arr.)
Métro: Porte de Vanves
Season: Oct.–Mar.

Cirque d'Hiver Bouglione
110 Rue Amelot (11th arr.)
Métro: Filles-du-Calvaire
Season: Oct.–Jan.

Bercy-Palais Omnisport (Palace of Sport)
8 Boulevard de Bercy

Opened in 1984, the complex has accommodation for 17,000 spectators.
tel. 43 42 01 23
Circuses by various promoters.

Curiosities

Paris sewers
Les Egouts de Paris
Entrance opposite 93 Quai d'Orsay, (1st arr.)
Metro: Alma
Open: Mon., Weds. and last Sat. in month 2–5 p.m. Entrance fee. Closed on public holidays, and on the days preceeding and following them.

Catacombs
See entry in A to Z.

Currency/Currency Regulations

Currency
The unit of currency is the French franc (F) which is made up of 100 centimes. There are banknotes for 20, 50, 100, 200 and 500 francs, and coins in denominations of 1, 2, 5 and 10 (100 from autumn 1990) francs and 5, 10, 20 and 50 centimes.

Currency Regulations
There are no restrictions on the import of French or foreign currency. The export of foreign currency in cash is permitted up to a value of 50,000 francs or to any higher amount which has been declared on entry into France. Up to 5000 French francs may be exported. Eurocheques can be used up to a value of 1400 French francs. Visitors are recommended to carry their currency in the form of travellers' cheques or Eurocheques.

Banks, the larger hotels, good-class restaurants, car-rental firms and many shops accept most international credit cards (Access, Visa, Diners' Club, American Express, etc.)

The current rates of exchange can be obtained from banks, travel bureaux, etc. or from national newspapers.

Customs Regulations

Visitors to France are allowed the usual duty-free allowances of alcohol and tobacco, etc. For goods bought in ordinary shops in Britain or another EEC country (i.e. duty and tax paid) the allowances are 300 cigarettes or 150 cigarillos or 75 cigars or 400 g of tobacco; 1½ litres of alcoholic drinks over 38·8° proof or 3 litres of alcoholic drinks not over 38·8° proof or 3 litres of fortified or sparkling wine, plus 5 litres of still table wine; 75 g of perfume; and 375 cc of toilet-water. For goods bought in a duty-free shop, on a ship or on an aircraft, the allowances are two-thirds of these amounts (250 g of tobacco); the allowances of tobacco goods are doubled for visitors from outside Europe.

The duty-free allowances on return to Britain are the same as those for British visitors to France.

Department Stores (Grands Magasins)

La Samaritaine
19 Rue de la Monnaie (1st arr.)
Métro: Pont-Neuf.

Aux Trois Quartiers
17 Boulevard de la Madeleine (1st arr.)
Métro: Madeleine.

Les Galeries Lafayette
40 Boulevard Haussmann (9th arr.)
Métro: Chaussée d'Antin; RER: Auber.

Filiale (branch) Maine-Montparnasse
22 Rue du Départ (14th arr.)
Métro: Montparnasse-Bienvenue.

Le Bazar de l'Hôtel de Ville
52 Rue de Rivoli (4th arr.)
Métro: Hôtel de Ville.

Au Bon Marché
Rue de Sèvres/Rue de Bac (7th arr.)
Métro: Sèvres-Babylone.

Le Printemps
64 Boulevard Haussmann (9th arr.)
Métro: Havre-Caumartin; RER: Auber.
Branches: 63 Rue Malte (11th arr.)
           Avenue des Ternes (17th arr.)

Marks & Spencer
35 Boulevard Haussmann (9th arr.)
Métro: Havre-Caumartin

Diplomatic and Consular Offices in France (Ambassades)

United Kingdom

Embassy
35 Rue du Faubourg St-Honoré (8th arr.)
tel. (1) 42 66 91 42
Consular section: tel. 42 60 33 06

Consulates-General
16 Rue d'Anjou (8th arr.)
tel. (1) 42 66 91 42

United States of America

Embassy
2 Avenue Gabriel (8th arr.)
tel. (1) 42 96 12 02 and 42 61 80 75

Consulates-General
(Consular Section of Embassy)
2 Avenue Gabriel (8th arr.)
tel. (1) 42 96 12 02 and 42 61 80 75
(Visas Section of Embassy)
2 Rue St-Florentin (8th arr.)
tel. (1) 42 96 12 02 and 42 61 80 75

Electricity

Canada

Embassy
35 Avenue Montaigne (8th arr.); tel. (1) 47 23 01 01

Consular Section
4 Rue Ventadour (8th arr.); tel. (1) 40 73 15 83

Electricity (Courant electrique)

Most electrical connections in Paris have been changed to 220 V but some hotels still have 110 V sockets. When sockets are unmarked it is better to ask.

Excursions (Excursions)

Visitors to Paris usually have little time for excursions except to Versailles and Fontainebleau.

The following places near Paris are of interest:

Breteuil (Park, Château)
Open: Park: daily
10 a.m.–6 p.m.;
Château: Mon.–Sat. 2–
6 p.m., Sun. 11 a.m.–6 p.m.

35 km (22 miles) SW; take N306 to Saint-Remy-lès-Chevreuse, N838 left to Les Molières, D40 right towards Cernay, turn off to the right after approx. 5 km (3 miles).
RER-line B: Saint-Remy-lès-Chevreuse then by bus to the château.
Restored 17th c. château. Historical attraction and appropriate setting for concerts and events of the Festival Estival de Paris (see Calendar of Events).
The park of the château was laid out by Le Nôtre.

Champs (Park, Château)
Open: 10 a.m.–5 p.m.,
closed Tues.

20 km (13 miles) E; take N34 to Neuilly-sur-Marne, D33 right to Noisy-le-Grand, D75 left to Champs-sur-Marne.
The Château of the Marquise de Pompadour, mistress of Louis XV, at Champs-sur-Marne (formerly a village) dates from the early 18th c. Its sumptuously decorated and panelled interior is a magnificent example of original "Louis Quinze".

Fontainebleau (Forest)

The Forest of Fontainebleau (Forêt de Fontainebleau) is a popular recreation area (c. 23,000 ha – 57,000 acres). Walks are signposted. The wild and romantic scenery of the famous "Gorges de Franchard" is used as a training ground for mountaineering.
(Information: Club Alpin Français, 7 Rue La Boëtie, 8th arr.; tel. 42 65 54 45.)

Meudon (Terrace, Museum, Woods)
Open: daily 8 a.m.–5 p.m.;
1 April–30 Sept. 8 a.m.–
8 p.m.

10 km (6 miles) SW; N10 to Pont de Sèvres, right: N187 to Meudon.
The "Terrasse de Meudon" (terrace of the former château) affords beautiful views of the Seine valley and Paris. Other attractions: "Bois de Meudon" (wooded resort), aviation museum and Meudon Museum (see Museums).

Sceaux (Museum, Park, Château)
Open: daily 8 a.m.–sunset
(between 5.15 and
10.15 p.m.)

10 km (6 miles) SW.
Tel. 6 61 19 03; RER-line B: Parc de Sceaux.
The former château built for Colbert, Minister of Finance, was destroyed during the French Revolution. The present château dates from the 19th c. and houses a museum (see Museums). In the Orangerie of the château, built by Jules Hardouin-Mansart

in 1685, chamber and solo concerts take place from July to October (Wed. at 9 p.m., Sun. and holidays at 5.30 p.m.). The park, designed by Le Nôtre, is one of the finest in the Ile-de-France.

Fashion Houses

Among celebrated Parisian couturiers are:

Balmain, 44 Rue François Ier (8th arr.).
Cardin, 27 Avenue de Marigny (8th arr.).
Carven, Rond-Point des Champs Elysées (8th arr.).
Chanel, 31 Rue Cambon (1st arr.).
Courreges, Rue François Ier (8th arr.).
Dior, 30 Avenue Montaigne (8th arr.).
Féraud, 88 Faubourg St-Honoré (8th arr.).
Givenchy, 3 Avenue George-V (8th arr.).
Grès, Rue de la Paix (2nd arr.).
Guerlain, 68 Champs-Elysées (8th arr.).
Hermès, 34 Faubourg St-Honoré (8th arr.).
Kenzo, 3 Place des Victoires (2nd arr.).
Christian Lacroix, 73 Rue du Faubourg St-Honoré (8th arr.).
Lanvin, 22 Faubourg St-Honoré (8th arr.).
Ted Lapidus, 23 Faubourg St-Honoré (8th arr.).
Laroche, 29 Avenue Montaigne (8th arr.).
Serge Lepage, 15 Rue Duphot (1st arr.).
Jean Patou, 7 Rue St-Florentin (8th arr.).
Paco Rabanne, 7 Rue du Cherche-Midi (6th arr.).
Nina Ricci, 39 Avenue Montaigne (8th arr.).
Saint-Laurent, 5 Avenue Marceau (16th arr.).
Scherrer, 51 Avenue Montaigne (8th arr.).
Ungaro, 2 Avenue Montaigne (8th arr.).
Ventilo, 27 bis Rue du Louvre (2nd arr.).

Galleries (Galeries)

Bama
40 Rue Quincampoix (4th arr.); tel. 42 77 38 87
Métro: Rambuteau
Open: Tues.–Sat. 2.30–7 p.m.
Avant-garde art.

Alain Blondel
4 Rue Aubry-le-Boucher (4th arr.); tel. 42 78 66 67
50 Rue du Temple (4th arr.); tel. 42 71 85 86
Open: Tues.–Fri. 11 a.m.–7 p.m. Sat. 2–7 p.m.
Realism and art of the 30s.

Crousel-Hussenot
80 Rue Quincampoix (3rd arr.); tel. 48 87 60 81
Métro: Rambuteau
Open: Tues.–Sat. 2.30–7.30 p.m.
Avant-garde art.

Beaubourg

163

Daniel Templon
30 Rue Beaubourg (3rd arr.); tel. 42 72 14 10
Métro: Rambuteau
Open: Tues.–Sat. 10 a.m.–7 p.m.
Representatives of the best known of New York, Germany and France.

Beaubourg
23 Rue du Renard (4th arr.); tel. 42 71 20 50
Métro: Rambuteau
Open: Tues.–Sat. 10.30 a.m.–1 p.m., 2.30–7 p.m.
Art by César and Yves Klein, Edouard Pignon and Joseph Beuys.

Farideh Cadot
77 Rue des Archives (3rd arr.); tel. 42 78 08 36
Métro: Arts et Métiers, Rambuteau
Open: Tues.–Sat. 10.30 a.m.–noon, 2–7 p.m.
Young French artists, also Wilden Salomé and Luciano Castelli from Berlin and the Americans Fischer, Hazzlitt, and Sonneman.

Durand-Dessert
3 Rue des Haudriettes (3rd arr.); tel. 42 77 63 60
Métro: Rambuteau
Open: Tues.–Sat. 2–7 p.m.
European avant-garde, including Richter, Morellet and Tosani.

Saint-Germain-des-Prés

Dina Vierny
36 Rue Jacob (6th arr.); tel. 42 61 32 83
Métro: Saint-Germain-des-Prés
Open: Tues.–Sat. 10 a.m.–noon, 3–7 p.m.
Drawings by Maillol, Matisse, etc.

Denis René
196 Boulevard Saint-Germain (7th arr.); tel. 42 22 11 02
Métro: Rue du Bac
Open: Tues.–Sat. 10 a.m.–1 p.m., 2.30–7 p.m.
Kinetic art and Neo-Constructivism.

Albert Loeb
10/12 Rue des Beaux-Arts (6th arr.); tel. 46 33 06 87
Métro: Saint-Germain-des-Prés, Mabillon
Open: Tues.–Sat. 10 a.m.–12.30 p.m., 5.30–6.30 p.m.
French paintings of the 60s and 70s.

Karl Flinker
25 Rue de Tournon (6th arr.); tel. 43 25 18 73
Métro: Mabillon
Open: Tues.–Sat. 10 a.m.–1 p.m., 2.30–7 p.m.
Older generation representational painters.

8th Arrondissement

Bernheim Jeune
27 Avenue Matignon (8th arr.); tel. 42 66 60 31
Métro: Franklin D. Roosevelt
Open: Tues.–Sat. 10.30 a.m.–12.30 p.m., 2.30–6.30 p.m.
Art of the turn of the century.

Ariel
140 Boulevard Haussmann (8th arr.); tel. 45 62 13 09
Métro: Saint-Augustin, Miromesnil

Galerie des Colonnes, part of a complex designed by Ricardo Bofill

Open: Mon.–Fri. 10.30 a.m.–1 p.m., 2.30–6.30 p.m.
Art of the 50s and the new "Ecole de Paris".

Artcurial
9 Avenue Matignon (8th arr.); tel. 42 99 16 19
Métro: Franklin D. Roosevelt
Open: Tues.–Sat. 10.30 a.m.–7.15 p.m.
Art market sponsored by L'Oréal cosmetic firm.
Vitesse
48 Rue de Berri (8th arr.); tel. 42 25 48 13
Métro: George V
Art concerning car racing and sport (photos, sculptures, rare
models, etc.).

Art à la Bastille   11th Arrondissement
27 Rue de Charonne
Métro: Bastille
Association of 25 galleries showing modern Parisian art (including Nane Stern, Leif Stahle, Gallerie Keller).

Galerie des Colonnes   14th Arrondissement
Ensemble Ricardo Bofill
86 Rue de Château (14th arr.); tel. 43 27 11 86
Métro: Montparnasse
Open: Mon.–Sat. 11.15 a.m.–1.15 p.m. and 2–7 p.m.
Art of the 30s.

Viviane Esders   Photographic Galleries
12 Rue Saint-Merri (4th arr.); tel. 42 71 03 12

Métro: Châtelet, Rambuteau
Open: daily (except Mon. and Sat.) 2–7 p.m.
One of the most exclusive photographic galleries.

Zabriski
37 Rue Quincampoix (4th arr.); tel. 42 72 35 47
Métro: Rambuteau
Open: Tues.–Sat. 11 a.m.–7 p.m.
One of the best photographic galleries in the world.

Texbraun
12 Rue Mazarine (6th arr.); tel. 46 33 14 57
Métro: Mabillon
Open: Tues.–Sat. 2.30–7 p.m.
Photographic art of the 70s and 80s.

Agathe Gaillard
3 Rue du Pont-Louis-Philippe (4th arr.); tel. 42 77 38 24
Métro: Hôtel de Ville
Open: Tues.–Sat. 1–7 p.m.
One of the oldest photographic galleries in Paris, well known
and expensive.

Help for Handicapped

Comité National Français pour Réadaptation des Handicapés
(C.N.F.L.R.H.)
38 Boulevard Raspail
F 75007 Paris
tel. 45 48 90 13.

The brochure "Touristes quand même", published by the
C.N.F.L.R.H., contains a comprehensive list of hotels, etc.,
means of transport and public institutions which cater for the
handicapped. In addition, the "Guide National Officiel de
l'Hôtellerie Française – Les Hôtels de France" indicates by
the wheelchair symbol hotels which have facilities for the
handicapped.

Hotels (Selection)

Reservations

Hotel rooms can only be booked in advance directly from the
hotel.
In the official bureaus for hotel reservations (see Information;
Office de Tourisme) rooms can only be booked for the same
day.

Categories

Hotels in this guide are listed alphabetically in categories (from
four stars to one star).

****L
Luxury hotels

Bristol, 112 Rue du Faubourg Saint-Honoré (8th arr.),
tel. 42 66 91 45, telex 2 80 961, fax 42 66 68 68.
Claridge-Bellmann, 37 Rue François Ier (8th arr.),
tel. 47 23 54 42, telex 6 41 150, fax 47 23 08 84.
Crillon (de), 10 Place de la Concorde (8th arr.),
tel. 42 65 24 24, telex 2 90 204, fax 47 42 72 10.

George V, 31 Avenue George V (8th arr.),
tel. 47 23 54 00, telex 6 50 082, fax 47 20 40 00.
Grand Hôtel, 2 Rue Scribe (9th arr.),
tel. 42 68 12 13, telex 2 20 875, fax 42 66 12 51.
Inter Continental, 3 Rue de Castiglione (1st arr.),
tel. 42 60 37 80, telex 2 20 114, fax 42 61 14 03.
Jolly Hôtel Lotti, 7 Rue de Castiglione (1st arr.),
tel. 42 60 37 34, telex 2 40 066, fax 40 15 93 56.
Prince de Galles, 33 Avenue George V (8th arr.),
tel. 47 23 55 11, telex 2 80 627, fax 47 20 96 92.
Meurice, 228 Rue de Rivoli (1st arr.),
tel. 42 60 38 60, telex 2 30 673, fax 40 15 92 31.
Plaza-Athénée, 23–25 Avenue Montaigne (8th arr.),
tel. 47 23 78 33, telex 6 50 092, fax 47 20 20 70.
Ritz, 15 Place Vendôme (1st arr.),
tel. 42 60 38 30, telex 2 20 262, fax 42 60 23 71.
Royal Monceau, 35 Avenue Hoche (8th arr.),
tel. 45 61 98 00, telex 6 50 361, fax 45 63 28 93.
Scribe, 1 Rue Scribe (9th arr.),
tel. 47 42 03 40, telex 2 14 653, fax 42 65 39 97.
Sofitel Paris Invalides, 32 Rue Saint-Dominique (7th arr.),
tel. 45 55 91 80, telex 2 50 019, fax 47 53 90 50.
Warwick, 5 Rue du Berri (8th arr.),
tel. 45 63 14 11, telex 6 42 295, fax 45 63 75 81.
Westminster, 13 Rue de la Paix (2nd arr.),
tel. 42 61 57 46, telex 6 80 035, fax 42 60 30 66.

Alexander, 102 Avenue Victor Hugo (16th arr.),
tel 45 53 64 65, telex 6 10 373, fax 45 53 12 51.
Ambassador, 16 Boulevard Haussmann (9th arr.),
tel. 42 46 92 63, telex 6 50 912, fax 40 22 08 74.
Baltimore, 88 bis Avenue Kleber (16th arr.),
tel. 45 53 83 33, telex 6 11 591, fax 45 53 94 84.
Cayre-Copatel, 4 Boulevard Raspail (7th arr.),
tel. 45 44 38 88, telex 2 70 577, fax 45 44 98 13.
Château Frontenac, 54 Rue Pierre-Charron (8th arr.),
tel. 47 23 55 85. telex 6 49 994.
Commodore, 12 Boulevard Haussman (9th arr.),
tel. 42 46 72 82, telex 2 80 601, fax 47 70 23 91.
Concorde Lafayette, 3 Place de Général Koenig (17th arr.),
tel. 40 68 50 68, telex 6 50 892, fax 40 68 50 43.
Concorde-St-Lazare, 108 Rue St-Lazare (8th arr.),
tel. 42 94 22 22, telex 6 50 442, fax 42 93 01 20.
Edouard VII, 30 Avenue de l'Opéra (2nd arr.),
tel. 42 61 56 90, telex 6 80 217, fax 42 61 47 73.
Elysée-Marignan, 12 Rue de Marigan (8th arr.),
tel. 43 59 58 61, telex 6 44 018, fax 45 63 28 87.
François Ier, 7 Rue de Magellan (8th arr.),
tel. 47 23 44 04, telex 6 48 880, fax 47 23 93 43.
Garden Elysée, 12 Rue St-Didier (16th arr.),
tel. 47 55 01 11, telex 6 48 157, fax 47 27 79 24.
Holiday Inn, 10 Place de la République (11th arr.),
tel. 43 55 44 34, telex 2 10 651, fax 47 00 32 34.
Jeu de Paume, 54 Rue St-Louis-en-l'Ile (4th arr.),
tel. 43 26 14 18, telex 2 05 160, fax 43 26 14 18.
Lancaster, 7 Rue de Berri (8th arr.),
tel. 43 59 90 43, telex 6 40 991, fax 42 89 22 71.
Louvre, Place André Malreaux (7th arr.),
tel. 42 61 56 01, telex 2 20 412, fax 42 60 02 90.

**** First class hotels

Hôtel Crillon in the Place de la Concorde

Majestic, 29 Rue Dumont d'Urville (16th arr.),
tel. 45 00 83 70, telex 6 40 034.
Méridien, 81 Boulevard Gouvion-St-Cyr (17th arr.),
tel. 40 68 34 34, telex 2 90 952, fax 47 57 60 70.
Mériden Montparnasse, 19 Rue du Cdt-Mouchotte (14th arr.),
tel. 43 20 15 51, telex 2 00 135, fax 43 20 61 03.
Napoléon, 40 Avenue de Friedland (8th arr.),
tel. 47 66 02 02, telex 6 40 609, fax 47 66 82 33.
Nikko, 61 Quai de Grenelle (15th arr.),
tel. 40 58 20 00, telex 2 60 012, fax 45 75 42 35.
Normandy, 7 Rue de l'Echelle (1st arr.),
tel. 42 60 30 21, telex 6 70 250, fax 42 60 45 81.
Park Avenue et Central Park, 55 Avenue de Poincaré (16th arr.),
tel. 45 53 44 60, telex 6 43 862, fax 47 27 53 04.
Pavillon de la Reine, 28 Place des Vosges (3rd arr.),
tel. 42 77 96 40, telex 2 16 160, fax 42 77 63 06.
Pont-Royal, 7 Rue de Montalembert (7th arr.),
tel. 45 44 38 27, telex 2 70 113, fax 45 44 92 07.
Pullmann Windsor, 14 Rue Beaujon (8th arr.),
tel. 45 63 04 04, telex 6 50 902, fax 42 25 36 81.
Raphaël, 17 Avenue Kléber (16th arr.),
tel. 45 02 16 00, telex 6 10 356, fax 45 01 21 50.
Résidence Champs- Elysées, 92 Rue de la Boétie (8th arr.),
tel. 43 59 96 15, telex 6 50 695, fax 42 56 01 38.
Trémoille, 14 Rue de la Trémoille (8th arr.),
tel. 47 23 34 20, telex 6 40 344, fax 40 70 01 08.
Villa Maillot, 143 Avenue de Malakoff (16th arr.),
tel. 45 01 25 22, telex 6 49 808, fax 45 00 60 61.
Victoria Palace, 6 Rue Blaise-Desgoffe (6th arr.),
tel. 45 44 38 16, telex 2 70 557, fax 45 49 23 75.

Bretonnerie, 22 Rue Sainte-Croix-Bretonnerie (4th arr.),
tel. 48 87 77 63, telex 3 05 551, fax 42 77 26 78.
Claret, Boulevard de Bercy (12th arr.),
tel. 46 28 41 31, telex 2 17 115.
Cordélia, 11 Rue Greffulhe (8th arr.),
tel. 42 65 42 40, telex 2 81 760, fax 42 65 11 81.
Cyrnos, 154 Rue Montmartre (2nd arr.),
tel. 42 33 54 23, telex 2 40 638, fax 42 33 49 91.
Deux Iles, 59 Rue Saint-Louis-en-l'Ile (4th arr.),
tel. 43 26 13 35, fax 43 29 60 25.
Elysée (de l'), 12 Rue de Saussaises (8th arr.),
tel. 42 65 29 25, telex 2 81 665, fax 42 65 64 28.
Franklin et du Brésil, 19 Rue Buffault (9th arr.),
tel. 42 80 27 27, telex 6 40 988.
Gotty, 11 Rue de Trévise (9th arr.),
tel. 47 70 12 90, telex 6 60 330.
Grands Hommes, 17 Place du Panthéon (5th arr.),
tel. 46 34 19 60, telex 2 00 185, fax 43 26 67 32.
Keppler, 12 Rue Keppler (16th arr.),
tel. 47 20 65 05, telex 6 20 440, fax 47 23 02 29.
Lautrec Opéra, 8 Rue d'Amboise (2nd arr.),
tel. 42 96 67 90, telex, 2 16 502.
Lenox, 15 Rue Delambre (14th arr.),
tel. 43 35 34 50, telex 2 60 745, fax 43 20 46 64.
London, 32 Boulevard des Italiens (9th arr.),
tel. 48 24 54 64, telex 6 42 360, fax 48 00 08 63.
Louvre-Forum, 25 Rue du Bouloi (1st arr.),
tel. 42 36 54 19, telex 2 40 288.
Lutèce, 65 Rue St-Louis-en-l'Ile (4th arr.),
tel. 43 26 23 52, fax 43 29 60 25.
Marroniers, 21 Rue Jacob (6th arr.).
tel 43 25 30 60, fax 40 46 83 56.
Massenet, 5 bis Rue Massenet (16th arr.),
tel. 45 24 43 03, telex 6 20 692, fax 45 24 41 39.
Mercure, 27 Avenue des Ternes (17th arr.),
tel. 47 66 49 18, telex 6 50 679, fax 47 63 77 91.
Mercure Paris Montmartre,
1 Rue Caulaincourt (18th arr.),
tel. 42 94 17 17, telex 6 40 605, fax 42 93 66 14.
Montana Tuileries, 12 Rue St-Roch (1st arr.),
tel. 42 60 35 10, telex 2 14 404, fax 42 61 12 28.
Moulin Rouge, 39 Rue Fontaine (9th arr.),
tel. 42 81 93 25, telex 6 60 055.
Néva, 14 Rue Brey (17th arr.),
tel. 43 80 28 26, telex 6 49 041.
Notre-Dame, 1 Quai St-Michel (5th arr.),
tel. 43 54 20 43, telex 2 06 650.
Novotel Paris Les Halles, 8 Place de M-de-Navarre (1st arr.),
tel. 42 21 31 31, telex 2 16 389, fax 40 26 05 79.
Odéon, 3 Rue de l'Odéon (6th arr.),
tel. 43 25 90 67, telex 2 02 943, fax 43 25 55 98.
Pas-de-Calais, 509 Rue des Sts-Pères (6th arr.),
tel. 45 48 78 74, telex 2 70 476, fax 45 44 94 57.
Pavillon, 54 Rue Saint-Dominique (7th arr.), tel. 45 51 42 87.
Plaza Haussmann, 177 Boulevard Haussmann (8th arr.),
tel. 45 63 93 83, telex 648167. fax 42 89 33 00.
Pullmann St-Honoré, 15 Rue Boissy-d'Anglais (8th arr.),
tel. 42 66 93 62, telex 2 40 366. fax 42 66 14 98.
Regent's Garden Hotel, 6 Rue Pierre Demours (17th arr.),
tel. 45 74 07 30, telex 6 40 127, fax 40 55 01 42.

***Very comfortable hotels

Résidence St-Honoré, 214 Rue du Faubourg-St-Honoré (8th arr.), tel. 42 25 26 27, telex 6 40 524, fax 45 63 30 67.

Sainte Beuve, 9 Rue Ste-Beuve (6th arr.),
tel. 45 48 20 07, telex 2 70 182.

Sévingé, 6 Rue de Belloy (16th arr.),
tel. 47 20 88 90, telex 6 10 219, fax 40 70 98 73.

Splendid Etoile, 1 bis Avenue Carnot (17th arr.),
tel. 43 80 14 56, telex 2 80 773, fax 47 64 05 09.

Sts-Pères (des). 65 Rue des Sts- Pères (6th arr.), tel. 45 44 50 00, telex 2 05 424. fax 45 44 90 83.

Terminus Montparnasse, 59 Boulevard du Montparnasse (6th arr.), tel. 45 48 99 10, telex 2 02 636. fax 45 48 59 10.

Trianon Palace, 3 Rue de Vaurigard (6th arr.), tel. 43 29 88 10, telex 2 02 263. fax 43 29 15 98.

Varenne, 44 Rue de Bourgogne (7th arr.), tel. 45 51 45 55, telex 2 05 329.

** Good average hotels

L'Aiglon, 232 Boulevard Raspail (14th arr.),
tel. 43 20 82 42, telex 2 06 038, fax 43 20 98 72.

Albe, 1 Rue de la Harpe (5th arr.),
tel. 46 34 09 70, telex 2 03 328, fax 40 46 85 70.

Baldi, 42 Boulevard Garibaldi (15th arr.), tel. 47 83 20 10.

Bellevue, 46 Rue Pasquier (8th arr.), tel. 43 87 50 68.

Blanche, 69 Rue Blanche (9th arr.),
tel. 48 74 16 94, fax 49 95 95 98.

Champs-Elysée (des), 2 Rue d'Artois (8th arr.),
tel. 43 59 11 42, fax 45 61 00 61.

Cluny Sorbonne, 8 Rue V-Cousin (5th arr.),
tel. 43 54 66 66, telex 2 01 674.

Ducs d'Anjou, 1 Rue Ste-Opportune (1st arr.),
tel. 42 36 92 24, telex 2 18 681.

Eden Hotel, 90 Rue Ordener (18th arr.),
tel. 42 64 61 63, telex 2 90 504, fax 42 64 11 43.

Fénelon, 23 Rue Buffault (9th ar.), tel. 48 78 32 18.

Friant, 8 Rue Friant (14th arr.),
tel. 45 42 71 91, fax 45 42 04 67.

Istria, 29 Rue Campagne-Première (14th arr.),
tel. 43 20 91 82, telex 2 03 618, fax 43 22 48 45.

Jardin des Plantes, 5 Rue Linné (5th arr.),
tel. 47 07 06 20, telex 2 03 684.

Place des Vosges (de la), 12 Rue Birague (4th arr.),
tel. 42 72 60 46, fax 42 72 02 64.

Queen's Hotel, 4 Rue Bastien-Lepage (16th arr.),
tel. 42 88 89 35.

Résidence Etoile-Pereire, 146 Boulevard Pereire (17th arr.),
tel. 42 67 60 00.

Résidence Vert-Galant, 43 Rue de Croulebarbe (13th arr.),
tel. 43 31 63 05.

St-Germain-des-Prés, 36 Rue Bonaparte (6th arr.),
tel. 43 26 00 19.

Vieux Marais, 8 Rue du Plâtre (4th arr.),
tel 42 78 47 22, fax 42 78 34 32.

* Average hotels

Andrea, 3 Rue Saint-Bon (4th arr.), tel. 42 78 43 93.

Avenir, 52 Rue Gay-Lussac (5th arr.), tel. 43 54 76 60.

Bel Hôtel, 20 Rue Pouchet (17th arr.),
tel. 46 27 34 77, telex 6 42 396.

Central (le), 5 Rue Descartes (5th arr.), tel. 46 33 57 93.

Chevreuse (de), 3 Rue de Chevreuse (6th arr.),
tel. 43 20 93 16.

Clauzel, 33 Rue des Martyrs (9th arr.), tel. 48 78 12 24.
Familles (des), 216 Faubourg Saint-Denis (10th arr.),
tel. 46 07 76 56.
Family, 35 Rue Cambon (1st arr.), tel. 92 61 54.
Jules César, 52 Avenue Ledru-Rollin (12th arr.),
tel. 43 43 15 88, Telex 6 71 945.
Speria, 1 Rue de la Bastille (4th arr.), tel. 42 72 04 01.
Square (du), 87 Rue des Archives (3rd arr.), tel. 48 87 83 14.
Stella, 114 Rue Neuve-Saint-Pierre (4th arr.), tel. 42 72 23 66.
Vallée (de la), 84–86 Rue Saint-Denis (1st arr.),
tel. 42 36 46 99.

Inexpensive Accommodation

There are several places offering inexpensive accommodation specially for young people, some of which are listed below:

For Young People

12 Rue des Barres (4th arr.); tel. 42 72 72 09
Métro: Hôtel de Ville.

Accueil des Jeunes en France (AJF)

Plateau Beaubourg (AJF)
119 Rue St-Martin (4th arr.); tel. 42 77 87 80
Métro: Châtelet
Open: Mon.–Sat. 9.30 a.m.–7 p.m.
There is also an information office at the Gare du Nord.

Reservations

Hôtel de Ville (AJF)
16 Rue du Pont Louis-Philippe (4th arr.); tel. 42 78 04 82
Métro: Hôtel de Ville
Open: Mon.–Sat. 9.30 a.m.–12.30 p.m., 2.30–6.30 p.m.

Central de réservations et d'information
20 Rue Jean-Jacques Rousseau (1st arr.); tel. 42 36 88 18
Métro: Les Halles.

Union des Centres de Rencontres Internationales de France (UCRIF)

Some of these hotels, situated in the centre of Paris, date from the 17th century. The buildings were originally mansions or monasteries with green inner courtyards. Overnight accommodation costs about 60F per person.

Youth Hotels (Hôtels de la Jeunesse)

Le Fauconnier
11 Rue du Fauconnier (4th arr.)
Métro: Pont-Marie, Saint-Paul.

Le Fourcy,
6 Rue de Fourcy (4th arr.), tel. 42 74 23 45
Métro: Pont-Marie.

Centre International Paris, Opéra
11 Rue Thérèse (1st arr.), tel. 42 60 77 43
Métro: Pyramides.

C.I.S.P. Kellerman
17 Boulevard Kellermann (13th arr.), tel. 45 80 70 76.
Métro: Porte d'Italie.

C.I.S.P. Maurice-Ravel
8 Avenue Maurice-Ravel (12th arr.), tel. 43 43 19 01.

Le D'Artagnan
80 Rue Vitruve (20th arr.), tel. 43 61 08 75

Youth Hostels (Auberges de la Jeunesse)

Information

Métro: Porte de Bagnolet
(half board obligatory).

Jules Ferry

8 Boulevard Jules Ferry (11th arr.), tel. 43 57 55 60
Métro: République
(no groups).

Silence Rule

Between 1 and 6 a.m.

Information (Renseignements)

Information Bureaux in Paris

Office de Tourisme de Paris
127 Avenue des Champs-Elysées (8th arr.); tel. 47 23 61 72
Open: main season Mon.–Sat. 9 a.m.–9 p.m., Sun. and public
holidays 9 a.m.–8 p.m.; low season 9 a.m.–8 p.m., Sun. and
public holidays 9 a.m.–6 p.m.
Information, brochures, hotel reservations (not by telephone)
for Paris and surroundings. This head office is often extremely
busy and it is advisable to apply to the branch offices for
information and hotel reservations, but most brochures are
obtainable at the head office only.

The branch offices dealing with hotel reservations and brochures are located in the four railway stations and the Congress
Centre at Porte Maillot.

At Stations

Gare du Nord
18 Rue de Dunkerque, tel. 45 26 94 82
Open: main season Mon.–Sat. 8 a.m.–10 p.m.; Sun. 1–8 p.m.;
low season daily (except Sun.) 8 a.m.–8 p.m.

Gare de l'Est (arrivals hall); tel. 46 07 17 73
Open: main season Mon.–Sat. 8 a.m.–10 p.m.; low season
Mon.–Sat. 8 a.m.–1 p.m., 5–8 p.m.

Gare de Lyon (main line exit); tel. 43 43 33 24
Open: main season Mon.–Sat. 8 a.m.–10 p.m.; low season
Mon.–Sat. 8 a.m.–1 p.m., 5–8 p.m.

Gare d'Austerlitz (main line arrivals); tel. 45 84 91 70
Open: main season (Apr.–Oct.) Mon.–Sat. 8 a.m.–10 p.m.; low
season Mon.–Sat. 8 a.m.–3 p.m.

In Congress Centre

Service Comité Parisien des Congrès; tel. 47 20 12 55.

Eiffel Tower

Tour Eiffel; tel. 45 51 22 15
Open: May–Sept. 11 a.m.–6 p.m.

Services Touristiques of the
RATP

RATP tourist information centres
RATP, Paris's public transport undertaking (see Public transport), has two tourist information centres (Services touristiques) supplying general information and tourist tickets for
bus, Métro, RER. They also book short weekend trips.
53 bis, Quai des Grands-Augustins (6th arr.); tel. 43 46 42 03
Métro: Pont-Neuf, Saint-Michel
Place de la Madeleine, next to the flower market (8th arr.);
tel. 42 65 31 81
Métro: Madeleine.
(Times of opening: see Travel bureaux.)

Electronic route finder, operated by buttons. You give the required address and receive a printed slip giving the most convenient bus and métro services.

SITU

Comité Régional de Tourisme
101 Rue de Vaugirard (6th arr.); tel. 42 22 74 43
Non-verbal information only and brochures for the Région Ile-de-France (surroundings of Paris).

About the Ile-de-France Region

The following organisations specialise in helping young travellers:
Centre d'Information et de Documentation de la Jeunesse (CIDJ); 101 Quai Branly (15th arr.); tel. 45 66 40 20
Métro: Bir Hakeim
Open: 9 a.m.–7 p.m., closed Sun.
Information of every kind regarding accommodation, events, jobs.
Service Parisien d'Accueil aux Etudiants Etrangers
6 Rue Jeyn Calvin (5th arr.); tel 47 07 26 22
Métro: RER Luxembourg
Open: Mon–Fri. 9 a.m.–6 p.m.
Bureau for receiving foreign students: general information regarding accommodation, events, studying in France.

Specially for Young People

Libraries (Bibliothèques)

Bibliothèque Nationale
5 Rue de Richlieu (2nd arr.), tel. 42 61 82 83
Métro: Palais-Royal, Bourse
Open: daily, except Suns. and public holidays noon–6 p.m.
Prints, magazines, manuscripts, etchings, maps, plans, coins, oriental manuscripts; in addition the National Library puts on temporary exhibitions on the history of books and art.

National Library

To relieve pressure on the Bibliothèque Nationale the Bibliothèque de France will come into being in 1995 on the Tolbiac site of 7 ha (17 acres) in the 13th arrondissement. This library will house all material published after January 1st 1945. (Architect: Dominique Perrault.)

Bibliothèque de France

Bibliothèque Historique de la Ville de Paris
24 Rue Pavée (4th arr.), tel. 42 74 44 44
Métro: Saint-Paul
Open: daily (except Suns. and public holidays) 9.30 a.m.–6 p.m.
Admission free
Situated in the Marais quarter and housed in an old patrician mansion, the Hôtel Lamoignon.

History of Paris

Archives Nationales
60 Rue des Francs-Bourgois (4th arr.), tel. 42 77 11 30
Métro: Saint-Paul, Rambuteau, admission free
Also housed in an old patrician mansion, the Hôtel de Rohan-Soubise, in the Marais quarter.

National Archive

Bibliothèque du Centre National d'Art et de Culture Georges Pompidou
Rue Rambuteau (4th arr.), tel. 42 77 12 33
Métro: Rambuteau, Hôtel de Ville, Châtelet

Library of the Centre Pompidou

Lost Property

	Open: daily (except Tuesday) noon–10 p.m. See A to Z: Centre Pompidou.
Forney Library	Bibliothèque Forney Hôtel de Sens, 1 Rue du Figuier (4th arr.), tel. 42 78 14 60 Métro: Saint-Paul Open: Tues.–Fri. 1.30–8 p.m., Sat. 10 a.m.–8 p.m.
Mazarine Library	Bibliothèque Mazarine in the Palais de l'Institut, 23 Quai Conti (6th arr.), tel. 43 54 89 48 Métro: Pont Neuf Open: Mon.–Fri. 10 a.m.–6 p.m.
Library of St Geneviève	Bibliothèque Sainte-Geneviève 10 Place du Panthéon (5th arr.), tel. 43 29 61 00 Métro: Luxembourg Open: Mon.–Sat. 10 a.m.–10 p.m.
Library of the Chamber of Commerce	Bibliothèque de la Chambre de Commerce 16 Rue Châteaubriand (8th arr.), tel. 45 61 99 00 Métro: Charles-de-Gaulle/Etoile Open: Mon. 2–6 p.m., Tues.–Fri. 9.30 a.m.–6 p.m., Sat. 9.30 a.m.–2 p.m. Economics library.
Library of the Museum of Anthropology	Bibliothèque du Musée de l'Homme Place du Trocadéro (16th arr.), tel. 47 04 53 94 Métro: Trodadéro Open: Mon. and Wed.–Sat. 10 a.m.–5 p.m. See A to Z: Musée de l'Homme.

Lost Property (Bureau des Objets Trouvés)

Lost Property	Bureau des Objets Trouvés: 36 Rue des Morillons (15th arr.); tel. 45 31 14 80 Métro: Convention. Open: Mon.–Fri. 8.30 a.m.–5 p.m. (Thurs. until 8 p.m.) The loss of a passport should be reported to the nearest police station and a "déclaration de vol" requested. This, with two passport photos, should be taken to the appropriate consulate (see Diplomatic and Consular Offices in France). A travel document valid for three days will be issued on payment of a fee.

Markets (Marchés)

Street markets (Rues commerçantes)	Rue de Buci (6th arr.) Métro: Odéon.
	Rue Cler (7th arr.) Métro: Ecole-Militaire.
	Rue de Poteau (13th arr.) Métro: Jules-Joffrin.
	Rue Legendre (17th arr.) Métro: Villiers.

Rue Lepic (18th arr.)
Métro: Abbesses, Blanche.

Rue Montorgueil (1st arr.)
Métro: Halles.

Rue Mouffetard (5th arr.)
Métro: Cardinal-Lemoine.

Marché d'Aligre, Place d'Aligre (12th arr.)   Covered markets (Marchés
Métro: Bastille or Ledru-Rollin.   couverts)

Marché Château d'Eau, Rue Château d'Eau (10th arr.)
Métro: Château d'Eau.

Marché Enfants-Rouges, 39 Rue de Bretagne (3rd arr.)
Métro: Filles-du-Calvaire.

Marché Saint-Quentin, Boulevard du Magenta (10th arr.)
Métro: Gare de l'Est.

Porte de Clignancourt   Flea Markets
See A–Z Marchés aux Puces.   (Marchés aux Puces)

Porte de Montreuil (20th arr.)
Métro: Porte de Montreuil
Open: Sat., Sun., Mon.

Porte de Vanves (14th arr.)
Métro: Portes de Vanves
Open: Sat., Sun. 7 a.m.–7 p.m.

Place Louis-Lépine (4th arr.)   Flowers
Métro: Cité   (Marchés aux Fleurs)
Open: 8 a.m.–7 p.m.; closed Sun.

Place de la Madeleine (8th arr.)
Métro: Madeleine
Open: 8 a.m.–7 p.m.; closed Mon.

Place des Ternes (17th arr.)
Métro: Ternes
Open: 8 a.m.–7 p.m.; closed Mon.

Avenue Gabriel, Avenue Marigny (8th arr.)   Stamps
Métro: Champs-Elysées-Clemenceau   (Marchés aux Timbres)
Open: Thur., Sat., Sun., public holidays 10 a.m.–6 p.m.

Carreau du Temple, 1 Rue Dupetit-Thouars (3rd arr.)   Clothing
Métro: République   (Marché de la Friperie)
Open daily: 9 a.m.–noon, Mon. 9 a.m.–7 p.m.

Place Louis-Lépine (4th arr.)   Birds
Métro: Cité   (Marché aux Oiseaux)
Open: Sun. 8 a.m.–7 p.m.

Quai de Mégisserie (1st arr.)
Métro: Châtelet, Pont-Neuf
Open: 9 a.m.–7 p.m.; closed Sun.
Lots of bird and animal stalls along the Seine.

Material (Marché aux Tissus)	Marché Saint-Pierre, Place Saint-Pierre (18th arr.) Métro: Anvers Open daily; closed Sun.
Wholesale market in Rungis	Mon.–Fri. noon–3 p.m. (for visits) (Information: tel. 46 87 35 35) Buses: 185, 285 Porte d'Italie Rail: Gare d'Austerlitz.

Medical Emergencies

Emergency Doctor	S.O.S. Doctor (24-hour service); tel. 47 07 77 77.
On Call	S.O.S. Docteur Nuit; tel. 43 37 77 77.
	Service de Garde des Médecins de Paris (8 p.m.–8 a.m.); tel. 45 33 99 11.
	General Practitioners (médecins généralistes de Paris); tel. 45 42 37 00.
Urgent Cases	AUMP (Association pour les urgences médicales de Paris); tel. 48 28 40 04.
	SAMU (Service Aide d'Urgence); tel. 45 67 50 50.
Emergency admission to hospital	Ambulance de l'Assistance Publique; tel. 43 78 26 26 (24-hour service).
Dental Emergency	S.O.S. dentaire (8 p.m.–8 a.m.); tel. 43 37 51 00.

Museums (Musées)

Note	The "Carte musées et monuments" (for 1, 3 or 5 days), which is obtainable from museums and métro stations, is valid for admission to more than 60 museums and monuments in the city.
Musée de l'Affiche	18 Rue de Paradis (10th arr.) Métro: Château d'Eau Open: Mon., Wed.–Sun. noon–6 p.m. Poster museum.
Musée de l'Air et de l'Espace	Aéroport du Bourget RER: line B to Le Bourget-Drancy, then bus 15e Open: 1 May–30 Oct. 10 a.m.–6 p.m.; 1 Nov.–30 April 10 a.m.–5 p.m.; closed Mon. Air and space travel.
Musée-Association "Les Amis d'Edith Piaf"	5 Rue Crespin du Gast (11th arr.) Métro: Ménilmontant Mon.–Thurs. 1–6 p.m. (only by prior arrangement) Photos, letters, drawings and other mementoes of the popular entertainer.
Musée des Antiquitiés National de France	See A–Z – Saint-Germain-en-Laye.
Musée de l'Armée	See A–Z – Musée de l'Armée.

See A–Z – Palais de Tokyo.

Musée d'Art et d'Essai

42 Rue des Saules (18th arr.)
Métro: Lamarck-Caulaincourt
Open: Sun.–Thur. 3–6 p.m. (except Aug. and Jewish festivals)
Museum of Jewish art. Cult objects from Poland
In the Hôtel de Saint-Aignan in the Marais quarter an Institute of Jewish Art is to be established which will also house the collection of Jewish art now in the Cluny Museum.

Musée d'Art Juif

See A–Z – Musée d'Art Moderne de la Ville de Paris.

Musée d'Art Moderne de la Ville de Paris

22 bis, Rue Gabriel Péri
932 Saint-Denis
Métro: Saint-Denis
Bus 156 from Porte de la Chapelle
Open: Mon. and Wed.–Sat. 10 a.m.–5.30 p.m., Sun. and public holidays 2–6.30 p.m.
Exhibition in the Carmelite monastery, which dates from the time of Louis XII, of articles connected with the Carmelite order and also mementoes of the 1871 commune, archaeological finds and modern works of art.

Musée d'Art la Ville de Saint-Denis

293 Avenue Daumesnil (12th arr.)
Métro: Porte Dorée
Open: 9.45 a.m.–noon, 1.30–5.20 p.m.; closed Tues.
Art from black Africa and Oceania; aquarium.

Musée National des Arts Africains et Océaniens

(Pavillon de Marsan) 107 Rue de Rivoli (1st arr.)
Métro: Palais-Royal, Tuileries
Open: Wed.–Sat. 12.30–6 p.m., Sun. 11 a.m.–6 p.m.
Dubuffet, Middle Ages, Renaissance, toys noon–6 p.m. (Louis XIV and Louis XVI collections until 7 p.m.)
History of decorative arts (furniture and everyday objects from the Middle Ages to the early 20th c.).

Musée des Arts Décoratifs

109 Rue Rivoli (1st arr.)
In the top three storeys of the Pavillon de Marsan in the north wing of the Louvre.
Métro: Palais Royal
Open: Wed.–Sat. 12.30–6 p.m., Sun. 11 a.m.–6 p.m.
Clothes, costumes and accessories of three centuries (from the age of the Sun-King to the outbreak of the Second World War) including valuable gowns by Chanel, Dior, Cardin, Worth, Schiaparelli and Corrèges.

Musée des Arts de la Mode

11 Rue Berryer (8th arr.)
Métro: Etoiles, Ternes, George V
Open: 11 a.m.–6 p.m.; closed Tues.

Centre National d'Arts Plastiques

6 Avenue du Mahatma-Gandhi, Jardin d'Acclimation (16th arr.)
Métro: Sablons, Porte Maillot; Bus: 73
Open: 10 a.m.–5.15 p.m.; closed Tues.
Museum of French popular art.

Musée National des Arts et Traditions Populaires

47 Rue Raynouard (16th arr.)
Métro: Passy, Muette
Open: 10 a.m.–5.40 p.m.; closed Mon.
Library: 10 a.m.–6 p.m.; closed Sun.

Maison de Balzac

Museums

Home of Honoré de Balzac containing numerous documents and a library of works by and about Balzac.

Ecole Nationale Supérieure des Beaux Arts

17 Quai Maalaquais (1st arr.)
Métro: Saint-Germain-des-Prés
Open: daily (except Tues.) 1–7 p.m.
Temporary art exhibitions.

Musée Bossuet

5 Place Charles de Gaulle, 771 Meaux
50 km (30 miles) E of Paris
Rail: from Gare de l'Est
Open: 10 a.m.–noon, 2–6 p.m.; closed Tues. and Fri.
Archaeology, art and history of the region in the former palace of Bossuet, Bishop and Court Preacher to Louis XIV.

Atélier-Musée Henri Bouchard

25 Rue de l'Yvette (16th arr.)
Métro: Jasmin
Open: Wed. and Sat. 2–7 p.m.
Closed: the last 14 days in each quarter
Studio of the sculptor Henri Bouchard (1875–1960).

Musée Bourdelle

16 Rue Antoine-Bourdelle (15th arr.)
Métro: Montparnasse-Bienvenue, Falguière
Open: 10 a.m.–5.40 p.m.; closed Mon.
Works by the sculptor Antoine Bourdelle (pupil of Rodin) and temporary exhibitions of modern sculpture.

Musée Nissim de Camodo

63 Rue de Monceau (8th arr.)
Métro: Villiers
Open: 10 a.m.–noon, 2–5 p.m., closed Mon. and Tues.
18th c. Rococo furniture and tapestries, costume exhibition.

Musée Carnavalet

See A–Z – Musée Carnavalet.

Centre National d'Art et de Culture Georges Pompidou

See A–Z – Centre Pompidou.

Musée National de Céramiques de Sèvres

Place of Manufacture, 92 Sèvres
Métro: Pont de Sèvres, then Bus 171, 179, 169
Open 10.30 a.m.–noon, 1.30–5.15 p.m.; closed Tues.
Extensive collection of porcelain throughout history and from many countries.

Musée Cernuschi (Musée d'Art Chinois de la Ville de Paris)

7 Avenue Vélasquez (8th arr.)
Métro: Villiers, Monceau
Open: 10 a.m.–5.40 p.m.; closed Mon.
National Museum of Chinese Art.

Musée de la Chasse et de la Nature

Hôtel Guénégaud des Brosses, 60 Rue des Archives (3rd arr.)
Métro: Rambuteau, Hôtel de Ville
Open: 10 a.m.–12.30 p.m.; 1.30–5.30 p.m.; closed Tues. and Fri.
Hunting and weapons, Flemish and German paintings of the 16th and 17th c.

Musée du Cinéma Henri Langlois

Palais de Chaillot, Place du Trocadéro (16th arr.)
Métro: Trocadéro
Open: 10, 11 a.m., 2, 3, 4 p.m. only with guide; closed Tues.
History of cinema in documents, costumes and apparatus.

Musée de l'Hôtel de Cluny

See A–Z – Musée de l'Hôtel de Cluny.

25 Boulevard des Capucines (2nd arr.)
Métro: Opéra, Madeleine
Open: 10 a.m.–5.40 p.m.; closed Mon.; Entrance fee
A sumptuously furnished museum with Rococo interiors
established by the Cognacq-Jay family (founders of La Sama-
taritaine Department Store). (Moving to the Hôtel de Donon in
the Marais during 1990.)

Musée Cognacq-Jay

See A–Z – Musée Conde.

Musée Conde

Hôtel de Vigny, 10 Rue du Parc Royal
Métro: Chemin Vert
Open: Mon.–Fri. noon–5 p.m.

Centre National de
Documentation du
Patrimoine-inventaire
Général

6 Place de Furstemberg (6th arr.)
Métro: Saint-Germain-des-Prés
Open: 10 a.m.–5.15 p.m.; closed Tues., Dec. 25th and Jan. 1st
Sketches and paintings by the master of the French Romantic
movement.

Musée National Eugène
Dalacroix

59 Avenue Foch (16th arr.)
Métro: Dauphine
Open: Sun. and Thurs. 2–5 p.m.
Chinese and Japanese art.

Musée National d'Ennery

42 Avenue des Gobelins (13th arr.)
Métro: Gobelins
Open: guided tours through the studios: Tues., Wed., Thurs.
2.15, 4.45 p.m.
State factory where tapestries (Gobelins) are still being made
by the same method as in past centuries.

Manufacture National des
Gobelins

See A–Z – Grand Palais.

Galeries Nationales du
Grand Palais

10 Boulevard Montmartre (9th arr.)
Métro: Montmartre
Open: daily 10 a.m.–7 p.m.
Very popular waxworks presenting historical tableaux and
celebrities.

Musée Grevin

See A–Z – Les Halles.

Grevin Forum

See A–Z – Musée Guimet.

Musée Guimet

43 Avenue de Villiers (17th arr.)
Métro: Villiers
Open: daily (except Mon.) 10 a.m.–noon, 2–5 p.m.
Works by the Alsatian painter Jean-Jacques Henner (1829–
1905).

Musée Henner

Hôtel de Soubise, 60 Rue des Francs-Bourgeois (3rd arr.)
Métro: Rambuteau, Hôtel de Ville
Open: 2–5 p.m.; closed Tues.
History of France from the Merovingian period (7th and 8th c.)
until the Second World War.

Musée de l'Histoire de
France

See A–Z – Musée Carnavalet.

Musée de l'Histoire de Paris

See A–Z – Musée de l'Homme (Musée National d'Histoire
Naturelle).

Musée d l'Homme

Museums

Musée Français de l'Holographie

Forum des Halles, level 1, 15–21 Grand Balcon
Métro: Châtelet-Les Halles
Open: Mon.–Sat. 10.30 a.m.–7 p.m., Mon., Sun., public holidays 1–7 p.m.
This new museum of the laser age houses the precursors of the hologram (three-dimensional photographic images).

Maison Victor Hugo

Hôtel de Rohan-Guéménée, 6 Places des Vosges (4th arr.)
Métro: Bastille, Saint-Paul, Chemin-Vert
Open: 10 a.m.–5.40 p.m.; closed Mon.
The poet Victor Hugo lived in this house in the Place des Vosges (see A–Z) between 1832 and 1848. Since 1903 it has been a museum exhibiting mementoes, furniture, illustrations of his works and 400 of his drawings.

Musée de l'Ile-de-France

Château de Sceaux, 92 Sceaux
RER line B: Parc de Sceaux
Open: Mon., Fri. 2–5 p.m., Wed., Thurs., Sat, Sun. 10 a.m.–noon, 2–5 p.m.
The history of the Ile-de-France in documents, paintings, coins, ceramics and other craft objects.

Musée Instrumental du Conservatoire Supérieur de Musique de Paris

14 Rue de Madrid (18th arr.)
Métro: Europe
Open: Wed.–Sat. 2–6 p.m.
Temporary exhibitions of musical instruments.

Musée Jacquemart-André

158 Boulevard Haussmann (8th arr.)
Métro: Saint-Philippe-du-Roule
Open: 1.30–5.30 p.m., closed Mon. and Tues.
18th c. European paintings and Italian Renaissance paintings; temporary exhibitions.

Jardin des Plantes

See A–Z – Jardin des Plantes.

Musée du Jeu de Paume

See A–Z – Jeu de Paume.

Musée Kwok On

41 Rue des Francs-Bourgeois (4th arr.)
Métro: St-Paul
Open: Mon.–Fri. noon–6 p.m.
Asian theatre.

Musée National de la Légion et des Ordres de Chevalerie

Hôtel de Salm, 2 Rue de Bellechasse (7th arr.)
Métro: Solférino
Open: 2–5 p.m., closed Mon.
Orders of chivalry from the Middle Ages until the present day (insignia and documents).

Musée du Louvre

See A–Z – Louvre.

Galeries Nationales du Luxembourg

See A–Z – Palais du Luxembourg.

Musée de la Marine

See A–Z – Musée de la Marine.

Musée Marmottan

2 Rue Louis Boilly (16th arr.)
Métro: Muette
Open: 10 a.m.–5.30 p.m., closed Mon.
Principally the collection "100 Masterpieces of Claud Monet and his Impressionist friends". In October 1985 9 paintings were stolen; 5 Monets, 2 Renoirs, a picture by Berthe Morisot

Orangerie: Claude Renoir as a clown . . .   *. . . and Picasso's "Woman in a white hat"*

("Jeune fille au bal") and one by Naruse ("Portrait de Monet"), valued at several million francs. Among the pictures by Monet that disappeared was the prize of the collection "Impression, soleil levant", to which Impressionism owes its name, as well as "Camille Monet et sa cousine sur la plage à Trouville", "Portrait de Jean Monet", "Portrait de Poly, pêcheur de Belle-Isle" and "Champ de tulipes en Hollande". The stolen Renoirs were the "Baigneuses" and "Portrait de Monet".

195 Rue Saint-Jacques (5th arr.)
Métro: Luxembourg
Open: 10 a.m.–5.30 p.m., closed Mon.
Film presentations, etc. about the work of Jacques Cousteau.

Centre de la Mer et des Eaux

Maison d'Armande Béjart, 11 Rue des Pierres, below the terrace (see Excursions), 92 Meudon
RER line C
Open: Wed.–Sun. 2–6 p.m.
The pretty house which the poet François Rabelais lived in when he was a priest, was bought by Molière's widow, Armande Béjart, after his death. Richard Wagner, Auguste Rodin and the author Louis-Ferdinand Céline later stayed here. The present museum houses mementoes of those who lived here as well as Meudon glassware, documents relating to the former Château of Meudon and Redouté roses.
In the park are sculptures by contemporary artists – Arp, Bourdelle, Stahly, etc.

Musée d'Art et d'Histoire de Meudon

Palais Gallièra, 10 Avenue Pierre Ier de Serbie (16th arr.)
Métro: Iéna

Musée de la Mode et du Costume

Open: 10 a.m.–5.40 p.m.; closed Mon.
Museum of fashion (civilian uniforms and fashionable dress from 1735 until the present day).

Monnaie de Paris

See A–Z – Monnaie de Paris.

Musée de Montmartre

12 Rue Cortot (18th arr.)
Métro: Lamarck-Caulaincourt
Open: Tues.–Sat. 2.30–6 p.m., Sun. 11 a.m.–6 p.m.
History of the "Free Commune" of Montmartre.

Musée des Monuments Français

See A–Z – Musée des Monuments Français.

Musée National Gustave Moreau

14 Rue de la Rochefoucauld (9th arr.)
Métro: Trinité
Open: 10 a.m.–12.45 p.m., 2–5.15 p.m., closed Tues.
The former home and studio of the Symbolist painter houses a unique museum containing about 1000 paintings and 7000 drawings.

Musée de la Femme et Collection d'Automates de Neuilly

12 Rue du Centre, 92 Neuilly
Métro: Pont-de-Neuilly
Open: 2.30–5 p.m.; closed Tues., public holidays, July and Aug.
Collection of old automata which are set in motion once daily at 3 p.m. Museum of Womankind.

Musée Notre-Dame de Paris

10 Rue du Cloître (4th arr.)
Métro: Cité
Open: Wed., Sat., Sun. 2.30–6 p.m.
History of the Ile-de-la-Cité.

Musée de l'Orangerie des Tuileries

Jardin de Tuileries, Place de la Concorde (1st arr.)
Métro: Concorde
Open: 9.45 a.m.–5.15 p.m.; closed Tues.
Collection of Jean Walter and Paul Guillaume. Works by the Impressionists Renoir, Cézanne, Derain, Soutine, Picasso. "Les Nymphéas" by Claude Monet.
Open daily, except Tues. 9.45 a.m.–noon, 2–5.15 p.m.

Musée d'Orsay

See A–Z – Musée d'Orsay.

Palais de la Découverte

See A–Z – Palais de la Découverte.

Palais de Tokyo

See A–Z – Palais de Tokyo.

Musée du Petit Palais

See A–Z – Petit Palais.

Musée français de la Photographie

78 Rue de Paris, 91 Bièvres
Rail: from the Gare de Lyon
Open: daily 9 a.m.–noon, 2–6 p.m.
Museum of photographic history.

Musée National Picasso

See A–Z – Musée Picasso.

Musée des Plans-Reliefs

See A–Z – Musée d'Armée.

Musée de la Poste

34 Boulevard de Vaugirard (15th arr.)
Métro: Montparnasse-Bienvenue, Falguière, Pasteur
Open: 10 a.m.–5 p.m.; closed Sun. and public holidays

History of the postal service and philately. Library and photographic library.

1 bis, Rue des Carmes (5th arr.)
Métro: Maubert-Mutualité
Open: Mon., Thur. 2–5 p.m., Fri. 9 a.m.–4.30 p.m.
Criminal history museum of the Préfecture of Police.

Musée de la Préfecture de la Police

See A–Z – Saint-Germain-en-Laye.

Musée de la Préhistoire

Maison de Radio-France, 116 Avenue du Président Kennedy (16th arr.)
Métro: Ranelagh, Passy, Mirabeau
Open: 10–11.30 a.m., 2–4.30 p.m.; closed Mon.
History and news of radio and television of the studios of Radio-France. Tours of the studios daily (except Suns. and public holidays) 10.30, 11.30 a.m., 2.30, 3.30 and 4.30 p.m.

Musée de Radio-France

Château d'Ecouen, 95 Ecouen
Métro: Saint-Denis-Porte de Paris
Rail: from Gare du Nord
Open: 9.45 a.m.–12.30 p.m., 2–5.15 p.m.; closed Tues. and public holidays
One of the most beautiful Renaissance château in the Région Ile-de-France.

Musée National de la Renaissance

See A–Z – Musée Rodin.

Musée Rodin

178 Boulevard Saint-Denis, 92 Courbevoie
Métro: Pont-de-Levallois
Open: Wed., Thur., Sat., Sun. and public holidays 2–6 p.m.
Fine museum of dolls and toys. Sculpture by Antoine Carpeaux (19th c.).

Musée Roybet Fould
Poupées anciennes

16 Rue Chaptal (9th arr.)
Métro: Pigalle
Open: daily (except Mon.) 9 a.m.–5.40 p.m.
Memorabilia of the writer Erenest Renan, the painter Ary Scheffer and the poetess George Sand.

Musée Renan Scheffer

Quai Saint-Bernard (5th arr.)
Métro: Gare d'Orléans-Austerlitz, Jussieu
Open: during the day
Sculpture by Arman, Brice, César, Etienne-Martin, Schoffer, Stahly, Zadkine, etc.

Musée de Sculpture ein plein Air de la Ville de Paris

1 Rue de la Perle (3rd arr.)
Métro: Chemin-Vert, St-Paul
Open: 10 a.m.–noon, 2–5 p.m.; closed Sun., Mon. and public holidays also in August
Old locks and works of art in wrought iron.

Musée de la Serrurerie
(Musée Bricard)

12 Rue Surcouf (7th arr.)
Métro: Latour-Maubourg, Invalides
Open: 11 a.m.–6 p.m.; closed Sun. and public holidays
Museum of the state tobacco industry.

Musée-Galerie de la SEITA

270 Rue Saint-Martin (3rd arr.)
Métro: Réaumur–Sébastopol
Open: Tues.–Sat. 1–5.30 p.m., Sun. 10 a.m.–5.15 p.m.
Technological museum, astronomy, automata, early cars and

Musée National des Techniques

trains (models), agricultural and industrial technology (metallurgy, chemistry), printing techniques, photography, weaving and spinning.

Musée National des Thermes	See A–Z – Thermes.
Musée Vivant du Cheval	Grandes écuries de Chantilly, 60 Chantilly Rail: from Gare du Nord Open: 10.30 a.m.–6.30 p.m.; closed Tues. Everything to do with horses: horses in art, bridles, saddles, harness, carriages, coaches. Demonstrations with live horses with commentary by an instructor (3.15 and 5.15 p.m.).
Musée du Vin	5 Square Charles Dickens (16th arr.) Métro: Passy Open: daily 2–6 p.m. Wine museum in a 13th/14th c. vault.
Musée Zadkine	100 bis, Rue d'Assas (6th arr.) Métro: Vavin, Notre-Dame des Champs, Port-Royal Open: 10 a.m.–5.40 p.m.; closed Mon. Works of the sculptor Ossip Zadkine are displayed in the garden, house and studio where he worked from 1928 until his death in 1967.

Music

Concert Halls
(Salles de Concert)

Paris is a metropolis that is famous for its music. Concerts are given almost daily in one or other of its concert halls. Details of these can be found in "7 à Paris" and "Pariscope".

Salle Pleyel
252 Faubourg Saint-Honoré (8th arr.); tel. 45 63 88 73
Métro: Ternes.

Salle Gaveau
45 Rue La Boëtie (8th arr.); tel. 45 63 20 30
Métro: St-Augustin.

Centre International de Paris, Palais des Congrès
Porte Maillot (17th arr.); tel. 46 20 22 22
Métro: Porte Maillot.

Salle Cortot
78 Rue Cardinet (17th arr.); tel. 49 24 80 16
Métro: Courcelles.

Théâtre des Champs-Elysées
15 Avenue Montaigne (8th arr.); tel. 47 23 47 77
Métro: Franklin D. Roosevelt.

Palais de Chaillot
Place du Trocadéro (16th arr.); tel. 47 27 81 15
Métro: Trocadéro.

Radio-France
116 Avenue du Président Kennedy (16th arr.); tel. 45 24 15 16
Métro: Ranelagh, Passy, Mirabeau.

Especially in the following churches: Notre-Dame, Saint-Eustache, Saint-Sulpice, Sainte-Chapelle, Madeleine, Saint-Germain-des-Prés and Saint-Louis-des-Invalides in the Hôtel des Invalides
(See entries in A–Z)

Church Concerts

The three main venues for opera and light opera are:

Opera and Light Opera

Opéra
Place de l'Opéra (9th arr.); tel. 48 42 57 50
Métro: Opéra.
Since 1990 used only for ballet and celebrity recitals.

Salle Favart (Opéra comique)
5 Rue Favart (2nd. arr.); tel. 47 42 57 50
Métro: Richelieu-Drouot.

Théâtre Musical de Paris
1 Place du Châtelet (1st arr.); tel. 42 61 19 83
Métro: Châtelet.

Since 1990 all opera performances, previously given in the Opéra (see above), have taken place in the new opera house at the Bastille which was opened on July 14th 1989.
Information: 11 bis, Avenue Daumesnel (12th arr.); tel. 43 42 92 92.

Bastille Opera

La Péniche Opéra
Quai de Jemappes (10th arr.); tel. 42 45 18 20
Métro: Jaurès
Opera, drama with music, musicals, plays; especially attractive for a young audience.

Musicals, Ballet

Espace Marais
23 Rue Beautreillis (4th arr.); tel. 42 71 10 19
Métro: Place de la Bastille
Modern ballet in a small theatre in the Marais quarter.

French and International singing stars as well as pop groups can be heard in the Music Halls.

Music Halls

Bobino
Rue de la Gaîté (14th arr.); tel. 43 22 26 39
Métro: Edgar-Quinet.

Olympia
28 Boulevard des Capucines (9th arr.); tel. 47 42 25 49
Métro: Madeleine, Opéra.

Chez Louisette
Marché Vernaison, Allée No. 10,
Flea market of Saint-Ouen (18th arr.)
Métro: Porte de Clignancourt
Sat., Sun., Mon.

Nostalgic Chansons

Night-life

Its "Cabarets and Revues" have made Parisian night-life famous throughout the world.

Cabarets and Revues

Paris by night

Some addresses are:

Alcazar
62 Rue Mazarine (6th arr.); tel. 43 29 02 20.

Crazy Horse Saloon
12 Avenue George-V (8th arr.); tel. 47 23 32 32.

Folies Bergère
32 Rue Richer (9th arr.); tel. 42 46 77 11.

Lido
116 Avenue des Champs-Elysées (8th arr.); tel. 45 63 11 61.

Moulin Rouge
Place Blanche (18th arr.); tel. 46 06 00 19.

Paradis Latin
28 Rue du Cardinal-Lemoine (5th arr.); tel. 43 25 28 28.

L'Apocalypse
Rue du Colisée (8th arr.); tel. 42 25 11 68
Open: daily 10.30 p.m.–8 a.m.

Casita Club
167 Rue Montmartre (2nd arr.); tel. 42 36 57 50
Open: Wed.–Sun. 10.30 p.m.–5.30 a.m.

Club 79
79 Champs Elysées (8th arr.); tel. 47 23 68 75
Open: discothèque Fri., Sat. 10 p.m. until morning; Sun.–
Thurs. 9.30 p.m.–3 a.m.

Le Corso
1 Avenue de Clichy (17th arr.); tel. 43 87 91 73
Open: daily 10.30 p.m. until morning.

La Coupole
102 Boulevard du Montparnasse (14th arr.); tel. 43 20 14 20
Open: from 9.30 p.m. (Fri., Sat. records, otherwise band.)

Flash Back
Corner 37 Rue Grégoire de Tours/18 Rue des Quatre Vents (6th
arr.); tel. 43 25 56 10
Open: daily (except Mon.) from 11 p.m.

Galaxy Club
40 Rue des Blancs-Manteaux (4th arr.); tel. 42 71 43 22
Open: Fri., Sat. from 11 p.m.

La Scala de Paris
188 bis, Rue de Rivoli (1st arr.); tel. 42 60 45 64
Open: daily 10.20 p.m. until morning.

Wagram
39 Avenue de Wagram (17th arr.); tel. 43 80 30 03
Open: Fri., Sat. 10 p.m. until morning.

Whisky à Gogo
57 Rue de Seine (6th arr.); tel. 46 33 74 99
Open: daily 10 p.m. until morning.

Who's Club
13 Rue du Petit-Pont (5th arr.); tel. 43 25 13 14
Open: Wed.–Sun. 10 p.m. until morning.

Deux Anes   Chansonniers
100 Boulevard de Clichy (18th arr.); tel. 46 06 10 26
Open: daily 9 p.m. until early morning; Sun. 3.30 p.m. until
early morning.

Caveau de la République
1 Boulevard St-Martin (3rd arr.); tel. 42 78 44 45
Open: daily 9 p.m. until early morning; Sun. 3.30 p.m. until
early morning.

Some suggestions for jazz fans: Jazz Clubs

Caveau de la Huchette
5 Rue de la Huchette (5th arr.); tel. 43 26 65 05
Métro: St-Michel
Open: daily 9.30 p.m.–2.30 a.m.

Chapelle des Lombards
19 Rue de Lappe (1st arr.); tel. 43 57 24 24
Métro: Bastille
Open: Wed.–Sat. from 10.30 p.m.

Cloître des Lombards
62 Rue des Lombards (1st arr.); tel. 42 33 54 09
Métro: Châtelet
Open: concerts daily 8.30–10.30 p.m.; 10.30 p.m.–4 a.m.

Slow Club
130 Rue de Rivoli (1st arr.); tel. 42 33 84 30
Métro: Châtelet, Pont-Neuf
Open: daily 9.30 p.m.–2.30 a.m.; Fri. to 3 a.m.; Sat. to 4 a.m.

Le Petit Journal
71 Boulevard St-Michel (5th arr.); tel. 43 26 28 59
Métro: Luxembourg
Open: Mon.–Sat. until 2 a.m.

Bars

Alexandre-Bar
53 Avenue George-V (8th arr.); tel. 47 20 17 82
Open: until 2 a.m.

Ascot
66 Rue Pierre Charron (8th arr.); tel. 43 59 28 15
Open: Mon.–Sat. 6 p.m.–4 a.m.

Bunny's Girls
14 Rue Fontaine (9th arr.); tel. 42 82 08 26
Open: Mon.–Sat. until 2 a.m.

Cambridge
17 Avenue de Wagram (17th arr.); tel. 43 80 34 12
Open: Mon.–Sat.

Capricorne
5 Rue Molière (1st arr.); tel. 42 96 20 27
Open: Mon.–Sat. 10 p.m. until morning.

Duplex
25 Rue Michel-le-Comte (3rd arr.); tel. 42 72 80 86.
Open: 8 p.m.–2 a.m.

La Caravelle
4 Rue Arsène-Houssaye (8th arr.); tel. 43 59 14 35
Open: day and night

Le Casanova
11 Rue Danielle-Casanova (1st arr.); tel. 42 61 48 26
Open: Mon.–Sat. noon–2 a.m.

Le César
4 Rue Chabanais (2nd arr.); tel. 42 96 81 13
Open: 2 p.m. until morning (topless waitresses).

Le 23
Avenue du Maine (Chez Hippolyte: 15th arr.); tel. 54 44 64 16
Open: 8 p.m. until morning.

Le Charivari
325 Rue St-Martin (3rd arr.); tel. 42 78 80 29
Open: 9 p.m.–2 a.m.
(3 restaurants, 5 bars, cabaret and discothèque).

Striptease

A host of striptease joints, bars, sex shops and porno cinemas
are located on the southern fringe of the Butte de Montmartre
(see A–Z, Montmartre) between Place Pigalle and Place Clichy,
and in the Rue Saint-Denis (1st arr.).

Parking (Parkings)

1st and 2nd Arrondissement

Parking Saint-Honoré. 58 Place du Marché-Saint-Honoré.
Parking Vendôme. Place Vendôme.

Bourse, Place de la Bourse.
Halles Garage, 10 bis, Rue Bailleul.
Paris Parking, Place du Louvre.
Parking St-Martin, Corner Rue Réamur/Rue St-Martin.
Pont-Neuf, Place Dauphine.
Pyramides, 15 Rue des Pyramides.

Parking Centre Beaubourg, Rue Rambuteau (underground garage of the Centre Pompidou).
Parking Sully, 5 Rue Agrippa-D'Aubigné.
Parking Notre-Dame, Place du Parvis Notre-Dame.
Centre de Paris, 11 Rue Béranger.
Lobau, Rue Lobau (entrance).
Pont-Marie, Rue Geoffrey-Lasnier.

3rd and 4th
Arrondissement

Parking Soufflot, 22 Rue Soufflot.
Parking Saint-Sulpice, Place Saint-Sulpice.
Parking Mazarine, 27 Rue Mazarine.
Parking Montparnasse-Raspail, 138 bis, Boulevard du Montparnasse.
Garage St-Germain, 29 Rue de Poissy.
Lagrange. Rue Lagrange, Place Maubert.

5th and 6th
Arrondissement

Parking Invalides, Esplanade des Invalides (opposite 23 Rue de Constantine).
L'Abbaye, 30 Boulevard Raspail.
Joffre, Place Joffre.

7th Arrondissement

Parking Concorde, Place de la Concorde (opposite Rue Boissy-d'Anglas).
Garages de Paris, 25 Place de la Madeleine.
Bergson, Place St-Augustin.
Berri-Ponthieu, 66 Rue de Ponthieu.
Elysée-La Boétie, 87 Rue de la Boétie.
Elysées-Ponthieu, 25 Rue de Ponthieu.
Parc Berri Washington, 5 Rue de Berri (50 m (55 yd) from the Champs-Elysées).
Porte Maillot, Place de la Porte Maillot.
Vernet, 16 Rue Vernet.
Parking Champs-Elysées-George-V, Rue de Galilée (opposite 130 Avenue des Champs-Elysées).

8th Arrondissement

Parking Galéries Lafayette, 54 Boulevard Haussmann.
Parking Paramount Opéra, 4 Rue de la Chaussée–d'Antin.
Parking Olympia, 7 Rue Caumartin.
Parking Anvers, 41 Boulevard de Rochechouart.
Bleue, 7 Rue Bleue.
Opéra, 4 Rue de la Chaussée–d'Antin (entrance).
Paris Nord Auto, 71 Rue de Dunkerque.
Parking Lambel, 107 Rue St-Lazare.
Parking Bergson, Rue Labourde.

9th Arrondissement

Parking Gare du Nord, 18 Rue de Dunkerque.
Garage Pierre-Dupont, 3 Rue Pierre-Dupont.
Lancry, 63 Rue de Lancry.
Paris-Temple, 83 Rue du Faubourg-du-Temple.
Perier, 60 Rue René-Boulanger.
St-Martin, 184 Rue du Faubourg St-Martin.

10th Arrondissement

Parks and Gardens

14th Arrondissement   Grand Garage Raspail, 14 Rue Campagne-Première.
                             Parking Edgar Quinet, Boulevard Edgar Quinet.

18th Arrondissement   Grand Garage de la Place Blanche, 4 Rue Coustou.

Parks and Gardens (Jardins, Parcs)

Jardins Albert-Kahn   92 Boulogne-Billancourt, 6 Quai du 4 Septembre
                             Métro: Porte de Saint-Cloud, Porte d'Auteuil
                             Buses: 52, 72
                             Open: daily 15 March–15 Nov. 9.30 a.m.–12.30 p.m., 2–7 p.m.
                             Different types of gardens in one park.

Jardin Fleuriste de la Ville de   3 Avenue de la Porte d'Auteuil (16th arr.)
Paris   Métro: Porte d'Auteuil.
                             Open: daily 1 April–30 Sept.: 10 a.m.–6 p.m.; 1 Oct.–31 March:
                             10 a.m.–5 p.m.
                             Civic nurseries with plants on display in the open and in green-
                             houses.

Parc des Buttes-Chaumont   19th Arrondissement
                             Métro: Buttes-Chaumont, Botzaris.
                             City park on one of the highest points in Paris.

Parc Monceau   Boulevard de Courcelles (8th arr.)
                             Métro: Monceau.
                             The "aristocrat" of Paris's public parks.

Parc Montsouris   Boulevard Jourdan (14th arr.)
                             RER: Cité Universitaire.
                             Very pretty little park opposite the Cité Universitaire Interna-
                             tionale.

Parc de Saint-Cloud   Rue de Saint-Cloud, 92-Saint-Cloud
                             Métro: Boulogne-Porte de Saint-Cloud.
                             Open: 7 a.m.–9 p.m. (accessible by car).
                             Classical gardens laid out by Le Nôtre (Paris A–Z, see Ver-
                             sailles).

Adventure Park Mirapolis   In May 1987 the first adventure park "Mirapolis" (building costs
                             about £50 million) was opened in Cergy-Pontoise in the north-
                             west of Paris.
                             This new leisure park is dominated by a 35 m (115 ft) high
                             concrete figure of the gluttonous giant Gargantua which was
                             featured by Rabelais. It is the second largest statue in the world,
                             exceeded in height only by the famous New York Statue of
                             Liberty. In the belly and limbs of this hero of French folk-lore are
                             a restaurant and boutiques. A day in the fairy-tale world of this
                             magical Parisian township costs about £8. Among the 36 attrac-
                             tions, which incorporate the most modern technical innova-
                             tions and which are spread over an area of 90 ha (222 acres), are
                             a time-machine, King Arthur's Round Table, a magic castle and
                             wild water trips.

Parc Astérix   On the A1 motorway, 38 km N of Paris in the département of
                             Oise, is a signpost to the Parc Astérix, opened in 1989. There are
                             five different magical worlds for the young and the young in
                             heart to discover in this 18 ha (45 acre) site. The busy Via

Antiqua leads to Astérix Village, where there are houses associated with the comic-strip hero and his friend Obélix. Then comes the Roman Town with the Ave. Caesar roundabout and the Dolphinarium. Finally you reach the 200-m-long Paris Road, covering about 1000 years of history, up to the cinematic era.

At Melun, to the south-east of Paris, a Utopian futuristic world "Colony Earth" is to be built, and finally in 1993 "EuroDisneyland" (see A–Z) is to be established at Marne-la-Vallée.

Future projects

Pets

Dogs and cats can be taken into France if they have a certificate of vaccination against rabies not less than a month or more than a year old. (In view of the quarantine regulations on re-entry into Britain most British visitors will, of course, leave their pets at home.)

Certificate of Vaccination

Police (Police)

There are police emergency telephones (tel. 17) all over Paris.

Emergency Telephones
(Police-Secours)

9 Boulevard du Palais; tel. 42 60 33 22.

Police Prefecture

Post (PTT)

Weekdays 8 a.m.–10 p.m.; tel. 42 80 67 89.

Information

Stamps (timbres) can be bought in post offices and tobacconists (bureaux de tabac).

Stamps

Head Post Office
52 Rue du Louvre (1st arr.)
Métro: Sentier, Les Halles, Louvre.
The only post office which is open day and night.

Times of Opening: Weekdays 8 a.m.–7 p.m., Sat. 8 a.m.–noon.

Postal Rates:
Letters within France cost 2F or (for faster delivery) 2·20F; to Britain 2·20F; to the United States (air mail, up to 5 grams) 4·20F; to Canada (air mail, up to 5 grams) 2·80F.
Postcards cost 2F within France and to Britain and Canada; to the United States 2.80F.

Programmes of Events

"L'Officiel des Spectacles", "7 à Paris" and "Pariscope": three weekly publications listing events for the forthcoming week, starting with Wednesday, and available at all kiosks.

Weekly Programmes

The "Office de Tourisme de Paris" in the Champs Elysées (see Information) has plenty of leaflets giving details of current events.

Publications of Office du
Tourisme

191

A street musician in the Place des Vosges

Maison d'Information Culturelle	26 Rue Beaubourg (3rd arr.); tel. 42 74 27 07 Open: 10 a.m.–8 p.m., closed Sun. The Office of Cultural Information provides free information about all the events taking place in Paris.
Programme of Events in English	By dialling tel. 47 20 88 98 you can hear a recorded message giving information about all kinds of events such as concerts, exhibitions, ballet, etc.

Public Holidays (Jours fériés)

1 January (Jour de l'An); 1 May (Fête de Travail); 14 July (Fête Nationale); 15 August (Assomption); 1 November (Toussaint); 11 November (Fête de l'Armistice 1918); 25 December (Noël); plus Ascension day, Easter Monday, Whit Monday.

Public Transport (Transports publics)

Information	RATP provides a 24-hour service concerning public transport in Paris (Métro, bus, RER). Tel. 43 46 14 14, daily 6 a.m.–9 p.m.
Buses	Since there are only 56 bus routes in Paris (143 in the suburbs) it is slightly more difficult to use the bus, but the journeys are also more enjoyable because the individual tourist can get better acquainted with the Paris that lies above ground.

Bastille Métro Station, with the Guerchet-Jeannin mosiac of the French Revolution

The tickets are the same as for the Métro and can be purchased from the bus driver.

However, a ticket is only valid for a specific section without changing. Within the city one ticket is valid for up to two sections; otherwise two tickets must be cancelled.

Ten-trip "carnet": the same as for the Métro.

Seine-Bus (see Boat excursions, Bateaux-Bus).

The Métro system is the most effective means of transport for the visitor because it covers the whole City, is relatively low-priced and it is easy to find one's way.

When using the Métro remember that although the lines are numbered they are generally referred to by the name of the station at the end of the line, so that if, for example, you want to travel from Cité in the direction of Montparnasse you follow the signs for "Porte d'Orléans" which is at the end of the line. Blue signs indicate the direction ("Direction") and stations where you can change trains ("Correspondances") are indicated on the platform by a yellow illuminated sign.

The maps inside the coaches show the stations on the line you are travelling on and indicate where you have to change (Correspondances) to connect with other lines.

Single ticket (ticket/billet): valid for one journey of any length including changes and obtainable from ticket offices at Métro

Métro

Tickets

193

stations. It is necessary to feed this into the automatic barriers at the entrance where it is magnetically checked and cancelled.

They are comparatively expensive and frequent users of the Métro would do better to get a tourist season ticket (see below) or a ten-trip "carnet". A single ticket works out about 40% cheaper if bought in a "carnet" of 10 tickets. One asks for "un carnet, s'il vous plaît".

Tourist tickets ("Formule I" and "Paris Visite") – see below.

RATP

RATP (Régie Autonome des Transport Parisiens), which is part State-owned, is Paris's most important transport undertaking with 36,000 employees and three forms of transport – Métro, buses, RER.

RER

There are four RER (Réseau Express Régional) express lines: RATP (see entry) operates the A and B lines and SNCF (see entry) operates lines C and D.

Line A from Saint-Germain-en-Laye to Boissy-Saint-Léger or Marne-la-Vallée; Line B from Saint-Rémy-les Chevreuse to Châtelet-Les Halles.
Gare du Nord-Roissy;
Line C: Gare d'Orléans–Austerlitz–Versailles.
Line D: Châtelet–Les Halles–Villiers–Le Bel Gonesse.

Fares

The fare depends on the length of the journey. For RER sections within the city the Métro tariff and tickets are valid. A fresh ticket is required to change from one RER line to another. Tickets are obtainable from automatic machines in RER stations.

Ten-trip "carnet": see Métro (above).

Tourist season ticket: see below.

SNCF

The French national railways, SNCF (Société Nationale des Chemins de Fer Français), operate the international and inter-city lines (Grandes Lignes), the commuter trains (Banlieue) and the C and D RER lines.

Fares depend on the length of the journey. Single tickets only and season tickets for the week or the month are available. Single tickets can be obtained from ticket offices and automatic machines in the stations.

Tourist Tickets (Formule I,
Paris Sésame)

Formule I
This ticket is valid for one day on all buses, the Métro and RER in two or three zones.
Paris-Viste
With this ticket, which is valid for 2, 4 or 7 days, the holder can make unrestricted use of all RATP services (Métro, RER – as far as the Gare du Nord station – all buses except special and minibuses).

Tourist tickets can be bought at:
Services touristiques de la RATP, 53ter, Quai de Grands-Augustins, tel. 43 46 43 03; Place de la Madeleine, tel. 42 65 31 18; at 80 Métro stations, 7 SNCF stations, several banks and from the Office du Tourisme (see Information).

To use the ticket, feed the individual coupons into the automatic barriers at Métro and RER stations.

On buses just show the ticket to the bus driver (do not insert it into the bus ticket machine because it cannot then be used again!).

The Métro runs every day from 5.30 in the morning until 1.15 at night. Trains run at 1½ minute intervals in the rush hour and at 5 to 10 minute intervals the rest of the day and at weekends.

Buses generally run between 6.30 a.m. and 9 p.m. at 5 to 10 minute intervals in the rush hour and at up to 30 minute intervals the rest of the time. Very few lines operate on Sundays and public holidays.

Trains on the RER system, which operates from 5.30 a.m. until 12.30 at night, run at 2–7 minute intervals during the rush hours, but at other times visitors must be prepared for a longer wait.

Ten bus routes, operating at night ("Noctambus"), run every 30–60 minutes between 1 and 5.30 a.m. from the Place du Châtelet.

Noctambus

Users of the Métro are warned against pickpockets who have their eye particularly on open handbags.

Warning

Railway Stations (Gares)

The six main stations are linked to the Métro-system (the names of the station and the Métro are the same).
The Gare du Nord, Gare de l'Est, Gare de Lyon and Gare d'Austerlitz have a tourist office operated by the City of Paris (see Information) and apart from Montparnasse, at present under reconstruction, they all have exchange bureaux (see Information – Banks).
The Gare du Nord has a special reception bureau for young people.

Gare d'Austerlitz (also Gare d'Orléans)
55 Quai d'Austerlitz (13th arr.)
Information: tel. 45 84 16 16; Reservations: tel. 45 84 15 20
Trains for S and SW France, Spain, Portugal.

Gare de l'Est
Place du 11 Novembre 1918 (10th arr.)
Information: tel. 42 08 49 90; Reservations: tel. 42 40 11 27
Trains for E France, S Germany, Luxembourg, N Switzerland, Austria.

Gare de Lyon
20 Boulevard Diderot (12th arr.)
Information: tel. 43 45 92 22; Reservations: tel. 43 45 93 33
Trains for S, SE and Central France, Italy, Switzerland and the Alps.

Gare de l'Est

Gare Montparnasse
17 Boulevard Vaugirard (15th arr.)
Information: tel. 45 38 52 29; Reservations: tel. 45 38 52 39
Trains for W France (particularly Brittany).

Gare du Nord
18 Rue de Dunkerque (10th arr.)
Information: tel. 42 80 03 03; Reservations: tel. 48 78 87 54
Trains for N France, N Germany, Belgium, Great Britain and the Netherlands.

Gare Saint-Lazare
13 Rue d'Amsterdam (8th arr.)
Information: tel. 45 38 52 29; Reservations: tel. 43 87 91 70
Trains for Normandy and Great Britain.
Notice: The squares outside the station have been recently embellished with two heavy works of art by the sculptor Armand. The lighter one, 7 m (23 ft) high weighing 3 tonnes, is a stack of clocks on a concrete plinth; the other is 18 m (59 ft) high, weighs 16 tonnes and consists of boxes.

Gare (Aérogare) des Invalides
Quai d'Orsay (7th arr.)
No longer has international rail connections but serves the RER line C (see Public Transport) to Orly airport (see Airports).

Seat Reservations

At all stations: Mon.–Sat. 8 a.m.–10 p.m. and Sun. 8 a.m.–7 p.m.

Information

Telephone information for all stations: daily 8 a.m.–8 p.m.; tel. 42 61 50 50.

In France tickets must be cancelled by the passenger before departure.

Restaurants (Selection)

Les Ambassadeurs (Hôtel Crillon)
10 Place de la Concorde (8th arr.); tel. 42 65 24 24
Métro: Concorde.

Luxury Restaurants

Bristol (Hôtel Bristol)
112 Rue du Faubourg St-Honoré (8th arr.); tel. 42 66 91 45
Métro: Châtelet-Les Halles.

L'Espadon (Hôtel Ritz)
15 Place Vendôme (1st arr.); tel. 42 60 38 30
Métro: Madeleine, Tuileries, Concorde.

Jules Verne
Champ de Mars-Tour Eiffel (2nd platform, 7th arr.);
tel. 45 55 61 44
Métro: Ecole Militaire, Bir Hakeim, Trocadéro.

Lasserre
17 Avenue Franklin-D-Roosevelt (8th arr.); tel. 43 59 53 43
Métro: Franklin-D-Roosevelt
Closed: Sun. midday, Mon. and August.

Laurent
41 Avenue Gabriel (8th arr.); tel. 47 23 79 18
Métro: Franklin-D-Roosevelt, Champs-Elysées
Closed: Sat. p.m., Sun. and bank holidays.

Lucas-Carton (Alain Senderens)
9 Place de la Madeleine (8th arr.); tel. 42 65 22 90
Métro: Madeleine
Closed: Sat. and Sun., July 29th–Aug. 22nd, Dec. 23rd–Jan. 2nd.

Maxim's
3 Rue Royale (8th arr.); tel. 42 65 27 94
Métro: Madeleine
Closed: Sun.

Régence (Hôtel Plaza Athenée)
25–27 Avenue Montaigne (8th arr.); tel. 47 23 78 33
Métro: Franklin-D-Roosevelt

Robuchon (Ex-Jamin)
32 Rue de Longchamp (16th arr.); tel. 47 27 12 27
Métro: Iéna
Closed: Sat., Sun. and July

Taillevent
15 Rue Lamennais (8th arr.); tel. 45 63 39 94
Métro: George V
Closed: Sat., Sun., public holidays, 2 weeks at Easter, last week in July, last week in August.

La Tour d'Argent, an exclusive restaurant

Le Pré Catelan
Route de Suresne, Bois de Boulogne (16th arr.);
tel. 45 24 55 58
Métro: no convenient station
Closed: Sun. evening, Mon., 2 weeks in February.

La Tour d'Argent
15 Quai de la Tournelle (5th arr.); tel. 43 54 23 31
Métro: Maubert-Mutualité
Closed: Mon.

Guy Savoy
28 Rue Duret (16th arr.); tel. 45 00 17 67
Métro: Argentine
Closed: Sat., Sun., first 2 weeks in January.

Nouvelle Cuisine
(New Cuisine)

Le Bourdonnais
113 Avenue de la Bourdonnais (7th arr.); tel. 47 05 47 96
Métro: Ecole Militaire
Closed: Sun. and Mon.

Carré des Feuillants
14 Rue de Castiglione (1st arr.); tel. 42 86 82 82
Métro: Opéra
Closed: midday Sat., Sun. and weekends July and August.

le Duc
243 Boulevard Raspail (14th arr.); tel. 43 20 96 30
Métro: Raspail
Closed: Sat., Sun. and Mon.

Michel Rostang
20 Rue Rennequin (17th arr.); tel. 47 63 40 77
Métro: Ternes
Closed: Sat. midday Oct.–Mar.; Sat. Apr.–Sept., Sun. and public holidays, last week in July–last week in Aug.; Christmas
week and 1 week in Feb.

Au Trou Gascon
40 Rue Taine (12th arr.); tel. 43 44 34 26
Métro: Daumesnil
Closed: Sat., Sun and Sept.

Ambassade d'Auvergne
22 Rue du Grenier-St-Lazare (3rd arr.); tel. 42 72 31 22
Métro: Rambuteau.

Cuisine Traditionelle
(Traditional Cuisine)

l'Ami Louis
32 Rue du Vertbois (3rd arr.); tel. 48 87 77 48
Métro: Temple
Closed: Mon., Tues., July/Aug.

La Coquille
6 Rue du Débarcadère (17th arr.); tel. 45 74 25 95
Métro: Porte Maillot
Closed: Sun., Mon., public holidays, Aug.

Dodin Bouffant
25 Rue Frédéric-Sauton (5th arr.); tel. 43 25 25 14
Métro: Maubert-Mutualité
Closed: Sun., Aug., 2 weeks at Christmas.

Le Dôme
108 Boulevard de Montparnasse (14th arr.); tel. 43 35 25 81
Métro: Vavin
Closed: Mon.

Chez Edgard
4 Rue Marbuf (8th arr.); tel. 47 20 51 15
Métro: Franklin D. Roosevelt
Closed: Sun.

Pierre Traiteur
10 Rue de Richelieu (1st arr.); tel. 42 96 09 17
Métro: Palais Royal
Closed: Sat., Sun. and in Aug.

Auvergne:
La Lozère
4 Rue Hautefeuille (6th arr.); tel. 43 54 26 64
Métro: St-Michel
Closed: Sun., Mon., Aug.

Cuisine Regionale
(Regional Cuisine)

Burgundy/Lyons:
Benoit
20 Rue St-Martin (4th arr.); tel. 42 72 25 76
Métro: Châtelet
Closed: Sat., Sun. and Aug.

Bretagne:
Auberge de l'Argoat
27 Avenue Reille (14th arr.); tel. 45 89 17 05

Métro: Cité Universitaire
Closed: Sun., Mon. and in August.

Les Armes de Bretagne
108 Avenue du Maine (14th arr.); tel. 43 20 29 50
Métro: Gaîté
Closed: Sun. evening, Mon. 1 Jan. and 1st week in May and August.

Louis XIV
1 bis, Place des Victoires (1st arr.); tel. 42 61 39 44
Métro: Bourse
Closed: Sat., Sun., Aug.
(pavement terrace).

Moissonnier
28 Rue des Fossés-St-Bernard (5th arr.); tel: 43 29 87 65
Métro: Jussieu, Cardinal Lemoine
Closed: Sun. evening, Mon., Aug.

Le Train Bleu
20 Boulevard Diderot, Gare de Lyon, 1st floor (12th arr.);
tel. 43 43 09 06
Métro: Gare de Lyon
Open: daily.

Chez la Vieille
37 Rue de l'Arbre-Sec (1st arr.); tel. 42 60 15 78
Métro: Pont-Neuf
Open: only midday
Closed: Sat., Sun., Aug.

Alsace:
Bofinger
5 Rue de la Bastille (4th arr.); tel. 42 72 87 82
Métro: Bastille
Open: daily (pavement terrace).

Brasserie Flo
7 Cour Petites-Ecuries (10th arr.); tel. 47 70 13 59
Métro: Château-d'Eau
Open: daily.

Brasserie de l'Ile St-Louis
55 Quai de Bourbon (4th arr.); tel. 43 54 02 59
Métro: Pont-Marie
Closed: Wed., Aug.

Chez Jenny
39 Boulevard du Temple (3rd arr.); tel. 42 74 75 75
Métro: République
Open: daily.

Jura:
Chez Maître Paul
12 Rue Monsieur-le-Prince (6th arr.); tel. 43 54 74 59
Métro: Odéon, Luxembourg
Closed: Sun., Mon., Aug.

Normandy:
Pharamond
24 Rue de la Grande-Truanderie (1st arr.); tel. 42 33 06 72
Métro: Les Halles
Closed: Sun., Mon. midday, mid July–mid Aug.
(pavement terrace).

Provence:
Chez Augusta
98 Rue de Tocqueville (17th arr.); tel. 47 63 39 97
Métro: Villiers
Closed: Sun. and in August.

Chez Toutoune
5 Rue de Pontoise (5th arr.); tel. 43 26 56 81
Métro: Maubert-Mutualité
Closed: Sun., Mon., 10 Aug.–10 Sept.
(pavement terrace).

Sologne:
La Sologne
8 Rue de Bellechasse (7th arr.); tel. 47 05 98 66
Métro: Solférino
Closed: Sat., Sun., Aug.

South-west France/Bordeaux:
Josephine
117 Rue du Cherche-Midi (6th arr.); tel. 45 48 52 40
Métro: Falguière
Closed: Sun. and in August.

Lamazère
23 Rue de Ponthieu (8th arr.); tel. 43 59 66 66
Métro: Franklin D. Roosevelt
Closed: Sun. and in August.

Louis Landes
157 Avenue du Maine (14th arr.); tel. 45 43 08 04
Métro: Gaîté
Closed: Sun., Mon. and at midday.

Sud-Ouest
40 Rue Montagne-Ste-Geneviève (5th arr.); tel. 46 33 30 46
Métro: Cardinal Lemoine
Closed: Sun. and in Aug.

Relais des Pyrenées
1 Rue du Jourdain (20th arr.); tel. 46 36 65 81
Métro: Jourdain
Closed: Sat., Aug.

Les Trois Piloux
61 Rue de Meaux (19th arr.); tel. 42 08 08 48
Métro: Laumière
Closed: Sun., Mon., Aug.

Au Cochon d'Or
31 Rue du Jour (1st arr.); tel. 42 36 38 31
Métro: Les Halles
Closed: Sat. midday, Sun.

Cuisine Bistro
(Bistro Cuisine)

Chez Georges
1 Rue du Mail (2nd arr.); tel. 42 60 07 11
Métro: Sentier
Closed: Sun., public holidays.

Gerard
4 Rue du Mail (2nd arr.); tel. 42 96 24 36
Métro: Sentier
Closed: Sat. midday, Sun., Aug.

Chez Pauline
5 Rue Villedo (1st arr.); tel. 42 92 20 70
Métro: Pyramides
Closed: Sat. evening, Sun.

Le Ruban Bleu
29 Rue d'Argentueil (1st arr.); tel. 42 61 47 53
Métro: Pyramides
Closed: Mon., Tues. evening, Sat., Sun., Aug.

Chardenoux
1 Rue Jules-Vallès (11th arr.); tel. 43 71 49 52
Métro: Charonne
Closed: Sat., Sun., public holidays, Aug.

A Sousceyrac
35 Rue Faidherbe (11th arr.); tel. 43 71 65 30
Métro: Faidherbe-Chaligny
Closed: Sat., Sun., Easter week, Aug.

Aux Charpentiers
10 Rue Mabillon (6th arr.); tel. 43 26 30 05
Métro: Mabillon
Closed: Sun.

Polidor
41 Rue Monsieur-le-Prince (6th arr.); tel. 43 26 95 34
Métro: Odéon, Luxembourg
Closed: Sun., Mon., Aug.

Chez René
14 Boulevard St-Germain (5th arr.); tel. 43 54 30 23
Métro: Cardinal Lemoine
Closed: Sat., Sun., Aug.

La Fontaine de Mars
129 Rue St-Dominique (7th arr.); tel. 47 05 46 44
Métro: Ecole Militaire
Closed: Sat. evening, Sun., Aug. and 1 week at Christmas.

l'Artois
13 Rue d'Artois (8th arr.); tel. 42 25 01 10
Métro: St-Philippe-du-Roule
Closed: Sat., Sun., 14 July–15 Sept.

Au Petit Montmorency
5 Rue Rabelais (8th arr.); tel. 42 25 11 19
Métro: St-Philippe-du-Roule
Closed: Sat., Sun., Aug.

Le Roi du Pot-au-Feu
34 Rue Vignon (9th arr.); tel. 47 42 37 10
Métro: Madeleine
Closed: Sun., public holidays, July
(pavement terrace).

Le Petit Marguery
9 Boulevard de Port-Royal (13th arr.); tel. 43 31 58 59
Métro: Gobelins
Closed: Sun. evening, Mon.

La Boutarde
4 Rue Boutarde, Neuilly; tel. 47 45 34 55
Métro: Pont de Neuilly
Closed: Sat. midday, Sun.

Au Cochon d'Or
192 Avenue Jean-Jaurès (19th arr.); tel. 42 45 46 46
Métro: Porte de Pantin
Open: daily.

Auberge du Bonheur
Bois de Boulogne, Allée de Longchamp (15th arr.);
tel. 47 72 40 75
Closed: Feb.

Restaurants with Terraces

La Colombe en l'Ile de la Cité
4 Rue de la Colombe (4th arr.); tel. 46 33 37 08
Closed: Sun., midday Mon.

Le Tourtour
20 Rue Quincempoix (4th arr.); tel. 48 87 82 18
Open: until 0.30 a.m.

Prunier Traktir
16 Avenue Victor Hugo (16th arr.); tel. 45 00 89 12
Closed: Mon., Tues.

Au Diable des Lombards
64 Rue des Lombards (1st arr.); tel. 42 33 81 84
Always open.

Pierre
Place Gaillon (2nd arr.), tel. 42 65 87 04
Closed: Sat. midday, Sun. and 1st week in May and August.

Le Récamier
4 Rue Récamier (7th arr.), tel. 45 48 86 58
Closed: Sun.

Shopping

As drugstores are open every day, including Sunday, from
9 a.m. until 2 in the morning, they facilitate shopping in the
evening and on Sundays.

Drugstores

Publicis Champs-Elysées
133 Avenue des Champs-Elysées (8th arr.)
Métro: Charles-de-Gaulle/Etoile.

Shopping

Publicis Saint-Germain
149 Boulevard St-Germain (6th arr.)
Métro: St-Germain-des-Prés.

Publicis Matignon
1 Avenue Matignon (8th arr.)
Métro: Franklin D. Roosevelt.

Pub-Renault
53 Avenue des Champs-Elysées (8th arr.)
Métro: Franklin D. Roosevelt.

Shopping Arcades

The covered shopping arcades, now again very fashionable, existed in Paris as early as the beginning of the 19th century. There are many in the area of the Boulevard des Italiens. They normally close at 9 or 10 p.m.

Galerie Vivienne
4 Rue des Petits-Champs (2nd arr.)
Métro: Richlieu-Drouot.

Passage des Pavillons
6 Rue du Beaujolais (1st arr.)
Métro: Pyramides.

Galerie Vero-Dodat
19 Rue J.-J.-Rousseau (1st arr.)
Métro: Louvre.

Passage du Caire
2 Place du Caire (2nd arr.)
Métro: Sentier.

Passage Choiseul
Rue St-Augustin (2nd arr.)
Métro: Quatre-Septembre.

Passage des Princes
97 Rue de Richlieu (2nd arr.)
Métro: Richelieu-Drouot.

Passage Jouffroy
10 Boulevard Montmartre (9th arr.)
Métro: Richelieu-Drouot.

Passage Verdeau
10 Boulevard Montmartre (9th arr.)
Métro: Richelieu-Drouot.

Passage des Panoramas (2nd arr.)
Métro: Richelieu-Drouot.

Shopping Centres

Forum des Halles
underground shopping arcades
see A to Z: Halles.

Centre Maine-Montparnasse
17 Rue de l'Arrivée (15th arr.)
Métro: Montparnasse.

Shopping arcade in the Forum des Halles

Les Boutiques de Paris
Palais des Congrès – Porte Maillot (17th arr.)
in the basement of the Congress building
Métro: Porte Maillot.

Les Quatre temps
Parvis de la Défense
see A to Z: Défense.

The galleries on the Champs-Elysées (8th arr.)
Lido, Passage des Champs, Berri, Claridge, Rond-Point des
Champs-Elysées
Métro: George V and Franklin D. Roosevelt.

Only foreigners are permitted to purchase duty-free goods. A   Duty-free shops
minimum purchase in one and the same shop amounting to
2400 francs for nationals of an EEC country and to 1200 francs
for those from other countries is necessary. The receipts must
be produced at the frontier when leaving the country; the
duty-free amount will then be notified to the purchaser's private bank account. As well as the large department stores
numerous boutiques operate this concession.

Eiffel Shopping
9 Avenue du Suffren (7th arr.)
Métro: Bir-Hakeim.

For You
380 Rue St-Honoré (1st arr.)
Métro: Concorde.

Exclusive boutiques in the Palais des Congrès

Liza
194 Rue de Rivoli (1st arr.)
Métro: Palais-Royal.

Michel Swiss
16 Rue de la Paix (2nd arr.)
Métro: Opéra.

Paris – Opéra 2
16 Avenue de l'Opéra (2nd arr.)
Métro: Palais-Royal.

Raoul et Curly
47 Avenue de l'Opéra (2nd arr.)
Opéra.

Also the boutiques at the airports.

Window shopping

Pleasant window shopping can be enjoyed in the district on the right bank of the Seine in the Rue du Faubourg St-Honoré and continuing along the Rue St-Honoré, the Avenue Montaigne and the Avenue Victor-Hugo. It is here that clothes are made and shown (see Fashion Houses). The finest jewellery can be admired (and purchased!) in the Place Vendôme, the Rue de la Paix and the Opéra quarter.

In the Rue de Passy there are numerous boutiques selling ready-made clothes.

On the left bank of the Seine, which is frequented by younger people and where the atmosphere is naturally jollier and livelier, most of the shops are in the Rue du Four, in Rennes and in the whole of the district of St-Germain-des-Prés.

See entry	Antiques
See entry	Department stores
See entry	Markets
See entry	Fashion Houses

Sightseeing (Conférences, Visites, Excursions)

Several organisations arrange guided visits daily to points in the city of particular cultural or historical interest. These visits last 1–1½ hours and the commentary is almost exclusively in French.

Guided Visits (Conférences)

62 Rue Saint-Antoine, (4th arr.); tel. 48 87 24 14 (not weekends) Métro: Bastille
Lectures by specialists about the history of Paris and its monuments.

Visites Conférences des Monuments Historiques

82 Rue Taitbout (9th arr.); tel. 45 26 26 77 (not Sun., public holidays)
Métro: Saint-Georges
A cultural society organising visits, conferences and excursions.

Paris et son Histoire

62 Rue Jean-Jacques Rousseau (1st arr.); tel. 42 33 01 53
Métro: Halles.

Michèle Mathilde Hager

56 Rue de l'Université (7th arr.); tel. 42 60 71 62
Métro: Solférino
Specialist in art and history; only in French.

Ann Ferrand

9 bis, Rue Labie (17th arr.); tel. 45 74 13 31
Métro: Argentine
Specialist in history, art and archaeology; only in French.

Elisabeth Romann

133 Rue Falguière (15th arr.); tel. 47 34 36 63
Métro: Pasteur
Only in French.

Les Amis de l'Histoire-Clio

46 Rue Cugnet, 92 Colombes; tel. 47 82 24 01
Courier service in your own vehicle or by bus; all languages.

Association des Guides-Interprètes et Conferenciers

35 Rue La Boétie (8th arr.); tel. 45 63 99 11
Métro: Saint-Augustin, Miromesnil
Courier service in your own vehicle or by bus; all languages.

Troismil

12 Rue Chabanais (2nd arr.)
Métro: Pyramides
Walks through parts of the city away from the tourist areas.

Paris Secret

Car Restaurant Panam 2002; tel. 42 25 64 39 (reservation compulsory)
In the restaurant-bus customers can enjoy a meal while making a two-hour tour of Paris.
Departures: 1, 8 and 10 p.m.
Corner of Rue de Rivoli/Rue de Castiglione (1st arr.).

Restaurant-Bus

Sightseeing Programme

Bel-Ami Bus	17 Rue de Clichy (9th arr.); tel. 42 85 72 79 Round tour in the "Bel-Ami", a luxury vintage Mercedes which has been restored in the style of the Belle Epoque with air-conditioning and a video show.
Excursions Outside Paris	Some travel agencies specialise in city tours but also arrange excursions to places outside Paris. Excursions of this kind (usually at the weekend) can also be booked at the RATP and SNCF travel bureaux:
Services Touristiques de la RATP	53 bis, Quai des Grands-Augustins (6th arr.); tel. 43 46 42 03 Métro: Pont-Neuf, Saint-Michel. Open: Mon.–Fri. 8.30 a.m.–noon, 1–4.45 p.m.; Sat., Sun., public holidays 8.30 a.m.–noon, 2–4.45 p.m. Place de la Madeleine, near the flower market (8th arr.); tel. 42 65 31 18 Métro: Madeleine Open: Mon.–Fri. 7.30 a.m.–6.45 p.m.; Sat., Sun., public holidays 6.30 a.m.–6 p.m.
Bureaux de Tourisme de la SNCF	In the Railway stations (see entry) Gare du Nord, d l'Est, de Lyon, d'Austerlitz. General Information: tel. 42 61 50 50.
Guided Tours by Coach	Paris-Vision 214 Rue de Rivoli (1st arr.); tel. 42 60 30 01 and 42 60 31 25 Métro: Tuileries. Cityrama 4 Place des Pyramides (1st arr.); tel. 42 60 30 14 Métro: Palais-Royal. American Express 11 Rue Scribe (9th arr.); tel. 40 73 42 90 Métro: Bourse. Cityrama/Théâtres-Voyages-Excursions 21 Rue de la Paix (2nd arr.); tel. 47 42 06 47 Métro: Opéra.
Sightseeing Flights	Viewing Paris from the air is expensive but well worth it.
Héli-France	Héliport de Paris 4 Avenue de la Porte de Sèvres (15th arr.) Métro: Balard Booking: tel. 45 57 95 11.
Hélicap	Héliport de Paris 4 Avenue de la Porte de Sèvres (15th arr.) Métro: Balard Booking in advance: tel. 45 57 75 51 Flights over the Défense quarter and Versailles.
Héli-Promenade	Tel. 46 34 16 18.
Boat Trips	See Boat trips.

Sightseeing Programme

Note	The recommendations below are intended to help the visitor whose first visit it is to Paris and who has only a short time at his

disposal, to plan his stay in the city in the most rewarding way. The names in italic print refer to the A to Z section.

The visitor who has only a few hours in Paris and nevertheless wishes to see the most important things is advised to join an organised bus tour (see Practical Information, Sightseeing).

Short visit

In good weather the inner city, around the *Ile de la Cité* can be explored on foot without too much effort. To cover longer distances the well organised public transport system (including the Métro, RER and buses; see Practical Information: Public Transport) and taxis are at the visitor's disposal.

One day

If the visitor begins his exploration of Paris at either the Gare du Nord or its near neighbour, the Gare de l'Est, he should make his way to the *Cité* along the Boulevard Sebastopol, one of the broad "traffic arteries" of Paris. Just before reaching the *Rue de Rivoli* two detours are recommended: one eastwards to the *Centre Pompidou* and the other to district of *Les Halles* which lies to the west. South of the Rue de Rivoli the oldest bridge over the Seine, curiously still called the *Pont Neuf*, links the open square of *Châtelet* with the *Ile de la Cité*. Here at the birthplace of the royal power of France time should be found for a visit to the Gothic *Cathedral of Notre-Dame*, the two-storied *Sainte-Chapelle* and the *Conciergerie*. On the left bank of the Seine, on the other side of the Cité lie the *Boulevard Saint-Michel*, the *Saint-Germain-des-Prés* quarter and the adjoining *Quartier Latin*, with the *Panthéon* to the east of the *Jardin de Luxembourg*.

To explore other well-known sights of Paris it is necessary to return to the Cité and follow the Quai des Tuileries, past the world-famous *Louvre*, which in the near future will be rebuilt as the "Grand Louvre" with a huge underground leisure centre. Further on, past the gardens of the *Tuileries* we come to the impressive *Place de la Concorde* with its obelisk, where begins the magnificent road called the *Champs Elysées*. The lower stretch of this road, as far as the Rond Pont, is flanked by park-like gardens; the upper part is characterised by high-class shops, hotels, cinemas and theatres. Here in one of the many restaurants or cafés the visitor can take a rest from the bustle of the town and watch the people strolling by. In the centre of the star-shaped Place Charles de Gaulle, known to most Parisians as the *Etoile*, stands the *Arc de Triomphe* and from here the Avenue Kleber leads to the twin-winged *Palais de Chaillot* which houses the *Musée de l'Homme*, the *Musée de la Marine* and the Musée du Cinéma. On the opposite bank of the Seine rises the *Tour Eiffel*, the landmark of the capital; it is 307 m/1008 ft high and can be seen from a considerable distance away. From the platform in good weather the best panorama of Paris can be enjoyed. From the foot of this iron construction, which celebrated its centenary in 1989, extends the Parc du *Champ de Mars*, adjoining which are the *Ecole Militaire* and the UNESCO building. Nearby can be seen the *Dôme des Invalides* with the tomb of Napoleon I and next to it the *Musée Rodin*.

There are many ways of ending a day in Paris. After enjoying the very properly esteemed French cuisine (see Practical Information: Restaurants) there are numerous possibilities for those who like the theatre, opera, ballet or concerts, for fans of

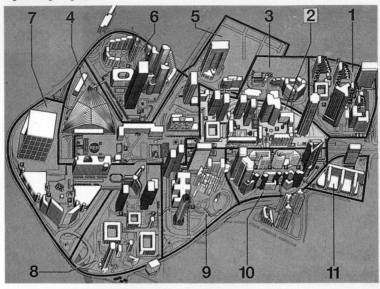

The eleven sectors of La Défense

experimental theatre in the typical café-theatres, for cinema-goers, for jazz lovers, for devotees of night clubs and for those who want to experience the "nuit folle" of Paris (see Practical Information: Theatres, Music, Nightlife).

Two days

The visitor who has two days at his disposal is recommended to visit on the second day one or more of the great museums. According to taste there are the famous *Louvre*, the new *Musée d'Orsay* on the opposite bank of the Seine, the *Musée Picasso* in the Quartier du Marais, the cultural centre *Centre Pompidou*, the *Musée de l'Hôtel de Cluny*, the *Musée Carnavalet*, the *Musée de l'Homme*, the *Musée Guimet* and the *Musée des Monuments Français* as well as numerous art exhibitions. After this time should be found for a stroll through the shopping districts; the "créateurs" of the smallest boutique to the palaces of haute couture lay great emphasis on stylish presentation (see Practical Information: Shopping). Ample ideas for further museum visits will be found in the Practical Information section: Museums.

An alternative suggestion is to spend the second day in further exploration of the city, using the centrally situated Louvre Museum as a starting point. From here we can follow the *Rue de Rivoli* in a south-easterly direction to the *Marais* quarter with the beautiful Place des Vosges, the *Musée Carnavalet* with exhibits illustrating the history of Paris, a whole row of patrician houses (once called "hôtels") and then on to the Place de la *Bastille*. It was here on 14 July 1789 that the prison of the same name was stormed; in 1989 the bicentenary was celebrated by the opening of the new Bastille Opera House.

On the other hand the great stores, Samartine, Belle Jardinière and BHV in the Rue de Rivoli are very attractive. They stand between the *Hôtel de Ville*, in neo-Renaissance style, opposite the *Ile Saint-Louis* and the Louvre. From the *Palais Royal* and the *Théâtre Français*, north of the Museum of Art, the fine building of the Paris Opera comes into view. A rewarding detour to the *Opera* goes across the unique *Place Vendôme*, the location of high-class jewellers and the famous Ritz Hotel.

Between the Louvre and the Place de la Concorde extend the extensive gardens of the *Tuileries*, where until 1986 the *Jeu de Paume* housed the Impressionist Collection. After a walk through the gardens we arrive at the great *Place de la Concorde* where we can decide whether to visit the *Palais Bourbon*, the pseudo-Grecian *Madeleine* Church or the *Champs Elysées*. Finally we can choose between the Romanesque-Byzantine Basilica of *Sacré Cœur* in Montmartre in the north of the city, which also provides a magnificent panorama of Paris, as does the Tour de *Montparnasse* south of the Seine.

After some intensive exploration of the most important sights of inner Paris a longer stay will give time for excursions in the immediate neighbourhood. The following are worth visiting: the Church of *Saint-Denis*, the *Bagatelle* Castle in the *Bois de Vincennes*, the Museum of Technology, the Parc de *la Vilette*, the *Maison-Lafitte* and the royal residences of *Versailles*, *Fontainebleau* and *Rambouillet*. Interesting contemporary architecture can be seen in Marne-la-Vallée ("Palacio d'Abraxas" by R. Bofil) and in *La Défense*, with the new "Grande Arche", and in Nogent-sur-Marne a visit to the restored Pavillon Baltard is recommended.

Three days

A visit to the *Zoo*, the Parc de *la Vilette* and to the new adventure park Mirapolis (see Practical Information: Parks) is especially appreciated by children.

The park-like Parisian cemeteries, where impressive monuments can be seen and where many famous personalities are buried, will repay a visit.

Tours to the more distant environs, perhaps to Breteuil to the Pompadour château, to Champs-sur-Marne, to *Chantilly*, Meudon, or to Sceaux where can be seen one of the finest gardens laid out by Le Nôtre, will, of course, take correspondingly longer (see Practical Information: Excursions).

Longer stay

Son et Lumière

"Son et Lumière" literally means "Sound and Light" and there are many "Son et Lumière" performances in places of particular interest to tourists throughout France. These usually present a kind of historical pageant, with words and music and highly theatrical lighting effects, of events connected with the particular building.
In Paris there is a "Son et Lumière" in French and English in the courtyard of the Hôtel des Invalides (see Paris A–Z, Hôtel des Invalides).

Flat-racing

Sport

Boxing and Wrestling	Cirque d'Hiver, 110 Rue Amelot (11th arr.) Métro: Filles-du-Calvaire.
	Pavillon de Paris, 211 Avenue Jean-Jaurès (19th arr.) Métro: Porte de Pantin.
Football and Rugby	Parc des Princes, 24 Rue du Commandant-Guilbaud (16th arr.) Métro: Porte de Saint-Cloud Paris's largest football stadium (capacity 50,000) is also used for other events (Pop concerts).
Tennis	Stade Roland-Garros, 2 Avenue Gordon-Bennett (16th arr.) Métro: Porte d'Auteuil Site of the French International championships.
Racecourses (Hippodromes)	Hippodrome d'Auteuil, Bois de Boulogne Métro: Porte d'Auteuil Steeplechasing; mid Feb.–end April, end May–mid July, mid Oct.–mid Dec.
	Hippodrome de Longchamp, Bois de Boulogne Métro: Porte Maillot, Porte d'Auteuil, then by bus Flat racing; May, Sept.–Oct. (see A–Z – Bois de Boulogne).

Hippodrome de Vincennes, Bois de Vincennes
RER A: Joinville le Pont
Métro: Château de Vincennes
Trotting; Jan.–end March, mid April–end Dec.

Hippodrome de Chantilly
18 Avenue du Général Leclerc, 60 Chantilly
Rail: from Gare du Nord to Champs de Courses
Steeplechasing and trotting; mid Feb.–Dec.
(see A– Z – Château de Chantilly).

Swimming Baths (Piscines)

Les Amiraux
6 Rue Hermann, La Chapelle
Métro: Simplon
Open: Mon. 2–7.30 p.m.; Tues.–Sat. 7 a.m.–7.30 p.m.; Sun. 8 a.m.–6 p.m.

Open-air baths

Butte-aux-Cailles
5 Place Paul Verlaine
Métro: Place Italie
Open: daily (except Mon.) 9 a.m.–7 p.m.

Cachan
2 Avenue de l'Europe
Buses: 184, 187
Open: Mon.–Sat. 10 a.m.–8 p.m. (Wed. until 10 p.m.); Sun. 9 a.m.–6 p.m.

Deligny
Pont de la Concorde, Quai Anatole France
Métro: Solferino
Open: daily 8 a.m.–8 p.m.
Deligny Swimming Bath, often called the "Paris Beach", is the oldest and best-known open-air bath in Paris.

Edouard-Pailleron
30 Rue Edouard-Pailleron
Métro: Boivar
Open: noon–1.45 p.m., 5–7.30 p.m.; Tues. and Thurs. until 9 p.m.; Sat. noon–7.30 p.m.; Sun. 8.30 a.m.–6 p.m.; in school holidays 9 a.m.–7.30 or 9 p.m.

Facilities for the
handicapped

Bernard Lafay
79 Rue de la Jonquère
Métro: Porte-de-Clichy
Open: Tues., Thurs., Fri., Sat. 7 a.m.–5.15 p.m.; Sun. 8 a.m.–5.15 p.m.

Jean Taris
18 Rue Thouin
Métro: Cardinal-Lemoine
Open: Tues. and Thurs. 7–8 a.m., 11.30 a.m.–1 p.m.; Wed. 7–8 a.m., 11.30–5.15 p.m.; Fri. 7–9 a.m., 11.30 a.m.–1 p.m., 5–7.30 p.m.; Sat. 7 a.m.–5.15 p.m.; Sun. and public holidays 8 a.m.–5.15 p.m.

Covered Baths

Chatillon-Malakoff, Stade Nautique
57 Rue Jean-Bouin
Métro: Chatillon – Etienne Dolet
Open: Mon.–Thurs. 10 a.m.–8 p.m.; Fri. 10 a.m.–10 p.m.; Sat. and Sun. 9 a.m.–7 p.m.

Molitor
Porte Molitor
Métro: Michel-Ange-Molitor
Open: Mon. and Thurs. noon–1.45 p.m., 5.30–7.30 p.m.; Tues. noon–1.45 p.m., 7.30–9 p.m.; Wed. 10 a.m.–7.30 p.m.; Fri noon–2 p.m., 7.30–9 p.m.; Sat. noon–7.30 p.m.

Aqua-Boulevard

Europe's largest swimming bath in the south of Paris is to be opened in 1990. A bath with artificial waves, designed to resemble a cruise liner, will occupy part of a site covering 3.5 ha (8 acres). There will also be tennis courts and a general purpose hall.

Taxis

Since 1937 the number of taxis in Paris has been restricted by law to 14,300. Consequently a taxi licence is hard to come by – and the same is often true of a taxi when you need one!

Fares

The fare is made up of a basic charge plus a time supplement. A higher basic charge is applied at the railway stations. Supplements for journeys to racecourses, stations, airports and for luggage.

The daytime rate (A) applies from 6.30 a.m. to 10 p.m. when the more expensive night rate (B) comes into force. Journeys outside the city boundaries are charged at the C rate.

Taxi-drivers expect a tip of 15%.

Minicabs

A selection of phone numbers: 42 03 99 99, 42 00 67 89, 45 83 16 05, 46 57 11 12, 47 39 33 35, 47 58 11 28, 42 70 41 41, 47 07 02 55.

Motorcycle-taxis

Since June 1985 motorcycle-taxis have been running in Paris. The vehicles have no taximeter; the fare must be negotiated before the journey begins.

Telephone

International Calls

At post offices (see Post) you can ask for an international line (communication internationale) or use a pay-phone for international calls. These pay-phones can also be found on the street and in the Métro stations and have more than one coin slot.
To make an international call:
1. Lift the receiver and insert at least 3 francs (1 minute).
2. Then dial the international prefix 19 and wait for the dialling tone.
3. Then dial the country code (UK – 44) followed straight away by the area code (omitting prefix "0") and then the local number.

4. A flashing black and white disc at the top left of the coin box indicates that more money needs to be inserted.
International calls can be made in many cafés.

The same procedure as for international calls but using the prefix 16 instead of 19 (wait for dialling tone) followed by the area code and local number.

Calls in France

At post offices and most cafés it is still generally necessary, for local calls, to ask for a phone token (*jeton*) which has to be inserted in the single slot before dialling the number (wait for the dialling tone). With the older type of phone you press a button when the subscriber answers and the coins then drop and make the connection.

Local Calls (City and Greater Paris)

For a local call the street pay-phones require 2×20 centimes if they are the older model and a 50-centime coin if they are the new type.

Telephone cards which can be obtained from post offices, bars and tobacconists, can now be used with many telephones.

Telephone cards

In kiosks where a blue bell sign is displayed calls can be received as well as made.

"Call-back" facility

There are two places where phone calls can be made to any where and at any time, day or night. These are:

Day and Night

the Head Post Office (see Post) and
the Post Office at: 8 Place de la Bourse (2nd arr.). Métro: Bourse.

Theatres (Selection)

Information and programme details of theatrical performances can be found in current publications of the Office de Tourisme (see Information). For additional information visitors should consult the weekly publications "L'Officiel des Spectacles", "Pariscope" and "7 à Paris".
Two theatre box offices (15 Place de la Madeleine, and RER station Châtelet-Les-Halles sell tickets at half-price for the current day's performances (Tues.–Fri. 12.45–7 p.m.).

Notice

Comédie Française
2 Rue de Richelieu (1st arr.); tel. 42 96 10 20
Métro: Palais Royal.

Classical

La Cartoucherie de Vincennes
Route de la Pyramide, Bois de Vincennes
Métro: Château de Vincennes, then bus 112. Three stages in a derelict powder factory:
Théâtre du Soleil (Ariane Mnouchkine); tel. 43 74 24 08
Théâtre de la Tempete; tel. 43 28 36 36
Théâtre de l'Aquarium; tel. 43 74 99 60
Atelier de Chaudron; tel. 43 28 97 04.

Classical and Modern

Théâtre de l'Odéon

Odéon
Place Paul-Claudel (6th arr.); tel. 43 25 70 32
Métro: Odéon
Two stages for the Classical Comédie Française and the home
of Giorgio Strehler's "Théâtre de l'Europe".

Théâtre de la Ville
2 Place du Châtelet (4th arr.); tel. 42 74 22 77
Métro: Châtelet
Among the directors here is Patrick Chereau.

Théâtre National de Chaillot
Place du Trocadéro (16th arr.); tel. 47 27 81 15
Métro: Trocadéro.

Théâtre National de la Colline
15 Rue Malte-Brun (20th arr.); tel. 43 66 43 60
Métro: Gambetta.

Boulevard Theatres
(Théâtres de Boulevard)

Amandiers de Paris
110 Rue des Amandiers (20th arr.); tel. 43 66 42 17
Métro: Ménilmontant.

Antoine
14 Boulevard de Strasbourg (10th arr.); tel. 42 08 77 71
Métro: Strasbourg-Saint-Denis.

Atelier
Place Charles Dullin (18th arr.); tel. 46 06 49 24
Métro: Anvers.

Bouffes Parisiens
4 Rue Montsigny (9th arr.); tel. 42 96 60 24
Métro: 4-Septembre.

Carré Silvia Montfort
106 Rue Brancion (15th arr.); tel. 45 31 28 34
Métro: Porte de Vanves.

Comédie des Champs Elysées
15 Avenue Montaigne (8th arr.); tel. 47 23 37 21
Métro: Alma.

Daunou
7 Rue Daunou (2nd arr.); tel. 42 61 69 14
Métro: Opéra.

Edouard VII
Place Edouard-VII (9th arr.); tel. 47 42 17 49
Métro: Opéra.

Le Dejazet
41 Boulevard du Temple (3rd arr.); tel. 48 87 97 34
Métro: Fille du Calvaire, République.

Fontaine
10 Rue Fontaine (9th arr.); tel. 48 74 74 40
Métro: Blanche.

Gaité Montparnasse
6 Rue de la Gaité (4th arr.); tel. 43 22 16 18
Métro: Gaité.

Théâtre Grevin
10 Boulevard Montmartre (18th arr.); tel. 42 46 84 47
Métro: Rue Montmartre.

Gymnase-Marie-Bell
38 Boulevard de Bonne-Nouvelle (10th arr.); tel. 42 46 79 79
Métro: Bonne Nouvelle.

Mathurins
36 Rue des Mathurins (8th arr.); tel. 42 65 90 00
Métro: Havre-Caumartin, Madeleine, Auber.

Michodière
4 bis, Rue de la Michodière (2nd arr.); tel. 47 42 95 22
Métro: Quatre-Septembre.

Montparnasse
31 Rue de la Gâté (14th arr.); tel. 43 20 89 90
Métro: Montparnasse, Edgar Quinet.

Nouveautés
24 Boulevard Poissonière (2nd arr.); tel. 47 70 52 76
Métro: Montmartre.

Palais-Royal
38 Rue Montpensier (1st arr.); tel. 42 97 59 81
Métro: Bourse, Palais Royal.

Theatres

Théâtre Renaud-Barrault
Avenue F. D. Roosevelt (8th arr.); tel. 42 56 60 70
Métro: Franklin D. Roosevelt.

Théâtre de l'Est Parisien
159 Avenue Gambetta (20th arr.); tel. 43 63 20 96
Métro: Saint-Fargeau.

Varietés
7 Boulevard Montmartre (2nd arr.); tel. 42 33 09 92
Métro: Montmartre.

Café Theatres

Bec Fin
6 Rue Thérèse (1st arr.); tel. 42 96 29 35
Métro: Palais-Royal.

Blancs-Manteaux
15 Rue des Blancs-Manteaux (4th arr.); tel. 48 87 15 84
Métro: Hôtel de Ville, Rambuteau.

Café d'Edgar
58 Boulevard Edgar Quinet (14th arr.); tel. 43 20 85 11
Métro: Edgar Quinet.

Café de la Gare
41 Rue du Temple (4th arr.); tel. 42 78 52 51
Métro: Hôtel de Ville.

Petit Casino
17 Rue Chapon (3rd arr.); tel. 42 78 36 50
Métro: Arts et Métiers.

Experimental Theatres

Cité Internationale Universitaire
21 Boulevard Jourdan (14th arr.); tel. 45 89 38 69
Métro: Cité Universitaire.

Théâtre de la Commune
2 Rue Edouard-Poisson; 93 Aubervilliers; tel. 48 33 16 16.

Théâtre de Paris
Rue Blanche (9th arr.); tel. 42 80 09 30
Métro: Blanche, Trinité.

Athenée Louis-Jouvet
4 Square de l'Opéra-Louis-Jouvet (9th arr.); tel. 47 42 67 27
Métro: Opéra.

La Bastille
76 Rue de la Roquette (11th arr.); tel. 43 57 42 14
Métro: Bastille.

Essaion
6 Rue Pierre-au-Bard (4th arr.); tel. 42 78 46 42
Métro: Rambuteau.

Bouffes du Nord
37 bis, Boulevard de la Chapelle (10th arr.); tel. 42 39 34 50
Métro: La Chapelle.

Ouvert
4 bis, Veron Cité (18th arr.); tel. 42 55 74 40
Métro: Blanche.

L'Escalier d'Or
18 Rue d'Enghien (10th arr.); tel. 45 23 13 10
Métro: Château d'Eau.

Lucenaire Forum Centre National d'Art et d'Essai
53 Rue Notre-Dame-des-Champs (6th arr.); tel. 45 44 57 34
Métro: Vavin, Notre-Dame-des-Champs
Eight separate stages.

Théâtre des Amandiers
7 Avenue Pablo-Picasso, 92 Nanterre; tel. 47 21 18 81
RER/SNCF Nanterre-Université.

Théâtre Gérard Philippe
59 Boulevard Jules Guesde, 93 Saint-Denis; tel. 42 43 00 59.

Centre d'Animation des Batignolles   Children's Theatre
77 Rue Trauffaut (17th arr.); tel. 47 37 30 75
Métro: Brochant
Open: daily 3 p.m.
Musical clowns, conjurors, Punch and Judy.

La Magie des Automates
8 Rue Bernard de Clairvaux (3rd arr.); tel. 42 71 28 28
Métro: Rambuteau
Open: 10.30 a.m.–6.30 p.m., closed Tues.
14 scenes with a light and sound show ("Son et Lumière").

Théâtre Guignol Anatole
Parc des Buttes-Chaumont (19th arr.); tel. 43 87 13 12
Métro: Laumière
Open: daily at 3.30 and 4.30 p.m.
Punch and Judy Theatre.

Théâtre Jerval
Relais du Bois, Croix Catelan, Bois de Boulogne (16th arr.);
tel. 47 37 30 75
Métro: Porte Maillot, Porte Dauphine, Sablons
Open: Wed., Sat. and Sun at 2.30 p.m.

Théâtre 3 sur 4
122 Boulevard du Montparnasse (14th arr.); tel. 43 27 09 16
Métro: Vavin, Raspail
Open: Wed. and Sun at 3 p.m.

Jardin d'Acclimatation   Puppet Theatres
Boulevard des Sablons, Bois de Boulogne (16th arr.)
Métro: Sablons
Open: Wed., Sat., Sun and public holidays at 3 p.m.; 3.15 p.m.
Punch and Judy show (see A–Z – Jardin d'Acclimatation).

Marionettes du Champ-de-Mars
Champ-de-Mars (7th arr.); tel. 46 37 07 87
Métro: Ecole Militaire
Open: Wed., Sat. and Sun at 3.15 and 4.15 p.m.

Marionettes du Luxembourg
Jardin du Luxembourg (6th arr.); tel. 43 26 46 47
Métro: Vavin, Notre-Dame-des-Champs
Opening times: variable.

Marionettes des Champs Elysées
Square Maringy (8th arr.); tel. 45 79 08 68
Métro: Champs Elysées.

Marionettes du Parc Montsouris
Parc Montsouris, Avenue Reilles/Rue Gazan (14th arr.);
tel. 46 65 45 95
Métro: Cité Universitaire, Glacière
(see A–Z – Parks).

Opera, Ballet	See Music.

Time

French Summertime – i.e. Central European Time (CET) plus 1
hour – operates from early April to late September.

Times of Opening (Heures d'ouverture)

Shops

Retail shops usually open from 9 a.m. to 7 p.m. Grocers generally open earlier. Each quarter has at least one shop which stays
open until 10 p.m. Shops normally only shut on Sunday but if
they open on Sunday they shut on Monday or Wednesday.
Butchers and grocers are open until noon on Sun. The bakers in
a quarter arrange for at least one of them to stay open all day
Sun. Most shops are closed for lunch from 1 to 3 p.m.

Department Stores

Open 9.30 a.m.–6.30 p.m. Mon. to Sat. Open on Wed. until
10 p.m.: Bazar de l'Hôtel de Ville (BHV) and Samaritaine. Many
department stores close at lunchtime.

Churches

Churches are normally open from 8 a.m. to 7 p.m. but close at
lunchtime from noon to 2 p.m.
Visitors should avoid sightseeing during Mass.

Museums

The opening times of museums are given in their entry in the
Paris A–Z section and under "Museums" in the "Practical Information" section.
NB: All "national" museums (Musée National de . . .) are
closed on Tues.

Post Offices

Mon.–Fri. 8 a.m.–7 p.m.; Sat. 8 a.m.–noon.

Parks and Gardens

Public parks and gardens are open until sunset from 10 a.m. in
the winter (1 Oct.–31 March) and from 8 a.m. in the summer
(1 April–30 September).

Tipping (Pourboire)

The menu card on the counter should state: "Service compris" (service included) or "Service non compris" or "Service en sus" (service not included). The rate for waiters is 12–15% but an extra tip is always welcome.

Cafés, Restaurants

Waiters, chambermaids, etc., but not the owner get a small tip.

Hotels

Usherettes insist on a tip (about 1F per person). Their earnings often consist solely of tips.

Cinemas, Theatres

15%.

Taxis

Tourist Information

See Information.

Traffic

Driving in Paris traffic calls for special skills besides experience. The driver needs to be agile and alert, to fit in with the traffic flow and to cope with the failure of other drivers to use their indicators. Nervous drivers should stay off the roads between 11 in the morning and 8 at night.

Lanes marked with broad white lines at the side of medium and arterial roads are for buses and taxis and may not be used by other cars before 8.30 at night. Besides risking a heavy fine, the offending driver will be furiously hooted at by bus and taxi drivers who will if necessary eject him from their territory!

Taxi and Bus Lanes

When parking on the flat leave the car in neutral with the handbrake off to avoid damage from other drivers attempting to park. Of course, this only applies where parking is permitted. (Street parking is normally limited to two hours.) Otherwise be sure to find an official car park or a multi-storey (see Parking). The police are strict with illegal parking. When vehicles are towed away it costs more than 500F to redeem them, not to mention unpleasantness with the authorities.

Parking on the Road

Although traffic from the right should have priority this cannot be relied upon when entering main roads or roundabouts.

Entering Main Roads

Travel Bureaus (Agences de voyages)

French Government Tourist Office
Head Office: 8 Avenue de l'Opéra (1st arr.); tel. 47 66 51 35
Métro: Palais-Royal.

In Paris

French Government Tourist Office
178 Piccadilly, London W1V 0AL; tel. (071) 491 7622 (emergencies).

In Great Britain

610 Fifth Avenue, New York, NY 10021; tel. (212) 757 1125.

In the USA

9401 Wilshire Boulevard, Beverly Hills, CA 90212; tel. (213) 272 2661, 271 6665.

645 N. Michigan Avenue, Chicago, IL 60611; tel. (312) 751 7800, 337 6301.

In Canada

1 Dundas Street W, Suite 2405, Toronto, Ontario M5G 1Z3; tel. (416) 593 4717, 593 4723, 593 6327.

1981 McGill College Avenue, Suite 490, Montreal, Quebec H3A 2W9; tel. (514) 288 4264.

Airline offices in Paris

Addresses and telephone numbers are obtainable from the Paris office of the airlines.

Aeroport de Paris, 291 Boulevard Raspail (14th arr.); tel. (1) 43 20 15 00.

Air France, 17 Avenue des Champs-Elysées (8th arr.); tel. (1) 43 35 61 61; reservation by phone can be made.

British Airways, 91 Avenue des Champs-Elysées (8th arr.); tel. (1) 47 78 14 14.

Air Inter, 17 Rue de l'Aude; tel. (1) 43 20 13 60.

TAT, Aérogare, B.P. 0237, Tours Cédex; tel. (1) 47 42 30 00

Pan Am, 1 Rue Scribe (9th arr.); tel. 42 66 45 45.

TWA, 101 Avenue des Champs-Elysées (8th arr.); tel. (1) 47 20 62 11.

Air Canada, 39 Boulevard de Vaugirard (15th arr.); tel. (1) 42 73 84 00.

Air France Abroad

158 New Bond Street, London W1Y 0AY; tel. (071) 499 9511 and 499 8611.

666 Fifth Avenue, New York, NY 10019.

1 Place Ville-Marie, Suite 3321, Montreal H3B 3N4, P.Q.

National Railways (Offices, Information)

British Rail
12 Boulevard de la Madeleine (8th/9th arr.); tel 42 66 90 53.

Société Nationale des Chemins de Fer Français (SNCF)
16 Boulevard des Capucines (9th arr.).

French Railways

179 Piccadilly, London W1V 0BA; tel. (071) 409 3518.

610 Fifth Avenue, New York, NY 10020; tel. (212) 582 2110.

2121 Ponce de Leon Boulevard, Coral Gables, Florida 33134; tel. (305) 445 8648.

11 East Adams Street, Chicago, Illinois 60603; tel. (312) 427 8691.

9465 Wilshire Boulevard, Beverly Hills, California 90212; tel. (213) 272 7967.

323 Geary Street, San Francisco, California 94102;
tel. (415) 982 1993.

1500 Stanley Street, Montreal H3A 1R3, P.Q.;
tel. (514) 288 8255–6.

Travel Documents

Visitors from Britain and most Western countries require only a valid passport (or a British Visitor's Passport) to enter France.

Passports

British and other Western driving licences and car documents are accepted in France and should accompany the driver.

Driving Licence/Car Documents

Although nationals of EEC countries do not need an international insurance certificate (green card) it is desirable to have one since otherwise only third-party cover is provided.

Green Card

All foreign cars visiting France must display an international distinguishing sign of the approved pattern and design showing the country of origin.

Country of Origin

Travelling to Paris

A number of companies operate car ferries between Great Britain and France and it is advisable to find out from your travel agent which is the most suitable crossing. The following are examples of the most convenient crossings for Paris:
Dover–Calais/Boulogne (75–105 min. by car ferry, 35 min. by Hovercraft) via St Omer and the Autoroute des Anglais (A26) to the Autoroute du Nord.
Folkestone–Boulogne (105 min.) via St Omer and the Autoroute des Anglais (A26) to the Autoroute du Nord.
Newhaven–Dieppe (4 hr) via Rouen to the Autoroute de Normandie.
Portsmouth–Le Havre (5½ hr) via the Tancarville Bridge to the Autoroute de Normandie.

By Car

Distances are shorter by the national roads (routes nationales) but the journey takes longer.

The present speed limits are 130 km per hour (80 m.p.h.) on motorways, 110 km per hour (68 m.p.h.) on expressways, 90 km per hour (56 m.p.h.) on national and departmental roads and 60 km per hour (37 m.p.h.) in built-up areas unless otherwise signposted.

Tolls are payable on the motorways.

French petrol prices are higher than the European average but they are standardised throughout France (including on motorways) by the Government.

Travel by coach is becoming increasingly popular and Paris is a favourite destination for city tours. Many companies offer a

By Coach

variety of inexpensive tours and there are regular coach services to Paris from London and certain other towns in Britain. Check with your local travel agent.

By Air

Buses and trains run between Paris and the three Airports (see entry).

NB: Taxis may only charge the single fare to or from the airport.

Several companies offer car hire (see entry) with or without driver.

By Rail

Exchange bureaux at the airports are open from 6 a.m.–11 p.m.

London Victoria–Paris Gare St Lazare (10 hr);
London Victoria–Paris Gare du Nord (7 hr).

Both stations in Paris have Information, Banks/Exchange bureaux, Taxis and connections with Public transport (see entries). Further details and reservations from the British Rail Travel Centres at Waterloo Station, London SE1 or Birmingham New Street (tel. 021–643 4444 ext. 2593).

Useful Telephone Numbers at a Glance

All Paris telephone numbers must be preceded by 1

Emergency Services:	Telephone No.
– AA London (from Paris)	19–44–(081)–954–7373
– Ambulance	43 37 51 00
– Breakdown (English-speaking service)	45 32 22 15
– Doctor (SOS Médecins)	43 37 77 77 and 47 07 77 77
– Fire brigade (Sapeurs-Pompiers)	18
– Police (Police Secours)	17
– RAC London	19–44–(081)–686–2525
– Vet (8 p.m.–8 a.m., SOS Vétérinaires)	48 71 20 61

Information (Renseignements):

Airports (Aéroports):	
– Charles-de-Gaulle/Roissy	48 62 22 80
– Orly	46 87 12 34
Automobile Club de France	42 66 43 00

Dialling Codes (indicatifs):	
– from UK to Paris	010 33 1
– from USA and Canada to Paris	011 33 1
– to UK from Paris	19 44
– to USA and Canada from Paris	19 1

Embassies (Ambassades):	
– Great Britain	42 66 91 42
– United States of America	42 96 12 02 and 42 61 80 75
– Canada	47 23 01 01

Events (English)	47 20 88 98
Lost Property (Bureau des Objets Trouvés)	45 31 14 80
Maison d'Information Culturelle	42 74 27 07
Railways (SNCF)	42 61 50 50
Road Conditions (Inter Service Routes)	48 58 33 33
Stations (Gares):	
– Main Office	42 61 50 50
– Gare de l'Est	42 08 49 90
– Gare du Nord	42 80 03 03
– Gare de Lyon	43 45 92 22
– Gare Montparnasse	45 38 52 29
– Gare d'Austerlitz	45 84 16 16
– Gare Saint Lazare	45 38 52 29
Tourist Information/Tourist Office	47 23 61 72

Index

Index

Notes

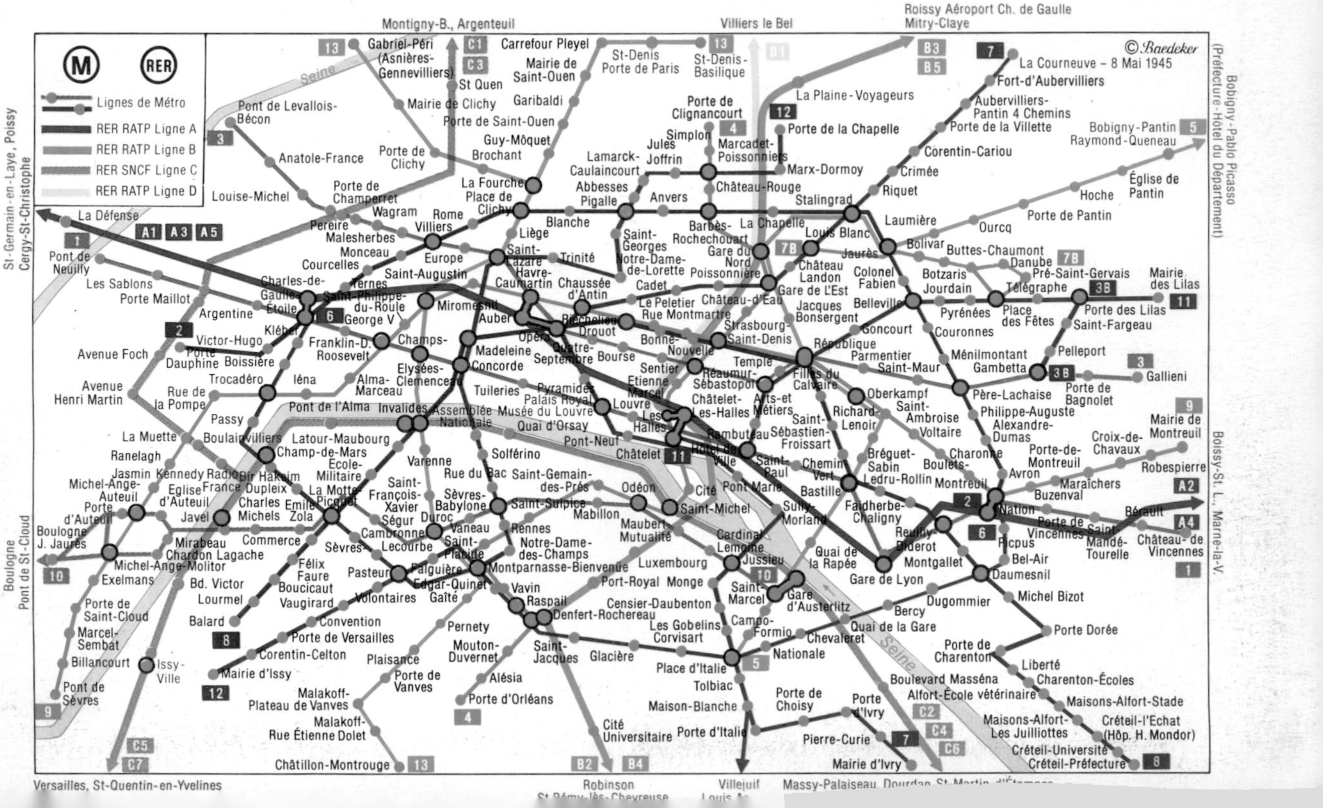